THE NEW CANADA

THE NEW CANADA

A Globe and Mail Report on the Next Generation

Erin Anderssen and Michael Valpy,
with
Alison Gzowski, Richard Palmer,
Margaret Philp, Ingrid Peritz,
Roy MacGregor, Matthew Mendelsohn,
Alanna Mitchell, Doug Saunders
and Ken Wiwa

A Globe and Mail / McClelland & Stewart Book

M&S

APR 27 2004

A Globe and Mail / McClelland & Stewart Book

National Library of Canada Cataloguing in Publication

Anderssen, Erin
The new Canada : a Globe and Mail report on the next generation /
Erin Anderssen and Michael Valpy ; with Alison Gzowski … [et al.].

ISBN 0-7710-0752-3

1. Young adults — Canada — Interviews. 2. Canada — Social conditions —
21st century. 3. Young adults — Canada — Attitudes. 4. Canada — Public
opinion. 5. Public opinion — Canada. I. Valpy, Michael, 1942-
II. Gzowski, Alison, 1959- III. Title.

FC51.N48 2004   971'.071   C2003-907194-4

We acknowledge the financial support of the Government of Canada through the Book Publishing Industry Development Program and that of the Government of Ontario through the Ontario Media Development Corporation's Ontario Book Initiative. We further acknowledge the support of the Canada Council for the Arts and the Ontario Arts Council for our publishing program.

Typeset in Minion by M&S, Toronto
Printed and bound in Canada

This book is printed on acid-free paper that is 100% ancient forest friendly (100% post-consumer recycled).

McClelland & Stewart Ltd.
The Canadian Publishers
481 University Avenue
Toronto, Ontario
M5G 2E9
www.mcclelland.com

1 2 3 4 5   08 07 06 05 04

CONTENTS

INTRODUCTION

THE NEW CANADA IS NOT THE PRODUCT of an immaculate conception. It did not arrive on the scene one sunny day fully formed and strutting its stuff. This new society we are creating in the northern half of the North American continent, in a land long ago dismissed by French philosopher Voltaire as "a few acres of snow," is the offspring of many decisions over many years. It has survived a long and, at times, difficult gestation and still has a ways to go before it can claim to have passed safely through its adolescence.

But let's be clear: There is a New Canada out there. If Canadians can't see it themselves, they certainly pay attention when others see it on our behalf. Thus, The Economist magazine captured our attention in the fall of 2003 when it put on its cover a moose in sunglasses under the headline "Canada's new spirit" and went on to laud our tolerance and cultural diversity and describe our major cities as vibrant, cosmopolitan places.

"This social liberalism," the *Economist* stated, "points to an increasingly self-confident country." The rest of the world looked on with awe as we modernized our economy, balanced our budgets and accepted strangers within our midst with a warm handshake rather than the shake of a fist. The *Boston Globe* declared Canada no longer is a cold country; it is a cool country. The Prime Minister of France booked a trip to see how we pulled it off, saying Canada "incarnates the values of the 21st century."

A new confidence has taken hold among Canadians and with it a new form of nationalism is flowering. This is not the exclusionary economic nationalism of old – not the "we must close the shutters against American influence" kind – nor is it the exclusionary ethnic form of nationalism so often evident in other places around the world.

1

Rather, Canada is indeed blazing the trail of 21st-century nations: globally engaged, socially liberal, culturally diverse. After years of struggling for an international identity, Canada has found its unique voice in the chorus of nations. While other countries struggle with issues of openness and tolerance, Canadians actually embrace their extraordinary diversity and celebrate it as a proud national symbol.

Charles de Gaulle famously pondered about France: How can you govern a country that has 246 varieties of cheese? Well, in the New Canada we manage to govern ourselves peacefully and prosperously with an even greater variety of national origins, races, religions, ethnicities, sexual orientations and mother tongues. And, by and large, we revel in it.

This unfolding reality of a new and different Canada kept showing up on the radar screens of *Globe and Mail* editors through the latter half of 2002. Something was happening out there, but exactly what wasn't clear. Statistics Canada had begun releasing reports from the 2001 census. The reports provided a series of snapshots of the Canadian population. We wondered about the portrait that would emerge if we set out to connect the dots of bald numbers.

There is a moment when an idea crystallizes. It is not the same as the moment when a new idea is born, such as the theory of relativity or gravity, or the discovery that a man named Elvis can sway his hips in a certain way and energize an entire generation. Rather, it is the moment when someone describes a reality, and that illumination allows others to see themselves clearly for the first time.

Such was the kind of crystallization that occurred with publication of *The Globe and Mail*'s New Canada series in June of 2003. Light bulbs suddenly went on and people thought, "Yes, of course, that is us."

Our embrace of multiculturalism presents the most obvious manifestation of the New Canada. But it goes well beyond the mere fact of scores of different ethnic groups co-existing peacefully in our global cities, however notable an achievement that may represent in international terms.

Our schools ring out with the sound of different tongues, giving our children an early and ever-lasting lesson in the very Canadian balance of individual expression and social peace. This New Canada of which we speak flows from the long cherished frontier value of freedom. The New Canada is about the freedom to be who you are and still belong to the larger group.

The same-sex marriage debate notwithstanding, Canadians increasingly accept the rights of individuals to choose the lifestyle of their liking. Younger Canadians, in particular, raised on the ideals of the Charter of Rights and Freedoms, have trouble comprehending the hang-ups of their elders with issues of personal choice. Among those under 30, 80 per cent believe the Charter should prohibit discrimination on the grounds of sexual orientation. And seven out of 10 believe gays should have the right to marry. History is speeding in a single direction on such matters.

Virtually nobody under the age of 30 thinks that a similar ethnic or racial background is an important consideration in choosing a spouse – even if that means holding two separate weddings to unite the couple, as Erin Anderssen shows us in her depiction of a Filipino-Sikh coupling in Chapter 2. It is no longer the way you look, but the way you think that makes the difference. Writer Ken Wiwa speaks in Chapter 4 of a "fusion generation" as the face of the New Canada, and in Chapter 14 later describes Toronto's ultra-diverse Bloor Street as "a long bill-board to tolerance."

The New Canada of which they write emerged out of a hospitable genetic pool. Over the past 20 years, Canada has experienced its third major immigration wave since Confederation. In the first, Ukrainians and other eastern Europeans settled the west. The high water mark for foreign-born residents of Canada – until 2001 – was 1931.

Immigration died down during the Depression and the Second World War. Then, starting in the post-war period, Canada attracted a wave of skilled and semi-skilled blue-collar workers from southern Europe. Many of the children of this second wave sit proudly today in our legislatures and Parliament.

And then the third wave – the one that has so demonstrably changed the look of our cities over the past generation. Chinese, Sri Lankans, Filipinos, Sikhs, Ismailis, West Indians, North and sub-Saharan Africans – an influx that has challenged our capacities but strengthened our fabric. Thanks to the education system and the media, integration occurs far faster than ever before – usually within the same generation for younger Canadians. As Queen's University professor Matthew Mendelsohn, a consultant on the New Canada series, points out, in France, Britain, Italy, the United States and elsewhere, anywhere from 30 to 50 per cent of people say that relations between different ethnic groups are a problem. In Canada, just 12 per cent think so.

This process of ethnic diversification is inevitably changing our world outlook – making us less parochial in all our dealings. When you see a *pure laine* Québécois boy strolling down Rue St. Denis with his Haitian-Canadian girlfriend and their Moroccan-Canadian schoolmates, it is hard to imagine them being overly agitated about the hanging of Louis Riel. They are connected to a vibrant world, not stuck in an historical rut.

Not that the New Canada does not have its grounding in our history. From early times, Canadians have possessed a certain genius for accommodation. As I stated at the outset, the New Canada did not burst from the womb fully formed. It emerged out of a long period of introspection about the meaning of being Canadian and a period of extraordinary uncertainty about whether this project we call Canada was truly worthy of the effort.

As a country, we took numerous false steps through the final quarter of the 20th century. Federalists and sovereigntists tangled endlessly about Quebec's role in Confederation. The provinces sparred with Ottawa over jurisdiction and finances. Public treasuries built up debts first in the tens of billions and then the hundreds of billions of dollars. The global economy intruded upon the protected Canada of Sir John A. Macdonald. Jobs – the touchstone of economic dignity – became scarcer and scarcer. Living standards fell, and with them so did quality of life. Even as our taxes inexorably rose, our physical infrastructure crumbled and the social-policy railroad that linked Canadians through shared values fell into disrepair and often disrepute.

Those were trying times – economically, socially and politically. There was nothing uniquely Canadian about this period of decline, but Canada, through a series of poor policy choices, fared worse than most. Yet out of this difficult experience there emerged a newly resilient citizenship, one forced to contemplate whether the very idea of Canada still merited their support.

Overwhelmingly, Canadians said yea.

In part, they so decided because they saw their economy recover. Governments mustered the courage to corral deficits and the private sector finally began churning out new jobs. Moreover, comfort grew with the global bogeyman. Canadians, so fearful of the free-trade agreements of the late 1980s and early 1990s, transmogrified into the world's greatest free-trade cheerleaders. They came to conclude – especially the younger among us – that along with greater risk, globalization offered greater opportunity economically and, just as important in an information age, more choice culturally. Canadians, largely residing in global cities, brushed up against global realities every day – from the workplace to the school yard to their favourite hockey team. Through the 1990s, they grew comfortable with the changes touching their lives.

Indeed, one of the major surprises about the New Canada is the overwhelming attachment its citizens feel toward it. The huge popularity of Molson's "I am Canadian" advertising campaign was instructive. Rightly, most attention was directed at the word "Canadian" – illustrating as it did the renewed strength of our pan-Canadian identity in a global world. Whether born here or abroad, citizens take enormous pride in their native or chosen land. Their national consciousness runs as deep as the Arctic ice.

But the "I Am" is also telling. Their sense of Canada is more individualistic than institutional. It derives not so much from the CBC or National Film Board as from their sense that this country can deliver both prosperity and fairness. In other words, the source of our new identity is not dictated by a government program, but rather from an appreciation of the country itself and its willingness to allow one and all to feel at home within its midst.

Canadians looked around the world and decided that their values of openness and tolerance and compassion indeed made their country a worthwhile project. Shocked by the thought of having almost lost Canada in the 1995 referendum, they became more heavily invested in it.

Our political and social systems played their part, too. The New Canada grows out of the structures and institutions and decisions of the old Canada. The foundation stones are a federal political system that demands compromise; a vast wide-open territory that required settlement through immigration; a duality of languages and culture that bred tolerance; and a proximity to the great seething cauldron of the United States that forced upon us an open economy and induced in us a longing for social cohesion.

Others might talk about us as the first post-modern nation or the first nation-state of the globalization era. But there is nothing deterministic about our place in the world: We are the product of particular sets of circumstances set in train many, many years earlier.

This was the New Canada that the editors and writers of *The Globe and Mail* confronted over and over again in our story meetings in late 2002 and early 2003. Month by month, stories would be raised signalling that the world around us was undergoing a transformative change. We talked in these meetings of the new confidence we were witnessing and of the remarkable success of the multicultural experience. In Toronto, our largest city and home base to *The Globe and Mail*, nearly half the population is born outside of Canada, the highest proportion of any city in the world. There were some tensions to be sure, but these were overwhelmed by expressions of harmony. The race riots that many had predicted a decade earlier had instead become inter-racial marriages.

We talked as well about the data showing Canada to be among the most highly educated populations in the world, and pondered what this might mean in terms of gender gaps, brain drain, jobs. We marvelled over the rapid progress being made in the area of gay rights. We fretted over changes in the nature of political participation. We wondered about the social impacts as technological change, long a force to fear, instead became a force of information enfranchisement.

But how to write the narrative of the New Canada? Catherine Wallace, lead editor on the project along with Cathrin Bradbury, proposed telling the story through a new generation – specifically Canadians in their 20s. They're old enough to vote, young enough to be idealistic; old enough to hold jobs, young enough to be in school; old enough to have children, young enough to be globe-trotting. Many come from countries that were never sources of immigration 20 years ago. Their Canada is the Canada of the future.

As Erin Anderssen and Michael Valpy wrote in the opening essay of the series: "They were babies when the Charter of Rights and Freedoms was signed in the rain in front of the Peace Tower, and now, as adults, they rank that piece of paper far higher than their parents do as a source of pride in their country. They live, as one young woman observed, what their parents had to learn."

Daily journalism is best at dealing with the small story – an event or development that occurs within a 24-hour period, between one day's edition and the next. Major trends like the New Canada are harder to grasp. But we decided to take whatever measures were necessary to tell this profound story of renewal and change, including assigning a team of great writers with a proven capacity to translate data into compelling human stories.

Between start and finish lay a great stretch of learning. Our reporters scoured the census material (Statistics Canada's analysts were tremendously helpful), looked at every piece of available polling about the attitudes of Canadians, and spoke to academics and experts who gave graciously of their time and research. Along the way, they asked two fundamental questions: a) who are we now, particularly the 3.9-million Canadians in their 20s and b) how do we differ from who we used to be, from one another and from citizens of other countries?

We forged a partnership with Andrew Parkin of the Centre for Research and Information on Canada, and Dr. Mendelsohn of Queen's University, both well-versed in the field of Canadian public opinion, and together we developed a survey to fill in the blanks – polling 2,000 Canadians, half of them in their 20s. Ipsos-Reid carried out our field work. The results helped us bring all the disparate elements together into one fascinating picture, and it marked our own crystallizing moment: The Canada of the twentysomethings – the Canada of tomorrow – is an astonishingly liberal, tolerant country. And, more interesting still, it is the product of older generations of Canadians who worked deliberately at injecting that liberal tolerance into the country's policies and legislation. We are, to borrow from Robertson Davies, bred in the bone.

In the process of peeling back the lid on the New Canada, Globe reporters made a number of fascinating discoveries:

• Young women are the vanguard of the New Canada – the most highly educated, the most socially liberal. As Michael Valpy notes in Chapter 17: "Nothing has put a more distinct imprint on the generation of Canadians in their 20s than the attainments, values and attitudes of its women."

• Within 10 years of their arrival, the values of new Canadians are nearly indistinguishable from the values of broader Canadian society.

• Our most ambitious citizens are arguably the "generation-and-a-halfers" – those young people who either arrived here in the arms of their immigrant parents or were born shortly thereafter. They possess a driving ambition to validate their parents' decision and struggles by succeeding in their new country.

• The attitudes of the young are very much the same as the attitudes of everyone under 55, only more so. The break point in worldview occurs among those who came of age in the 1960s – the era of Bob Dylan and anti-Vietnam War protests. From same-sex marriage to inter-ethnic marriage, our young people tend to be in agreement with their parents, but not necessarily with their grandparents.

• We are integrating our newest Canadians far better than the oldest Canadians, the aboriginal populations. Even as we bridge our new cleavages, our longest-standing one continues to bedevil us.

• Americans and Canadians truly are different – and are becoming more so. Even as our economic interests converge, our value systems diverge. This conundrum presents important challenges to our political and economic leaders.

The poster child for the New Canada series turned out to be a radiant young woman named Fahima Osman. A child-refugee from Somalia, she was poised to become her community's first Canadian-trained doctor when we interviewed her for our project. Her story of achievement, and the tremendous support from her wonderful family, inspired Canadians of all backgrounds. One even arranged an anonymous $5,000 scholarship to help her complete her studies.

After her story ran, Fahima wrote reporter Erin Anderssen to marvel at the response she was receiving. "But most importantly," she said, "you made my community very happy. There is hardly anything positive in the media about Somalis, and they were really proud of the story."

As this book went to press, Fahima was pushing forward on her chosen path, applying for a surgical residency.

Erin is somewhat of a new Canadian herself, just on the other side of 30. Working on the series left her with the image of a nation being shaped by a mass of individual choices, ones only made possible, paradoxically, because of our collective embrace as a nation of choice. "But the main message I take from the people I met," she says, "people like Fahima and the creative Calgarians, is this: We must not rest, as is the tendency it seems, on past achievements, but work hard to perfect what we have started. And then export it to the rest of the world."

The New Canada is a portrait of a nation with a mission. We trust this book – with four new chapters that did not appear in the original newspaper series – will be of interest to anyone wanting to understand our national embrace of a multicultural society, the outlook of our younger people and the way we relate to one another.

In other words, it is a book for anyone interested in getting to know the country we are fast becoming – the world's first 21st-century nation.

But let me leave the last word to Michael Valpy, the most senior member of our team, who credits his work on the series with helping him fall in love with his country again.

"I spent my 20s in the 1960s, at the apex of English-Canadian nationalism, a different kind of Canada-love, walled off and scared. I spent the next three decades convinced that all that was special about Canada was being lost to continentalism, a torrent of alien mass culture and the arrival of newcomers who would never meet my country's soul.

"New Canada opened up my eyes. For a few lovely weeks, I spent time with the finest generation of young adults any society has ever produced – young people with names like Ngo and Diaz, Gagné and Muraca, Bernabe and Kinsey and Strauss – passionate Canadians bonded by love of their land and a remarkable transcendent awareness of the greater Canadian common good, of values of equity, inclusiveness, acceptance of difference, decency and civility. And of a confident openness to the world.

"They live the Canada that I in my 20s was too fearful to imagine. It's very hard not to feel soppy about them."

Canadians no longer live in fear. They are too busy building the future.

Edward Greenspon, Editor-in-chief, *The Globe and Mail*

PART I

WHO WE ARE

FACE THE NATION

ERIN ANDERSSEN AND MICHAEL VALPY

It's become fashionable to say that Canada is changing, becoming more urban, ethnically mixed, competitive, secular and media-savvy. Ask anyone under 30, though, and you'll hear that the country has changed already. There is a new Canada, one with a clear identity, and for the young men and women now between 20 and 29 years of age it is the only Canada they have ever known. Not only will members of this generation soon be taking over positions of influence – in business, politics and culture – they already are leading broad Canadian thinking on such issues as race, sexuality, family and the media. They are the mainstream, only more so. We do indeed live in an altered state, but one very much built on the bones of the old.

THIS IS THE STORY OF THE CANADA we are becoming.

It will be fashioned by the now-grown children of immigrants from 210 countries, who are blending the roots of their past with the nation of their future. And by the young women who are outpacing their men

15

Photo by Patti Gower

in education, ambition and social vision, who have become the keepers of our national character. And by the couples who take love where it finds them, blind to the stale divides of race and religion and gender.

The 3.9-million Canadians today in their 20s defy a label.

They are the most fiercely educated generation ever produced by this country, yet evidence suggests that what drives them is not corporate success or material gain, so much as the goal of a balanced life. They are skipping election day in alarming numbers and lack faith in Ottawa, but they still expect a common fix for social problems and a state that will pay for daycare, social housing and nursing homes. They have abandoned religion, but place a premium on finding a spouse who shares their moral values. They still see big-picture racism, but not the colour of a person's skin. The women brace for a glass ceiling the men no longer notice. And for all their worshipping of American Idols, they think and live – more distinctly than ever – like Canadians.

There is one label they do carry: They are the most deeply tolerant generation of adults produced in a nation known for tolerance. They were babies when the Charter of Rights and Freedoms was signed in the rain in front of the Peace Tower, and now, as adults, they rank that piece of paper far higher than their parents do as a source of pride in their country. They live, as one young woman observed, what their parents had to learn.

They are the latest draft of a work in progress, a reflection of the Canada their parents began constructing half a century ago.

To craft a portrait of this newest group of Canadian adults, *Globe and Mail* writers and photographers sat down with their families at dinner, attended their weddings, visited their workplaces, poked into the inner workings of rural small towns and urban centres, brought high-school graduates of the 1990s together for reunions, attended university convocations and examined the generation's sense of civic engagement.

The Globe – with the Centre for Research and Information on Canada, and the Canadian Opinion Research Archive – extensively surveyed 20s Canadians and their elders on their idea of Canada, their thoughts and attitudes; dug deeper, with the assistance of Statistics Canada researchers, into the treasure trove of the country compiled in the 2001 census; and analyzed much of the academic research undertaken on this generation at universities across the country.

What emerges is a society no Canadian over 50 could have recognized as a child – a complex place, and not without shadows. Too many in this young generation grew up in poverty and too many have failed to leave that life behind. New immigrants do not make the same economic progress their predecessors did decades ago. Canadians can sometimes be better at talking about diversity than at changing the status quo. While young aboriginals are making progress in trade school and college, they still lag behind non-aboriginals on getting a university degree.

The gap is widening – in life choices and income – between Canadians who make it to university and those who don't. At the same time, some 20s are discovering they've been inappropriately educated for the workforce they're encountering – too many undergraduate degrees, too few electricians and plumbers.

This is what the census and polling reveal:

Canadians in their 20s are the smallest group of young adults in decades, accounting for only 13 per cent of the population. They have abandoned the country for the city in swarms, completing an urbanization that now has half the population living in the greater metropolitan areas of Vancouver, Edmonton-Calgary, Toronto and Montreal.

They take on the traditional trappings of adulthood years later than their parents did: Young Canadians, and particularly young men, now live at home until well into their 20s.

They are highly educated: Over the past 30 years, the proportion of Canadians in their 20s with a university degree has more than doubled, to 18 per cent in 2001, from 8 per cent in 1971. The number of twentysomethings in school has increased by more than 50 per cent, and the largest gains have been made by young women, raising questions both about the future nature of work and the future prospects of young men. Those without skills or education find themselves outside the walls of Canada's new knowledge economy, trapped in low-paid jobs and financially unable to begin adult lives or even find the money to upgrade their job-market qualifications.

They are not voting. Just 21 per cent of 20s Canadians marked a ballot in the last federal election – a harbinger, political scientists warn, of the generation's political behaviour as it ages. This is the result not of apathy, experts suggest, but of ignorance and alienation: There are those who don't know and don't care how the system works, and those who do know and think it works very badly.

What is clear is that Canadians in their 20s do not view traditional political institutions as the route to change or progress. Raised in the years since the Charter, they place a higher trust in the courts than in elected politicians. They put their faith in what they see working: While politicians have stalled on issues that young people support – from gay rights to the decriminalization of marijuana – the courts have stepped in and made rulings. They are the most likely to believe that the route to change lies with advocacy groups, not political parties. They are global in outlook, with the Internet as their public square.

They are also less involved in another traditional institution: the church. In 2001, 21.4 per cent of 20s said they had no religion, compared with 6.4 per cent in 1971. If they do attend a religious service, they do so far less frequently than their counterparts of an earlier generation, and the deity they worship is less likely to be Christian – a result of the country's increasing ethnic diversity. The Muslim faith, for instance, wasn't even counted separately in the 1971 census; and while its followers are still a relatively small number, it has made a leap since then to become the second-most-reported religion among 20s.

Just two decades ago – the point at which Statistics Canada began tracking visible minorities through the census – the percentage of people in their 20s who belonged to a visible minority was less than 5 per cent, roughly the same as for the whole population. In 2001, the number has tripled to more than 16 per cent, compared with 13 per cent of all Canadians. And their composition is different: The largest group among visible minorities in their 20s are South Asians; the largest for the population as a whole are Chinese. A sign of Canada's now varied origins: In 1971, the census tracked about 60 individual countries; in 2001, it asked about more than 200.

The growing diversity of 20s, and the fact that they are likely to live in or near the most multiethnic centres – the nation's cities and universities – has led to a steady increase in the number of mixed couples. The census looks only at intermarriage by race, not by ethnicity; but one in 20 young Canadian couples fits even this narrower definition. Mixed couples are more likely to have a university education, and are most often a match between someone from a visible minority and a white Canadian. In Vancouver, the city with the highest rate of intermarriage, the census puts the number of mixed couples at about 13 per cent of all pairs in their 20s.

And for the most part, these are not choices made in adversity: These couples are proud of the unions that are creating post-ethnic identities, and relatively free of concern for their children's futures. Said one groom on the eve of his wedding: "My mother cannot see the country that I do."

One in six Canadians in their 20s are immigrants, and one in five are the children of at least one immigrant parent. More than half of the second-generation, as they are known, live in Ontario. By education, they are among the most successful Canadians of their generation, pushed by working-class parents who were determined to find a better life for their children.

What is remarkable is how quickly immigrants buy into the Canadian way of life. Within 10 years of their arrival, their values are largely indistinguishable from the values of the broader Canadian society.

And with each generation, Canadians in general become more comfortable calling themselves Canadians. The youngest are most likely to do so, with 40 per cent of 20s listing at least part of their ethnic origin as Canadian in the 2001 census, compared with 32 per cent of those over 65.

It is clear that 20s remain fiercely proud of their country, or at least of the idea of what they believe their country to be. Their kind of patriotism views the nation in broader terms, with less attachment to their home provinces. They consider Canada's place in the world more important than settling old rivalries about language and national unity.

Their distinctiveness as Canadians is undiluted by the global ocean of American media and marketing that has washed over them since birth. More than older generations, they expect the global influence of their country to grow in the future.

They are more European than American – indeed, more happy and secure in their culture than young Europeans are. Young Americans remain more religious, more socially conservative, more materialistic. Canadians in their 20s are more interested in job security than big salaries; they would rather have more time with their families. They stack a good quality of life over a high standard of living.

Indeed, young Canadians are becoming less like Americans than ever. The reason is simple, says Michael Adams, president of the polling firm Environics and author of the book *Fire and Ice: The U.S., Canada and the Myth of Converging Values.* "Young Canadians," he said in an interview, "live in Canada."

In other words, the firsthand experience of the society they see around them – the culture they have absorbed from their parents and in their multicultural classrooms – is at odds with the secondhand experience they see portrayed in the U.S. media. American reality television may be popular entertainment this side of the border but the characters don't inhabit the real world of 20s Canadians. In a poll last year by the Centre for Research and Information on Canada, older Canadians were more likely than young ones to say they want the country to be more like the United States; that was a trend endorsed only by 8 per cent of 20s Canadians.

Hardly surprising from a Charter-raised generation. Take a look at how Americans and Canadians responded to this statement in an Environics survey: "The father of the family must be the master of his own house." In 1992, 42 per cent of Americans said the statement was true, compared with 26 per cent of Canadians. In 2000, 49 per cent of Americans agreed with it, compared with 18 per cent of Canadians. Mr. Adams calls this divergence the most astonishing polling result he has ever encountered.

Neil Nevitte, the University of Toronto political scientist who for 20 years has tracked values in Western Europe, the United States and Canada, credits Canada's egalitarian family structures and the high level of postsecondary education with helping to create young Canadians' ideology of tolerance, social justice and ecological concern.

Today's 20s are indeed the children of those who voted for successive 1960s and 1970s governments that enacted multiculturalism, decided the state had no place in the nation's bedrooms, crafted the Charter to elevate individual rights into Canada's supreme law and balance them against the rights of the collective, created the social programs that have allowed the great majority to grow up secure, healthy and well educated, and wove tolerance and respect for diversity into the schools, courts and law books.

If a ride on the Toronto subway is a trip through a hundred languages and the world's entire set of skin colours, it is because Canadians of older generations opened so widely the doors to the country.

If francophone Quebec has been transformed into a vibrant, multiethnic society that looks out confidently on the world rather than protectively in on itself, it is because *pure laine* Quebeckers – the parents and grandparents of today's young adults – put in place the foundations of that change.

If Canadians in their 20s overwhelmingly say yes to homosexuals being allowed to marry in law, it is because they were raised in Canadian families and educated in Canadian schools that assigned premium value to tolerance and social inclusiveness and independent thinking.

So 20s are really just a stronger version of the people who raised them, in a trend that promises even more tolerant generations to come. The real split in values and attitudes, the CRIC-*Globe* survey found, was with their grandparents who were, in almost every area, the least open to change.

"The Charter was not created to reflect Canada; but the Charter did create a new Canadian generation that reflects the Charter," said Queen's University political scientist Matthew Mendelsohn, who helped design the CRIC-*Globe and Mail* poll.

"It's tough to build a country to match a dream," Pierre Trudeau is once reported to have said. In fact, that appears to be what Canadians are succeeding in doing.

"It may turn out to be an anachronism," said Mr. Adams of Environics. In a world of six billion people, he says, a society defined by idealism, egalitarianism, personal fulfillment, tolerance and diversity "may be a dream that fails."

But not yet. When asked in the CRIC-*Globe* survey what made them proud to be Canadian, both young and old gave the same top two answers: Canada's No. 1 ranking by the United Nations, and the vastness and beauty of the land. But after that, it was young adults who gave higher rankings to the principles and policies constructed by a previous generation: multiculturalism, the Charter, and the belief that people coming from different cultures can live here in peace.

Because behind the numbers and surveys are people.

There are Yvonne Mugwaneza and Khalil Kanaan, determined to raise their children Roman Catholic and Muslim in faith, Rwandan, Lebanese and Canadian in cultures, and to teach them to speak English, French, Arabic and Kinyarwanda.

And Lonny Finkbeiner, a gun-loving self-proclaimed "redneck" in the Alberta oil patch who speaks bluntly about the equal society he seeks for his seven-year-old son.

And university graduate Alicia Gartrill, who works as a teller for a B.C. credit union because she likes its ethical mission to strengthen local community.

And First-Nations University valedictorian Damon Badger-Heit, 23, who hopes non-aboriginals in Saskatchewan aren't too terrified when they eventually become the minority in that province.

And two young women, Jennifer Woodill and Alex Vamos, lining up a sperm donor for their baby.

They are the new Canada.

THE NEW CANADA SURVEY

The New Canada poll was designed by the Centre for Research and Information on Canada, *The Globe and Mail*, and the Canadian Opinion Research Archive. The object was to provide an authoritative picture of the way the attitudes and values of Canadians are evolving.

The survey was carried out between April 21 and May 4, 2003, by Ipsos-Reid. A representative sample of 2,000 randomly selected Canadians were interviewed by telephone. A survey of this size has a margin of error of plus or minus 2.2 per cent, 19 times out of 20. Half of the respondents were between the ages of 18 and 30. The larger-than-usual sample of this age group means their results can be treated with greater confidence than is the case with standard surveys. The margin of error associated with the subsample of young Canadians is plus or minus 3.1 per cent, 19 times out of 20.

The survey team selected many questions that had not been asked in Canada in a long time, providing a portrait of how the country has changed since the 1960s and 1970s. The survey also contained a number of questions that had never before been asked in Canada, but that had been asked in the United States or Europe, providing insight into what makes Canada unique in the world.

The survey's two principal investigators, working in collaboration with the journalists at *The Globe and Mail*, were Dr. Matthew Mendelsohn, associate professor of political studies at Queen's University, the director of the Canadian Opinion Research Archive, and a researcher associated with CRIC; and Dr. Andrew Parkin, co-director of CRIC. CRIC is a program of the Canadian Unity Council; the council receives its funding from the government of Canada, provincial governments and the private sector.

In addition to the material in this book and posted on *The Globe and Mail*'s Web site (http://www.globeandmail.com/series/new-canada/index.html) survey results and technical information are available through the Web sites of CRIC (http://www.cric.ca) and the Canadian Opinion Research Archive (http://www.queensu.ca/cora).

Proud Canadians

On a scale of 1 to 10, please rate how much each of these makes you proud to be a Canadian:

Age 18 – 30

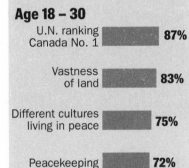

U.N. ranking Canada No. 1	87%
Vastness of land	83%
Different cultures living in peace	75%
Peacekeeping	72%
Charter of Rights and Freedoms	71%

Age 31+

Vastness of land	90%
U.N. ranking Canada No. 1	80%
Helping U.S. with planes post 9/11	78%
Peacekeeping	70%
Different cultures living in peace	69%

World stage

The percentage of people who feel Canada will have more influence on the world stage in years to come.

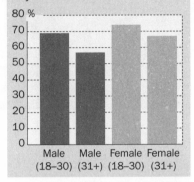

Government role

The percentage of people who feel it is the responsibility of the government to reduce differences between high and low incomes.

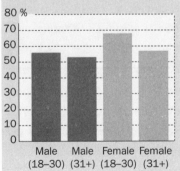

2

TWO WEDDINGS, ONE MARRIAGE

ERIN ANDERSSEN

*O*n an early summer weekend in Vancouver, Maricar Naval and
Parvinder Bains were joined in holy matrimony – twice. On Friday, there
was the Roman Catholic ceremony, at the church to which her Filipino
family is faithful. On Saturday, a traditional Sikh wedding, at the temple
of his family's choice. There were two wedding dresses, three receptions,
and two versions of the invitation. This is a story of Canada's new reality,
in which young people see no reason to let colour or culture block the way
to happiness, and families learn to adjust, though not always easily. But
most of all, like any modern marriage, it is a love story. On the night
between the two ceremonies, Par sent Maricar a dozen roses and this
note: "I will marry you once, I will marry you twice, I will marry you a
hundred times."

THE DANCE FLOOR IN THE BALLROOM OF Vancouver's
Fairmont Waterfront Hotel overflows with women in beaded saris and

men in dark suits. A half-dozen brightly coloured turbans bounce among brunette heads. Kool and the Gang is urging everyone around the world to celebrate. Somewhere in the middle, in her white strapless wedding dress, is Maricar Bains – until yesterday, Maricar Naval. By Philippine custom, she has money pinned all over her skirt and one bill lodged in her tiara, the price of a dance with the bride, paid even by her new father-in-law, who swung her first in an awkward bear hug. Her husband, Parvinder Bains, will soon be launched into the air by his groomsmen and danced around on their shoulders, laughing; moments ago, when he was waltzing with his mother, her tears made him cry. Maricar's father, a stately Filipino, is about to be dragged into an Indian dance by his new Sikh relatives.

A good party, the wedding planner decides with satisfaction, with the wine flowing and the buffet table wiped clean, and some furious dancing blurring lines, at last, between two families from two worlds.

They got to this point only after two separate weddings, three receptions and four costume changes – and before that, eight years of dating, a dozen family discussions about children and tradition, and one quiet religious conversion.

Par proposed on April 1, 2002. The following winter, more than 300 invitations – "a short novel," Maricar called it, crafted with the diplomatic care of an international treaty – were mailed around the globe. There were two versions of those as well.

On the first page of one, the honour of a guest's presence was requested at the Saturday, May 24, 2003, wedding at their temple, Akali Singh Sikh Gurdwara; on the other front page, in the same flowing script, guests were called to witness the ceremony Friday at St. Joseph the Worker Church. But as the last page in both cases politely added, everyone was welcome to both events. If they could have eloped to Hawaii, Par and Maricar joked wearily on the eve of their first wedding, they probably would have. But then "we never would have been able to come home."

When you meet these two families, you find they aren't that different. True, their skin tones are a few shades apart. The portraits of Sikh gurus hanging over the fireplace at the Bains home mirror the porcelain Catholic saints on the mantel at the Naval residence. While their husbands can chat in good English, Darshan Bains, a petite, soft-spoken woman who speaks mostly Punjabi, sadly cannot have a true conversation with Zenaida Naval, also a small, quiet woman, who speaks mostly Tagalog. But both families came to Canada for the same reason – to give their children a better life – and they echo the same wishes for their children now: to be married, happy and busy making grandkids.

Par's family arrived in 1978, when he was a toddler, leaving the small Indian village of Pajjadeota, outside Delhi, where Gurdev Singh Bains, a farmer and taxi driver, was married to Darshan in a match made by her brothers.

The Navals, who now travel between Canada and the Philippines, left Manila when Maricar was 13, to escape the political uncertainty when Ferdinand Marcos was forced from power. Macario Naval worked as a manager at a ceramics factory; he met Zenaida, a chemist at the plant and a talented chess player, when he beat her in a public match.

"Here, you can start from scratch and earn your own way," Mr. Naval said, sitting in the Richmond, B.C., home he has passed on to Maricar, on the eve of her first wedding day.

"All my family is Canadian now," observed Mr. Bains, standing with pride in the living room of his home on Vancouver's east side.

They do not expect their children to be like them. But it is clear they had their hopes about who the kids would marry. The Navals worry that their daughter will have a harder life, and that her children will experience more racism being half-Indian. "You have to face facts," her father told her the night they first met Par. "You two are from different cultures, and marriage is hard enough. Do you know what you're getting yourself into?"

Par's parents had always hoped that their only son would follow Sikh tradition and bring his wife home to live with them, and they grieve his decision to move out. They never speak of his choice to convert to Roman Catholicism. Their fear, they told Par, is that their culture, the less mainstream one, will lose out. Now and then, his mother still sighs, half in jest, "I should have worked harder to marry him off to a nice Indian girl at 22."

But in this modern Canada, nice Indian boys don't always fall in love with nice Indian girls. This country has become increasingly open to mixing in the bedrooms of the nation. In the 2001 census, about one in 20 Canadians under 30 is in a mixed pairing, but that is defined only in terms of race. The actual number of couples marrying across religious and cultural lines – the Jewish Canadian, say, who falls for an Irish Protestant – is far higher. At St. Joseph the Worker Church, Rev. Dennis Polanco considers at least 40 per cent of all the weddings he performs to be mixed. Vancouver, mind you, holds the record for youthful intermarriage in Canada, at more than 13 per cent, the census says, followed by Toronto and Montreal. The trend is mainly in the big cities because that is where most young immigrants live, and where universities bring them together.

Canadians' openness to falling in love across lines of race and religion sets this country apart from the United States. According to a 2000 poll, 30 per cent of white Americans were opposed to close family members marrying a black person – and 18 per cent were strongly opposed. When *The Globe and Mail* and the Centre for Research and Information on Canada asked a similar question in a poll for the New Canada, only 11 per cent of Canadians said the same thing – and among young Canadians, even the children of recent immigrants, the opposition virtually vanishes.

In fact, when it comes to what future spouses should share, Canadians under 30 are five times more likely to answer a common sense of humour, not matching ethnic backgrounds. Most mixed unions occur between one member of a visible-minority group and a white Canadian; among those in their 20s, the groups most likely to marry out are blacks, Latin Americans and Chinese Canadians.

Young Canadians did not just wake up suddenly tolerant. The poll clearly shows a sloping trend across the generations, from the baby boomers down. Older immigrants, such as the parents of Par and Maricar, give ethnic background the most weight. But even there, less than 40 per cent say it is important (45 per cent among all those over 60) and only about 10 per cent say it is very important.

Of course, answering a survey is one thing; having your Sikh son bring home a Roman Catholic Filipina is another. When Par first introduced Maricar to his parents, his mom hugged her without reservation – but they were only 22 then, and it was dating, not courtship; the Bains' friends were still hoping to arrange something with their eligible Indian daughters.

In the eight years since, both families have had time to adjust. And, especially on Par's side, his mother had heard the stories: The rumours of a Sikh daughter who committed suicide when her family refused her choice; the wedding her daughter attended where the parents sat sobbing in the back of the church while their child married a Christian. One niece didn't speak to her mother for two years when she refused to acknowledge her white boyfriend, who is now her husband. What it cost, Darshan Bains saw, was a strong relationship with their children. "This weighs on you," she said in Punjabi, with her daughter Tejinder Bains-Krupka translating. She decided it would not be her path. When Tej came home a few years ago with a Roman Catholic fiancé, they greeted him with the same hug at the door.

Rattan Singh Girn, the president of the Akali Singh Sikh Gurdwara temple, described parents' reactions to mixed marriage this way: "Internally, they don't want it, but they adjust." And some families better than others, he notes.

"The norm for us may always be that it's good to marry within your own tradition," Father Polanco said. "But that's not life any more."

The new life is here, at the Naval house on Evancio Crescent at 7:30 Friday morning, where Maricar's three closest friends lounge in sweats on wicker furniture in the living room, following a strict, printed schedule to get their hair done. They are debating, with great intensity, whether Par will cry at the wedding – Tuyen Riddell, the matron of honour, advises that if he faints, "Maricar, you'll catch him" – and teasing the bride on the complications her intricate dress may pose. Watching the hairdresser carefully pin Maricar's tiara, Ms. Riddell declares, "Aladdin is marrying the Filipino princess."

They know the story of Par and Maricar well, because they have been present from the beginning. It was a visiting cousin of Carol Majia-Laperle who sparked the trip to the Wild Coyote nightclub in the summer of 1994 that got them introduced. Suzanne Cabido fielded questions the next day from a smitten Par. Ms. Riddell, who is Vietnamese and the only non-Filipina in the room, met her Nova Scotian husband at the bar on the same night, and now he is one of Par's groomsmen. "And to think," she says, "that we joked about getting married together. Boy, would that have been complicated."

She means the logistics: Where do you fit a Vietnamese tea cere-mony between all those weddings and receptions? But the concept of race preventing you from marrying the one you love does not even register here. The children of new immigrants, they have all married outside their ethnic group – though minus, they admit, the complica-tion of two strongly different religions.

"Things would just happen," Ms. Majia-Laperle says. "It's actually the last thing on your mind when you are choosing a life partner." Ms. Majia-Laperle, who now goes to school in Arizona, fell for a Quebec exchange student, and Ms. Cabido's husband is Portuguese-Canadian. Her new relatives pronounced at first meeting that the babies would be beautiful. Ms. Majia-Laperle got used to the formal sit-down dinners, and her husband's boisterous brothers. This year, some of her family, who are moving to Canada, even lived with his parents in Montreal and "everyone survived."

When they are asked about race and equality, the room gets serious. They are not blind to the problems, they say. They are still conscious of not being white in a predominantly white society.

Ms. Riddell, an English teacher, lived first in Moose Jaw, Sask., where a church sponsored her family from Vietnam; she recalls the odd slur when they went shopping and her father's steadfast words: "You can't let that get in the way of living."

Ms. Cabido, a registered nurse, often attends patients who automatically assume that she is only an aide coming to give them a bath. "I say, 'Actually I am here to teach you how to take your medicine.' It happens so often I don't let it bother me." Ms. Majia-Laperle chose to hyphenate her name so people would not be surprised by her race.

But none of this, they say, is the kind of oppressive racism of the past, the internment camps and education barriers that haunted previous generations. They are free, Ms. Riddell explains, however people might judge them. "We can handle stereotypes." For their children, they are cautiously optimistic, imagining a country more fully living out the multicultural message it teaches. Their sons and daughters, they say, will think like them, only more so. They will be blessed, not hindered, Ms. Cabido says, by coming from two cultures.

"We're going to teach them the right way," she says. "To respect all cultures. 'Cause look at your mom and dad: We're happy."

The conversations of future in-laws may change too. Par and Maricar laugh now about how he had to explain to his parents that Maricar's family did not eat cats and dogs for dinner, and she had to deal with her folks' questions about turbans and whether Par carried a sword. To plan the wedding, they walked each set of parents through the different ceremonies, and divided the food and entertainment to represent both cultures evenly. Even so, they have heard grumbling, mostly relatives telling their parents one side was being favoured over the other.

"We think we did things pretty much down the middle," Par sighed as he sat down for a diner breakfast with Maricar the day before the first wedding. "In the end, as long as we're happy and our parents are . . ."

". . . reasonably happy," Maricar said, arching an eyebrow.

"What else can we do?"

They are already dreaming of their European honeymoon, which starts in three days.

The two balance each other: Maricar, a chief accountant with the Canada Customs Revenue Agency, is the practical one, the list maker. A devout Roman Catholic, she is the one who worried most about their different faiths; it took her two years to tell her parents that they were dating. Par, a substitute teacher, is the soft touch, the kind of guy who at family parties always has a kid in the crook of his arm. He was turned off by the way, even when he was dating Maricar, parents tried to orchestrate love by thrusting their Sikh daughters at him at parties. "I have to fall in love when I fall in love," he told his friends. Don't expect her to be Indian, he warned his parents. Raised in Canada, the sole brother to three strong-minded sisters, he wanted a wife he knew well and a relationship "that would be 50-50."

He is also the romantic, who made the rare choice to convert – his own choice, he says, but one made knowing it would ease things for the woman he wanted to marry. Father Polanco said it was not necessary: He could still have been married in the church, only without a full mass. But for Par, being Sikh was always more about culture than religion, and religion was important to Maricar. Every faith, he says, "believes in the same God. It just has a different messenger."

He began taking classes. A few years ago, on Easter vigil, he was baptized in a pool before the altar at St. Joseph's. Maricar was one of his sponsors. His family did not come. "I'd be lying if I said my parents weren't hurt. I was hurt," his sister says. "We needed to know he did it for the right reasons."

True to expectations, Par does cry at wedding No. 1. He is midway through his vows, having pledged to be true in sickness and health, when he has to stop to wipe his eyes. Laughter rumbles in the pews. His voice shakes as he finishes: "I will love and honour you with all my life."

On this Friday morning at St. Joseph's, the families have been seated by tradition: the groom's people to the right, the bride's to the left.

"We all come here before God as equal people," Father Polanco says. He addresses their differences from the start. Canada, he tells them, is the rare place where religions of the world live side by side. "We are pioneering a whole new way. We look to see what joins us, and what is more beautiful to join us than love?" Through Maricar and Par, he says, "we see something new happening in the world."

Following Philippine tradition, the couple are draped together in a veil, to represent unity, given coins for prosperity and a cord for togetherness. The priest calls for the families to share the peace. After a pause, Mr. Naval crosses the aisle to shake hands with Mr. Bains, and the rest of his family follows. How does Mr. Naval feel now? "I think I am adding someone to the family," he says later. "Why should I cry?"

Par, after all, is no longer a stranger. He has visited the Philippines, where Mrs. Naval plied him with mangoes and Mr. Naval took his money on the golf course and asked openly about his intentions. "He seems industrious," Mr. Naval said earlier, "and he likes kids, which is good." Ultimately, he says, "what is good for Maricar is good for us."

But Mr. Naval has also been reassured that Par is not traditional. This has been the topic of some discussion among the Navals. One of Maricar's uncles, Joremito Fajardo, explained: "I have read that their women do not interfere much in the affairs of the man. But the fact that Par grew up here, already that gives us a better feeling. Because we know you cannot treat Maricar like that."

That afternoon, when Par and Maricar arrive at the Mayfair Country Club in a cloud of bubbles, the room remains divided, a half-dozen round tables of Navals sitting together, another half-dozen for the Bains family. Only in the middle, among their friends from work, is there an easy overlap of culture. But toward the end of the reception, Mr. Naval ends up next to Mr. Bains, and the two men are suddenly talking and embracing. Their children notice right away. "Our dads are drunk," Par jokes to a friend. "So they communicate a lot better!"

At night, while having henna painted on her hands and feet for the next day's temple ceremony, Maricar lists that moment automatically as a highlight. Not too long ago, she says, "I could never have imagined them in the same room."

The flowers arrive an hour later. They are from Par, who is at his parents' home, being bathed in oil by his sisters, to purify him according to Sikh tradition. There are six red roses, for love, and six yellow roses, for friendship. "I will marry you once," the note reads, "I will marry you twice, I will marry you a hundred times."

On Saturday, the morning of the second wedding, it takes three tries for Par's cousins to get his turban tied properly, first stretching the burgundy cloth down the hall of the Bains home. Par has never worn one before, and, as with a necktie, it is hard for somebody else to put it on you. He repeatedly checks the clock, asking when his female cousins are due to arrive: It is their job to inspect him, ceremoniously apply a dab of kohl to his eyes and begin a series of family pictures. "Indians are normally very laid-back," he says. "But because there is another culture involved, we are trying to be on time."

The fears of Par's parents – his mother, in particular – are more personal than worrying about tradition. "I wanted him married," Mr. Bains says. "I wanted him to move forward." Through her daughter, Mrs. Bains says she is saddened by the language barrier between her and Maricar. "We'll never be able to have an intimate conversation. Everything else will sort itself out. But she is my fourth daughter and I will have trouble speaking to her."

Her greatest grief rests with the fact that Par and Maricar will not live with them after they marry. Par has promised to visit three times a week, but he is breaking custom to move into Maricar's house, 20 minutes away in Richmond.

Par's parents are not well. His mother, who used to pick berries in the summer, has painful arthritis in her hands and knees; his father, a retired scrap-yard worker, is on dialysis. "A little part of them," his sister

Tej confides, "is worried about who will take care of them." But mostly, it is about losing their son in a way they did not expect. Mrs. Bains has been weeping about it all week. "It will be okay," she says, firmly, resolutely. But then, with her son adjusting to the snug fit of his first turban and pacing the living-room floor anxiously a few steps away, his feet firmly planted in a different age, she begins to cry, pulling her daughter into tears beside her.

At the Akali Singh Sikh temple, wedding number two begins well before noon; it is bad luck, by Sikh custom, to have a wedding after 12 p.m.

Maricar sits with her bridesmaids in a side room, while outside by the front door, the male members of her family formally greet the male members of Par's and begin the marriage rite. She is dressed like the traditional Sikh bride: Her elegant red and gold lengha swirls around her feet, a veil covers her hair, and long gold bracelets dangle from her wrists nearly to her ankles. Around her neck, she wears a gift in gold from her mother-in-law.

While the families eat breakfast on the other side of the wall, she waits. Upstairs in the temple, they are divided by gender, men seated on the floor to the right, and women to the left. All heads are covered. Like Father Polanco, the president of the temple goes to great length to explain the service in English, "giving thanks to both families" gathered. Maricar and Par have distributed their own leaflet, advising everyone to wear pants, warning that people may wander around during the ceremony. The prayers are chanted in formal Punjabi, and one of Par's relatives directs Mr. Naval when the time comes for him to hand his daughter's palla or shawl to the groom, a symbol that they are now one person.

The most important part of the ceremony, the equivalent of the vows they spoke yesterday, happens when Par leads Maricar clockwise around the Guru Granth Sahib – the holy book. She has chosen four male cousins, who clasp her shoulders one after another when she passes; they are meant to represent, as the leaflet explains, that they will be present should she need a brother for support. Four times they circle the altar, pausing each time for a reading of the Lavaan, on the love between husband and wife. At the end of the ceremony, Maricar and Par remains seated on the floor, while relatives line up behind them and drop money on their laps.

They are now officially husband and wife to both sides of their family.

Directing guests to their dinner tables at the reception that evening, Sarah and Dalkit Dhillon speak wistfully about the ease with which Par's parents – their honorary aunt and uncle – have accepted their son's marriage.

It will be some time, they say, before it comes so easily in their own family. Their father has already presented them with a list of family names whose sons would be unacceptable; in his world, not only does he expect his daughters to marry Sikhs, he wants them married within their own farmer caste. There have been arguments about this; when Sarah, 21, was caught dating a Sikh man from another caste, her mother hinted that perhaps she should move out. Now, Sarah has "a lot of birthday parties" with her girlfriends, and dates him quietly. "I don't see him as a caste," she said. "I see him as Canadian."

"I'm going to raise my kids the Canadian way," Dalkit vows. "They'll be allowed to date. They'll be allowed to wear make-up. And they'll be allowed to choose." But until then, she says, "there is still a stigma. We hope it is changing." Sarah grimaces. "It has to change."

They place their hope in that change, at least in part, in Par and Maricar, whose care in giving their two cultures equal place is symbolized even in the Indian and Filipino dancers they arranged to perform at their reception.

The newlyweds talk confidently about teaching their kids both sides of their roots, to be baptized Roman Catholic but know the traditions of the Sikh culture, and to learn from their grandparents both

Punjabi and Tagalog. Their mothers and fathers, in the end, are united in their common goal – an older tradition – to soon see new grandchildren.

"They have their ways," said Tej, of her mother and father, "but I give them so much credit for the way they have handled it. It's not their ideal world, but they have accepted it."

And after that, what is left to do, but dance.

THREE TALES FROM POST-ETHNIC CANADA

Yvonne Mugwaneza-Khalil Kanaan
Marriage date: June 28, 2003, in Montreal

Seven years after they first met, he proposed by writing in a note the words he was too nervous to say. When Yvonne Mugwaneza's parents worried about his being Muslim and how he might treat his future wife, she told them, "Trust me." When Khalil Kanaan's mother fretted about the problems their children might face, her son would say, "Something great is going to come from Yvonne and me."

They were married at her parents' house in a private Muslim ceremony, and then again, by a judge in a hall before their friends. They moved in together for the first time, and began planning a family: Mr. Kanaan, 26, wants enough "for a soccer team." Ms. Mugwaneza, 24, is holding the count at two.

"We're going to teach them to always know where they came from," Ms. Mugwaneza says. "We're going to teach them to be strong." Those children will hear how their parents met as teenagers – how Mr. Kanaan fell for Ms. Mugwaneza when she was a high-school friend of his sister's, and wooed her at a party six months later. They never stopped to think about the races and religions that divided them, even when strangers stared at the movie theatre or, more recently, landlords didn't want to rent to them.

They may share the story of their first apartment: Mr. Kanaan had to go alone, say he was Italian and not mention Ms. Mugwaneza, holding his tongue when the landlady said she didn't rent to black people "because they are dirty." From the start, their mom will tell them, it was always as simple as this: "We work. We don't care what people say."

She and Mr. Kanaan plan to help their kids learn four languages: the English and French essential to a Canadian in Quebec, the Kinyarwanda of their mother's native Rwanda and the Arabic their father spoke growing up in Lebanon.

They will eat the food of their two diverse cultures, and learn about both faiths. They will, their parents insist, never have to choose between the two.

Their diversity will be a gift, a lucky charm in a global society and the post-ethnic nation their parents envision. Says Ms. Mugwaneza, with optimism: "Tomorrow will be different."

Nazaninam Afshari–Sotirios Stergiotoulos
Marriage date: June 28, 2003, in Toronto

Being a mixed couple means you get to celebrate at twice as many parties. Sotirios Stergiotoulos took his Muslim fiancée to his parents' home for Greek Orthodox Christmas. On the first day of spring, they rang in the Iranian New Year together.

"It's so much more fun," says Nazaninam Afshari, 23, whom everyone calls Nazy. "I get to celebrate his traditions and he gets to celebrate mine. [The differences] make our relationship more complete."

They discovered each other in the computer science building at York University and became friends while talking through recent breakups. "Everything just progressed naturally," says Mr. Stergiotoulos, 27, who goes by Steve.

Both arrived in Canada as teenagers. They both believe in God, but aren't "fanatical" about it. They both have big, tight families that like to throw big, boisterous parties. And on the small points, they are both open to compromise. "That is the Canadian opportunity," Ms. Afshari says. "You can keep your heritage but still move on with your life. And believe me, in a very magical way you can have both."

They were married outdoors in a ceremony that included readings from the Bible and the Koran. Neither family, they said, ever balked at their relationship. At some point, they may have an Iranian ceremony, so that they are officially married if they want to visit Ms. Afshari's native country. And they may eventually have a church wedding, in which case Ms. Afshari will convert to the Greek Orthodox faith – a step her parents have approved. "What's the difference if you call me Greek Orthodox or Muslim?" Ms. Afshari asks. "It would not make me any different as a person."

Their children will be raised to remember both branches of the families that created them. "They will be Canadian," Ms. Afshari says, "just with more history behind them."

Sabina Mehdi-Andre Holder
Marriage date: May 8, 2004, in Toronto

They are a study in opposites. Andre Holder is tall and laid-back; Sabina Mehdi is petite and fiery. They met when Mr. Holder had to correct Ms. Mehdi on the no-Internet rule in a computer lab at George Brown College, and she flew into a temper because she couldn't get a school project to print.

When they get looks in public, Mr. Holder shakes it off: "That's your business if you want to stare at me like that." Ms. Mehdi confronts: "What are you looking at?" Mr. Holder says she has the tongue of a rattlesnake, and calls her "Ugly Face" with ironic affection. She calls him "Dre" and teases him for being too quiet.

But the most obvious difference between them is the one they don't much notice. He is a Guyanese Roman Catholic who came to Canada when he was 12, and she is Muslim, born in Canada to Indian parents. "Canada is a very open society," says Ms. Mehdi, 28. "You date who you want to date."

And it's what their parents expected them to do. Mr. Holder's mother, Pamela, is happy that her 26-year-old son is marrying a strong woman who knows her own mind. She is not troubled by their differences. "I see people as human beings." Ms. Mehdi's parents would never have thought of trying to orchestrate a relationship with an Indian guy. "You are not a cow," her mother, Tyaba told her. "I'm not selling you off. Find your own, just make sure he's good to you." And her stepfather, Husain, who has been in her life as long as she can remember, would always tell her, "Love bears no colour and no religion."

Sabina's mother did warn her that it might not always be easy, raising children who are half-black, half-Indian. But she remembers her daughter telling her firmly, "If we don't try to change it, we will always have a problem."

In fact, the couple say the main disapproval has come from Mr. Holder's friends, often the black female ones who question why he is dating an Indian.

And while they are confident about where Canada is headed, they are not blindly cheerful about the future. Ms. Mehdi still remembers being told by a boy in Grade 9 that as pretty as she was, he could never bring her home to meet his parents.

She worries about their children being bullied, about perhaps having to work harder to defy a stereotype. "I will protect them," she says fiercely.

The couple will marry at a Catholic church, with a family member at her side performing the Nikah ceremony to represent the Muslim faith. She plans to wear a white dress for church and an Indian lengha for the reception.

They are still negotiating on their children's faith, though neither of them is very religious. But they will be careful, they say, to teach their children about both cultures, so they can blend them in their own unique way – a new group, Ms. Mehdi laughingly dubs them, of "Guyindians."

"Things evolve," she says, "and this is our evolution."

3

GAY LIKE ME

MARGARET PHILP

She came out of the closet in the late 1970s and felt so ashamed that she promptly took a vow of celibacy. Her daughter is also a lesbian – feisty, forthright and planning a wedding, honeymoon and kids with her female partner. While problems and prejudices still linger, the transformation of gay Canadian lives in the past quarter-century couldn't be more dramatic. And yet more remarkable, the vast majority of the mainstream under 55 is perfectly happy to hear it.

JENNIFER WOODILL WAS WALLOWING IN SELF-PITY, face drenched with tears, waiting for consoling words from her mother at the end of the long-distance telephone line. Except none came. The woman who could be counted on for her warm shoulder and wise counsel was being as prickly as a pin cushion.

There Ms. Woodill was, a righteous 25-year-old lesbian from Toronto marooned in the woods for two months at a posh summer camp in the United States, teaching guitar to the daughters of New Jersey's elite, all the while forbidden to breathe a word about her sexual orientation or to show a hint of affection for the camp's assistant director, who was her steady girlfriend.

Before the summer, she had lunged at the chance to pocket $5,000 for barely two months work in the glorious outdoors. It never crossed her mind that masquerading as a straight woman would feel like selling her soul. "I can't stand it here any longer," she sobbed into the receiver, like a homesick child. "I want to go home."

"Now you know what my life's been like," Marcia Perryman said simply, with all the sympathy of a callous shrug.

That telephone exchange on a steamy summer evening was the essence of the generation gap between a woman who came out as a lesbian 25 years ago and her lesbian daughter today.

Those years have been a lifetime in the evolution of gay rights in Canada – an evolution that in its speed and breadth is the most striking example of the acceptance of ethnic, religious and sexual diversity that Ms. Perryman's generation marched in the streets to establish, and that Ms. Woodill's generation takes as its birthright.

When middle-aged lesbians such as Ms. Perryman were the age their children are now, the gay-rights movement in Canada was in its infancy. Equality rights had not been enshrined in the Charter of Rights and Freedoms; sexual orientation was still grounds for discrimination; no one had dreamed of splashy gay-pride parades bringing city traffic to a halt with thousands of marchers. This was a gay generation compelled to live a heterosexual lie, heading for the altar in their 20s to smother their sexual leanings. Some treated their sexual orientation as though it were a nasty smoking habit that could be cured with cold-turkey abstinence. Those who knew better feared living outside the closet at a time when psychologists considered homosexuality a mental illness and the law regarded gay sex as a crime.

A generation later, gay households are counted in Canada's census, and high-profile court battles have been waged to award same-sex spouses almost all the trappings of common-law heterosexual life, from alimony to adoption – and marriage.

Instead of remaining closeted for decades, children are coming out in their adolescence. High schools and universities feature lectures against homophobia and offer clubs not only for gay students, but also for those who are bisexual, transgendered, or just wondering about their sexuality. Now that many of the thorny political battles waged by the first gay activists of the 1960s and 1970s have been won, the new generation has the time to refine what it means to be gay. Tossing out stereotypes, they are crossing from the margins to the mainstream, treading on heterosexual turf as though they own it. Couples are exchanging vows, and turning to fertility clinics and open-minded adoption agencies to start alternative families that their parents never imagined possible.

"There has been a fundamental shift in consciousness," says Ms. Perryman, who lives mostly in the closet with her partner in a farmhouse in a small town near Pembroke, Ont. "My generation of lesbians was more black and white. Our generation thinks of a bisexual person as someone who doesn't know what they're doing and should get on with it, and this new generation is much more conscious of the sexual continuum. For my generation of gay and lesbian people, because we are the first generation, it was much more important for us to define ourselves. The next generation is saying that the pigeonholes are much too small."

Ms. Perryman, 54, came out abruptly in the late seventies, a 29-year-old suburban housewife with two small children and no inkling she was gay until she was swept into the romance that would turn her cozy, conservative world on its head. In the next few years, she felt a shame so profound that she took a vow of celibacy. At her first gay-pride march, she self-consciously wore sunglasses and a hat to shroud her identity.

She shakes her head in wonder at her feisty, forthright daughter, now 28, who can no more imagine concealing her sexual orientation than she can her skin colour. As a lesbian in the blush of youth, there is nothing Ms. Woodill feels unentitled to. She and her partner, Alex Vamos, legally wed thanks to an historic Ontario court ruling that legalized same-sex marriages in Canada. They followed the ceremony with a romantic seaside honeymoon in Cape Cod. They live in a house in Toronto's trendy Beaches neighbourhood. And they have lined up a friend in New York willing to be sperm donor and part-time father to their children when they try to conceive.

"I would say my generation's theme in life is painful, and we've worked hard to provide liberation for the next generation of lesbians," Ms. Perryman says. "But I see them as much more hopeful. It's like our generation was begging at the table, and now they're sitting at the table going, 'Oh, yeah,' which is wonderful."

In the hurly-burly of change, fewer Canadians are batting an eye. Sixty-five per cent of people aged 18 to 30 support same-sex marriage, and just over 80 per cent agree the Charter should protect homosexuals from discrimination, according to the New Canada poll. Middle-aged Canadians, those between the ages of 35 and 54, are only slightly less open to same-sex marriage and prohibiting discrimination. Where the fault line lies is with those over age 55, where just over 60 per cent of people object to the prospect of same-sex marriage – almost matching the proportion of young people who support it.

Further, the lion's share of Canadians polled, regardless of their age, would be comfortable if a close family member announced they were gay: So say 70 per cent of people under 31 and 63 per cent of those older.

It seems hard to fathom, only a decade after gays were still fighting to preserve their jobs. And it's true that public opinion has not swung entirely over. Every gay and lesbian in Canada has a story of homo-phobia to tell. "It's important not to romanticize the ease of being a 20-year-old lesbian and gay person in many parts of this country," says David Rayside, a University of Toronto professor of political science and sexual-diversity studies. "A significant minority of my students admit to being uncomfortable at a party where there are same-sex couples, or uncomfortable if they knew their lab partner was gay."

•

Seven years ago, Jean-Yves Malenfant sat down with his three children to break the news that he was gay and had fallen in love with a man. Only two months before, the family had celebrated his 25th wedding anniversary with the small-town New Brunswick high-school sweetheart who was as madly in love with her husband as ever.

His sons cried. But his daughter, Sylvie, 16, known to everyone as Daddy's girl, took the news hardest. Bursting into tears, she shouted, "No. It's not true. Tell me that it isn't true."

These were painful moments but, for him, tinged with the relief of unloading a lifelong burden. "For the first time in my life," he says now, "I felt I was who I was. Even when I told my wife, I felt a big weight was lifted off my shoulders because I could be truthful."

He wonders now how it never crossed his mind that his daughter, ever the tomboy who seldom wore dresses, loathed Barbie dolls, loved sports and never gushed over boys, was a lesbian. When she confided in him a few years ago – the first person she told – he remembered her fierce response to his own declaration.

"He was so happy," recalls Sylvie, now 24 and with a new-minted masters degree in criminology from the University of Ottawa. "He told me, 'No matter if you're gay or not, you have the opportunity at your age to figure out who you are, and I think that's wonderful.'"

To figure himself out was a freedom that Mr. Malenfant never had. As a child, he was nagged by an attraction to men that he resolved to deny. "I thought I was the only one like that. I didn't know anyone who was gay around me. It was hard, growing up, feeling different, and not being able to look around and say, 'Maybe I'm like him.' I didn't feel like I had a choice. I had to have a straight life and get married and have kids. I met my wife, and I fell in love with her. I feel that I really was in love with her. I loved her the best way I could."

But as the years passed, it became more difficult to ignore the powerful urge to be with men. When he was 39 he had his first homosexual encounter, only to be plagued afterward by the guilt of cheating on his wife and, what was worse, in the arms of a man. He vowed it would never happen again. But some years later, when he was out of town at a conference, he met a man named Pierre who is now his partner of seven years.

"When I left to go back home, I was in love with that man," he says. "I knew going back home, things couldn't be the same as they were before."

Like her father, Sylvie discovered she was gay when she met someone, falling for a classmate in her first year of university after the woman confided her own attraction. It was like an epiphany. Never before had it dawned on her that she was a lesbian. She fretted about telling her mother. "How would I say to my mom what had hurt her so much for such a long time?" she wondered.

In the end, her mother guessed. "Are you gay?" she asked bluntly one day, after her daughter became distraught at news that a girlfriend had started dating another woman. "That's what I'm trying to figure out," was all Sylvie had the guts to respond. Her mother was indignant. "Homosexuality is hurting other people," she said. "Make sure you find out who you are before hurting someone else."

It would take her mother a few years to distinguish the pain her husband had inflicted from her daughter's revelation, but time has healed her wounds. And Sylvie, coming out to friends, has found that people treat her pronouncement as no big deal. Still, about to embark on her career, she refuses to use her first name in print, defaulting to her middle one.

"My dad, it took him 48 years to figure out, 'This is who I am.' I had the opportunity to explore who I was at 19 because people are more and more open-minded," she says. "Maybe I'm an optimistic person. But I think more and more, with knowledge, people are less fearful of coming out, and it means we're more present."

William White was a teenager easing out of the closet – "it was a gradual process, like I was almost emerging from a shell" – at the same time as his 48-year-old father bolted out of it with a suicide attempt that almost worked.

Like many gay people, William, now 21, had understood from an early age that he was different. At school in Halifax, where he still lives, he was a social outcast, teased and bullied by the popular children. When he caught himself fantasizing about the boys in his class, he would will himself to stare at the girls in a futile attempt to train his sexual orientation away from its natural leaning.

"In junior high, I had strange ways of thinking," he says. "It was not acceptable where I went. It was not a great time to discover things about yourself that don't make you popular when you're not popular to begin with. I was beginning to see stuff was not right. But it took me several years to understand what wasn't right. I have a hard time understanding it now, because I could walk up to anyone now and say, 'Hi. I'm William, and I'm gay.' Not that I'd do that. It wouldn't be socially appropriate. But I wouldn't have a problem with it."

A few years later, his depressed father would slash his wrists and neck at work, pushed over the edge by financial pressures, a job he loathed with a market-research company, two decades of living the lie of a gay man stuck in a crumbling straight marriage, and a nagging sense that he was unworthy as a father.

"I considered myself as a failure as a man and a father because I had these gay thoughts," Walter White says. "It was what I thought to be an evil, bad, immoral part of myself that I couldn't control. I thought I was less of a man than anyone else."

He and his wife had invested years in counselling to save their marriage. She sat by his hospital bedside for five weeks. Then he turned to her and said, "Well, I guess you know your husband is a homosexual?" After years of blaming herself for their marriage problems, her husband's revelation stung like a betrayal.

Walter emerged from hospital a changed man, bursting with plans to train for a new career and, for the first time in his life, describing himself as a bisexual. "It was an interesting parallel in our loves," says his son. "I was starting to go into the same place at the same time. He was repairing his life and I was shaping mine, but we were both doing the same thing."

Now, Walter lives in Halifax with his partner of three years, George, and holds a job he adores as a home-care worker for seniors, few of whom suspect he is gay. For his part, William juggles two jobs, managing a sandwich shop when not working as a landscape gardener. Everyone knows he is gay.

"I understand why my father tried to live mainstream and lived his life in a private section of his mind," William says. "But it's too hard to have a dual life in your head. I did on a micro scale what he did on a macro scale. What he took 20 years to do, I took two years to do. I couldn't do what my father did. He didn't share his feelings with my mom, and he built a life that was only half of his life. I could not build a huge mountain and watch it collapse."

Jennifer Woodill is sprawled on her ample denim-blue couch, bought when she and Alex Vamos moved into their new house. It isn't long before their wedding. The plans for their honeymoon are changing by the week. A resort in Algonquin Park was dropped for a bed-and-breakfast in Nova Scotia owned by a lesbian couple, itself then abandoned for a holiday in Provincetown, Mass.

For two women comfortable in their lesbian skins, it has been a rude awakening to realize that their sexual orientation would make them feel conspicuous at the luxury resorts they have pored over on the Internet – not the romantic retreat they had in mind. "I never feel bad about being gay," grumbles Ms. Vamos. "But with this honeymoon thing, it really feels like an obstacle." And so, the switch to a U.S. tourist town famous as a draw for gays and lesbians on vacation.

"It's very, very gay," Ms. Woodill says, trying to sound upbeat. "We can go there, and we'll be fine. I think it will be fun."

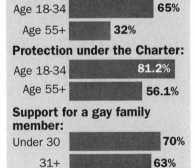

Gay support

A poll by the Centre for Research and Information on Canada and The Globe and Mail, asked 2,000 Canadians what they thought of same-sex marriages; protection, under the Charter of Rights and Freedoms, from discrimination; and how families would feel if one of their family members were gay.

In favour of same-sex marriage:

Age 18-34 **65%**

Age 55+ **32%**

Protection under the Charter:

Age 18-34 **81.2%**

Age 55+ **56.1%**

Support for a gay family member:

Under 30 **70%**

31+ **63%**

THE GLOBE AND MAIL

4

FUSION FOOD, FUSION GENERATION

KEN WIWA

It sounds like a set-up for a joke: A Muslim, a Hindu, a Buddhist and a Jew walk into a restaurant . . . But the punchline here is, they're the owners. A trendy bistro symbolizes the next stage in multiculturalism. Like many in their generation, this group of postnational entrepreneurs is neither particularly religious nor especially nostalgic for their family pasts. But they do feel a hankering for "an abiding idea based on our mutually disparate backgrounds" – as well as for excellent sushi.

IF EVER AN INTERSECTION WERE A SNAPSHOT of a social and cultural history of Canada, it would be the four corners of King and Bathurst Streets in downtown Toronto.

Anchoring the southwest corner is the Wheat Sheaf, the oldest tavern in the city and an enduring legacy of its Hogtown image. Southeast is a sports bar, a modern cousin of the Wheat Sheaf, but both catering to predominantly male and European tastes and culture.

Across King Street, facing these two monuments to Canadiana, are the new immigrants. On the ground floor of a condominium complex is a Second Cup franchise, with its accent on the coffee culture of the 1990s. And on the northeast corner, within the walls of a sober bank building still carrying the fading inscription Bank of Toronto, is the flashy new kid on the block – a restaurant serving sushi.

If you could choose a food that would suit a restaurant run by a Jew, a Muslim, a Hindu and a Buddhist, it would have to be sushi, fast becoming the signature dish of global culture.

This ethnic soup of immigrant investors hadn't even noticed the diversity of their religious backgrounds until it was pointed out to them. It is tempting to read the investor profile of Blowfish restaurant as one of those archetypical stories that hint at an effortless multiculturalism emerging out of Toronto's myth as meeting place. But it is a half-breed, a child of Canada's multicultural experiment, an example of the emerging demographic – of a fusion generation that is the face of new Canada. More visible in the country's big cities, it is a generation in the process of negotiating new spaces at the juncture of its cross-cultural past and its Canadian future.

Zark Fatah, at 28 the youngest Blowfish partner, is a product of this Canada. Born and raised here, he is a historical paradox. "My parents are from India and Pakistan. My mother is from Lahore and my father was born in Bombay, but raised in Karachi," he explains. "My mother is Christian and my father's Muslim. They were ridiculed and went through various problems, but because of their opposite backgrounds they didn't force their religion or culture on us, because they wanted us to grow up as Canadians. They wanted us to grow up with our own identity and not be moulded. Me and my brother grew up very Canadian, being independent and doing our own thing."

Mr. Fatah doesn't fit into many databases and he certainly doesn't fit old-Canada stereotypes of a successful, second-generation immigrant from South Asia; he is neither a lawyer nor an accountant, and he dropped out of high school. But he still emerged from what he considered the wastelands of suburban Toronto and, after an eventful career bartending in New York and Miami, he now runs a promotion company.

"I spent most of my years growing up in Scarborough. I always knew I didn't belong just from my attitude and my dress, and I just knew that I had to get out of there. So when I was 21, I finally moved downtown."

His story reminds you somewhat of Karim, the protagonist in *The Buddha of Suburbia*. Hanif Kureishi's award-winning novel of second-generation immigrants, set in London in the 1970s, tells the story of a bicultural Indian who propels himself out of the grey suburbs into the heart of the colourful metropolis.

Like Karim, Mr. Fatah has shape-shifted his way from the periphery into the pulsing centre being designed and fashioned on the iconoclastic lines and aesthetics of a fusion generation.

This new Canada could be described as a "mobile paradoxical space," which is how sociologists describe a place where people of mixed heritage can inhabit their paradoxes, and invent and reinvent their identities to fit whatever environment they may find themselves in. This sense of Canada as a place of limitless possibility is reflected in the New Canada poll, which indicates that Mr. Fatah's generation still rates the vastness of the land as one of the things that makes them most proud to be Canadian. Their need for space perhaps speaks to the anxieties of second-generation immigrants looking for a tabula rasa on which to impress and compose their emerging identities.

And cities like Toronto are the new Old West, frontier towns, the stage on which the new generation can play out its hopes, fears and ambitions, remaking Canada in its image. "You know, there's no racial boundaries, there's no limitations, it's a young country," Mr. Fatah says. "There are a lot of opportunities with its growing. You know, find your plot of land, make your stake and start building now. It's only going to get bigger and better."

With his postnational identity and with its fusion menu, Mr. Fatah and Blowfish are a window on that Canada, a Canada that will have to cater to a demographic other than the beer-and-hockey-night crowd. It is a demographic with overlapping categories, a Canada that nixes traditional databases and that daily challenges stereotypes and prejudices.

"Because I am somewhat mixed, people quite don't know where to place me," Mr. Fatah says. "They're not sure whether I am Italian, Spanish – I honestly get mistaken for many different things." But fluid as that identity is, it was still forged in the white heat of a rite of passage that will be familiar to many immigrants. "My first name is actually spelled Z-A-R-A-K. When I changed schools in Grade 3, for whatever reason, they had made a spelling mistake and the second A was dropped out of my name and I was introduced to the class as Zark . . . and that name stuck." Anglicizing foreign names is almost as old as the hills, but it offered Mr. Fatah a peg to hang his hat on. "Being in the promoting and marketing business, it's advantageous to have a unique name . . . Everyone wants to be unique and stand out – at least I do – but as more and more immigrants come to this country I will be less and less exotic."

For now, though, he is Noah aboard a Canadian cultural ark, the man responsible for bringing a cosmopolitan crowd of hyphenated stories to the Blowfish table.

"One of the beautiful things about living in Toronto or Canada is that we're so accustomed to racial diversity that it's so normal," Mr. Fatah says with conviction. "I met these two gentlemen from Manchester last weekend at my party and they're like, 'What is amazing is look around here, you have Asian, black, Indian, Italian, Greek, Jewish, Canadian, you have all these ethnicities, everyone is partying, no one is segregated to their corners. In England you'd never see that, people are so segregated and split up, and it's by their own choice that they keep to their own. Here everyone talks to everyone and that's a beautiful thing.'"

Press the Zarks of this world about racism and you get the impression that Canada is colourblind. "I don't even see that racism.

If anyone has ever discriminated against me racially, I've never even acknowledged it. Maybe I am naive but I don't even see that. My job is to network and befriend people all day and every day, and never does colour or race ever play. That doesn't even cross my mind, and my children, I think, will think that way as well. The more I travel, the more I appreciate and love Toronto. I don't think people here in Toronto realize what a great city we have, because maybe they haven't travelled enough. People always look down on Toronto . . . but I mean they really have no idea what a great city we live in."

It is tempting to describe the notion of a sushi restaurant being built by Canadian immigrants on the premises of an old Toronto banking institution as a silent revolution, but Blowfish is very much the product of immigrant experience.

The man chiefly responsible for Blowfish is Hanif Harji, a 32-year-old Hindu who came to Toronto as a five-year-old refugee from Idi Amin's dictatorship in Uganda. Soft-spoken and invariably immaculately suited, Mr. Harji is an experienced restaurateur who owns a string of Second Cups in the city. "I wanted to bring together a group of people who would add a tremendous amount of value, we all work together, we are all like-minded people, yet we come from totally different cultures," Mr. Harji says of his business partners, who also include Jo Siahou and chef G. Q. Pan.

It's interesting – and perhaps indicative of where the new Canada is headed – that this Utopia emerges not from a vision of effortless multiculturalism, but out of an economic impulse. "The idea of coming together from different backgrounds – it's just an issue of necessity," suggests Sang Kim, a Korean immigrant and Blowfish's culinary consultant. I have put it to him that Blowfish is more than a restaurant. I am half expecting him to confirm my pet theory of sushi as some kind of leitmotif for Canada.

"All food is fashion," Mr. Kim counters. "You're not going to have a kind of overwhelming philosophy that comes out of a group of guys coming together to make money. Businesses make no room for issues be it cultural, social, and political. You can riff on it over a beer and chat about this and that, but that cannot interfere with the fact that the guys are trying to run a successful business. To create a cultural icon out of four or five people from different backgrounds coming together to build something would mean that the foundations would have to be on an idea that's important. . . . I don't think we are on to something essential until we have an abiding idea based on our mutually disparate backgrounds."

Mr. Kim's view illustrates the soft centre of the fusion generation, the lack of a common thread in this colourful fabric. But, as he hints, the vision may come after the fact; while economic necessity will force Canada to embrace the shifts in its demography, new Canada will still have to find common cause from this fusion of values. So what sort of society might emerge from this generation?

"I think the next generation is going to be cooler or more open-minded," Mr. Fatah offers. "I live my life by my own set of morals and values that my parents instilled in me. I don't go to church; I can probably count the number of times on one hand that I have been to a church or mosque even. I definitely let my own conscience and values guide me. I have quite a lot of Jewish friends and they are religious in the sense that you know they have their family functions and get-togethers and they take their family functions seriously."

This acculturated and areligious mindset is not untypical of hyphenated second-generation Canadians raised without any decisive memory or nostalgia of their parents' country or home; but many Canadians in their 20s were raised on strong values yet are still drawn to the global metropolis.

Kristi Panko is a tall, blond, fourth-generation Canadian of Irish and Ukrainian extraction. The 27-year-old from Caledon, northwest of Toronto, is the manager of Blowfish and has been living in the city for only two months. Her history is as rooted as Mr. Fatah's is restless, and as she slips the moorings of Caledon to negotiate the multicultural forests of Toronto she is looking for something to anchor her in this bright new future. "My morals and values are very strong," she says. "I don't know whether they're – I mean, I guess they're not Canadian. I don't know if I would say I have Canadian morals, but I do have my own morals. I went to church as a child. I went to a Baptist church. I went for many years and it's something I feel I am missing out in my life now, but not enough to do anything about it."

Ms. Panko's concern for her moral centre is not just a factor of her own upbringing and new environment. It also reflects the results of the New Canada poll, which show that young women have a consistently higher awareness of social issues than do young men.

"The one thing that sticks in my mind about Toronto," she says, recalling her first winter in the city, "is the number of homeless people, especially in the climate we had this winter. It was so cold and I drove home one night and I remember I was freezing just walking from the office to the parking lot, and I was absolutely numb by the time I got to the car. And as I was driving, there was a man on the street, and the wind was so strong that blankets were blowing up over his head, and I thought, I don't know if this is the image we would want us to have in the city, a man out in the cold like that. That's something else."

As new Canada is influenced by the hopes and ideals of the fusion generation, those streets once dominated by the designs of a male and European heritage may have a very different profile in years to come.

5

BIRTH OF A NEW ETHNICITY

MATTHEW MENDELSOHN

As more young people consider themselves ethnically fractioned – a quarter this and half that – fewer will have a stronger connection to an ethnic group than to other Canadians. The very term 'ethnicity' is awkward, but it fits: We are creating a new multiracial, multicultural boundary-free ethnic group called Canadian.

SOCIAL CHANGE IS SOMETIMES DIFFICULT TO SEE. It's like looking at yourself in the mirror every day and not noticing that you're aging. But once in a while it's useful to pull out the high school year-book and take note of the transformation.

The survey we conducted for *The Globe and Mail*'s New Canada project asked people what makes them proud of Canada. Over all, things such as the beauty of the land, the country's high ranking by the United Nations and our role in peacekeeping came out at the top of the list. Among young Canadians, those in their 20s, other factors made them proud: multiculturalism, the Charter of Rights and Freedoms, bilingualism, having people from different cultural backgrounds living in peace.

These are the elements of the new Canadian mythology, one created in the period between the late 1960s and the early 1980s and codified as official in the Charter of Rights and Freedoms. Perhaps it is not surprising that these are sources of pride. After all, this is the only Canada that young people have ever known, and one quite different from that of their grandparents.

One of the biggest changes in Canada over the past twenty years has been the emergence of a more deeply entrenched pan-Canadian national identity. It was once thought that attachment to Canada was quite weak, with local attachments being more important. This is no longer the case. Waves of new immigrants from non-European countries chose to come to Canada, not to any particular province. Young Canadians, at least outside Quebec, are far more likely than older Canadians to define themselves as Canadian first, rather than in terms of their province.

The "I am Canadian" marketing phenomenon tapped into something real: Canadians are very proud of their national identity. With no trace of irony, they proudly yell about how modest they are, and patriotically proclaim that they have no patriotism. Despite our claim to a modest and deferential nationalism, our nationalism has become as emotional and assertive as anyone's. The introduction of the Charter of Rights was explicitly designed to unite all citizens in a pan-Canadian community, and it worked. Outside Quebec, a real national consciousness has been created – this despite simmering regional resentments and disaffection from the federal government.

The result has been the emergence over the past 20 years of a new ethnicity – simply Canadian. As more young people consider themselves ethnically fractioned – half of this and a quarter of that – fewer will have a strong connection to an ethnic group other than Canadian. In the 2001 census, when asked about the ethnic origins of our ancestors, fully 39 per cent of us said "just Canadian," and this number grows higher every year. The very term "ethnicity" is an awkward one, but it fits: We are creating a new multiracial, multicultural boundary-free ethnic group called "Canadian."

These are large and significant changes. Take immigration, for example. In 1946, almost half of all Canadians (46 per cent) said our immigration policy should ensure that Jews do not come to Canada. In 1961, 40 per cent of Canadians said that we should prevent the immigration of non-whites. Today, almost no one holds such views.

And, although many of us still consider our ethnic background important to us, virtually no one under the age of 30 thinks that a similar ethnic background is important when choosing a spouse or friends. Canadians date, marry, work and hang out with people from all kinds of backgrounds. What you believe, not where you come from, matters. For most Canadians, their ethnicity is a mark of personal identity, but in no way grounds for exclusion.

In surveys in France, Britain, Italy, the United States and other countries, anywhere from 30 to 50 per cent of people say that relations between different ethnic groups are a big problem; in Canada, just 12 per cent say this. In Canada, 81 per cent of those under 30 say immigrants are having a positive effect on our country, which is a significantly higher number than found among older Canadians, and significantly higher than young people in other countries, according to a major international study conducted for the Pew Research Center for People and the Press, an independent group based in Washington, D.C. In the United States, about one in three Americans say blacks and whites should not marry each other. In Canada, fewer than one in 10 hold that belief, and almost no one under 30 does. It is not merely starry-eyed back-patting to highlight these very real differences between Canada and other countries. They are real facts that define our national identity.

Canada integrates immigrants better than any other country in the world today. You might think we would rejoice in this, but instead some among us still choose to worry about multiculturalism, about "ethnic ghettos," and about whether immigrants retain too much attachment to their country of origin. Some – the Fraser Institute in its report *Canada's Immigration Policy: The Need for Major Reform*, for example – seek out an anti-immigrant backlash, fail to find it, but still warn ominously that it could come any day now. They seek out an anti-immigrant backlash that never materializes and refuse to acknowledge the reality of the country: People from different backgrounds are getting along better every year, not worse. While some remain uncomfortable with the changing face of Canada and project their own insecurities onto the country, young Canadians are simply not concerned.

Many Canadians do worry that immigrants are not adopting Canadian values quickly enough. However, immigrants come to share the same values as other Canadians relatively quickly. Our survey showed that within one generation, the children of immigrants have virtually identical values as other young Canadians. Moreover, even first-generation Canadians take pride in Canada for the same reasons as non-immigrant Canadians.

That's the good news. However, although Canadians' attitudes toward diversity have changed, this does not mean that we live in a colour-blind society. Most Canadians, regardless of ethnic background, continue to believe that racism exists, and this belief is higher among immigrants. For example, about 65 per cent of young visible-minority immigrants believe the police show bias in their treatment of blacks and aboriginals. This experience of lived racism is a reality. In particular, new immigrants are not doing as well economically as they used to. In 1980, after being in Canada for 10 years, immigrants were earning as much as native-born Canadians. Today, those who've been here 10 years only earn about 83 per cent as much as native-born Canadians. Some groups, particularly some visible-minority groups, are threatened with social exclusion. In our survey, 61 per cent of Canadians agreed that success depends more on "who you know" than on how hard you work. This sense that many opportunities may be closed to new immigrants is a potential source of tension in the New Canada.

Moreover, the issues of Quebec and aboriginal peoples have not been addressed in the New Canadian nation. The claims of these groups, to different rather than simply equal status, do not fit easily with the official ideology of individual rights articulated in the Charter. Non-aboriginal Canadians outside Quebec continue to ignore the fact that almost half of francophone Quebeckers would like to secede from Canada and that aboriginal peoples have outstanding land claims and treaty rights. English-speaking Canadians express great affinity with and solidarity for aboriginal peoples and francophone Quebec, but appear to be unwilling to make any sacrifices to do anything about this.

One of the most important changes in Canada over the past decade has been Canadians' embrace of trade and globalization as part of the New Canadian national identity. Canadians are more engaged with the world than ever before, more prepared to work abroad, and see this international engagement as key to Canadian prosperity. "Internationalism" has now been incorporated into Canadians' identity. Consistent with our multicultural nature, Canadians believe we have a moral obligation to other countries, we would like to encourage the adoption of Canadian values abroad, and we believe these can be furthered by trade and engagement with the world.

Comparing who we once were to who we are today can be startling. It is not so long ago in Canada that aboriginals on reserves couldn't vote, non-whites could not immigrate, and there were quotas to make sure there weren't too many Jews at Canadian universities. When your kids get hold of the old yearbook, they no doubt laugh at your funny hair and strange clothes. In much the same way, the beliefs of Old Canada are equally anachronistic.

The New Canada is the Canada that we hoped to create in the 1970s. The values in the Charter of 1981 may not have reflected who we were as a country then, but it is those values which have created who we are as a country today. This is exactly what we'd hoped for.

PART II

MOVING UP, FALLING BEHIND

6

DREAMCHILD

ERIN ANDERSSEN

One in five Canadians in their 20s are the children of immigrants. Driven to make good on their parents' sacrifices, they tend to excel beyond their peers. Fahima Osman is more exceptional yet: At 25, she is a year away from becoming the first Canadian-trained physician in Toronto's large Somali community. And that's only a start.

THE ENVELOPE ARRIVED ON A TUESDAY, a sunny and hot June 4, 2000, just before 1 p.m.

All the Osmans remember it: The day before, Fahima and her mother had gone to the end of their street in Markham, Ont., to the brown super-mailboxes, shoving the key into 10A slot with their hearts pounding, only to find it empty. They knew the mailman delivered just after noon. They knew McMaster University had sent their answer off on Friday. Fahima hadn't slept all night; she had borrowed a cellphone to call the long list of family waiting to hear. On Tuesday, her mom, Zahra, who considers herself "a lucky woman," insisted on being

Photo by Tibor Kolley

the one to open the mailbox and reach inside. It was a package so deliciously fat and bulging, they didn't even have to open it. There was no mistaking what it said. Screaming, Fahima tackled her mother in a hug and kissed her. Zahra started crying. Her daughter was going to medical school. "I used to wonder how people cried with joy," Fahima, now 25, recalls. "That day I found out."

The next big date is May 14, 2004, when Fahima Osman will have earned the right to put two long-dreamed-of letters before her name. And in that moment, the Somali refugee – whose parents had no formal schooling, whose father nearly drowned trying to flee a life of poverty, and whose high-school guidance counsellor once warned her not to aim so high – will have become an original: the first Canadian-trained medical doctor in the country's largest African community.

To reckon with how far Fahima has come, you have to look back more than 50 years, to an enterprising 10-year-old named Adam Osman, born to a long line of nomads in the desert. He spent his early years wandering in the dust with the sheep and camels, trading for water or food and living under makeshift canopies of branches and cloth. Years later, when his children refused to finish their suppers, he would tell them about getting rationed his one cup of milk every second day.

Adam's mother died when he was little, and his father remarried. As the second-oldest boy among 12 children, he was sent to make his way in the northern city of Hargeysa, working for a local merchant and farmer. At 15, he learned to drive a taxi and he saved enough money to bring two brothers into the city, and send the youngest to school. But he had ambition and he was clever, and with a bit more money, he managed to buy a one-way ticket to Yemen, where he paid 500 Yemen shillings – a fortune – to join 100 other stowaways on an unstable fishing boat bound for the United Arab Emirates. Finally, approaching land after days of motoring, the boat began to sink. Adam Osman could not swim. But while people churned helplessly in the water around him, he was pulled to safety by one of the other passengers and dropped on the beach.

His luck held in Abu Dhabi: He landed a job with a Canadian oil company, and worked himself up to a public-relations position that saw him organizing visas and ferrying around staff members. He paid for more siblings to go to school.

At 38, well past the age Somali men typically marry, he decided he was settled enough and sent home to his brothers and father to look for a wife. The name they produced was Zahra Ali, the 17-year-old daughter of the now-deceased merchant who had given him his first break.

Zahra was nervous about marrying someone so old, but she knew the way of these things. "I didn't have a choice," she says now. "I respected my family." She was married in white in Abu Dhabi. Two years later, in April, 1978, their first daughter, Fahima, was born.

By the late 1980s, the Canadian oil company had come up dry. Adam was given six months' notice, and with no job, he was not allowed to stay in the U.A.E. But the couple could not go home. They had six young children, and the political situation in Somalia was deteriorating, heading toward civil war. Zahra's family fell on the wrong side: "If we had gone back, they would have killed me," she explains, wiping a finger across her throat.

Her husband, who knew his way around bureaucracy, got them all visas to the United States, and they spent everything they had to fly to New York City. They went to Buffalo and crossed over to Canadian soil in July, 1989, carrying nothing but a few bags and a framed wedding picture, and declared themselves refugees. The children spoke some English, with heavy accents, but their mother none at all. On the ride to Toronto, she watched the taxi driver speak into his radio and worried they were being kidnapped. In the back seat was Fahima, springy curls falling down past her shoulders, at 11.

Their story was by no means the worst. In those years, a flood of Somali refugees – including many single mothers – came directly to

Canada, arriving poor and traumatized by violence and famine. Most settled in Toronto, where they are now believed to form the largest African community in Canada. How large is unclear. The 2001 census records fewer than 20,000 Torontonians who named Somali as their ethnic origin, but Farah Khayre, co-ordinator at the African Canadian Social Development Council, estimates the number at closer to 60,000. People move often, she says, and may list themselves as African or be nervous about sharing personal information. The community is very young (almost half below the age of 15) and very poor, with an average income per adult of about $15,000, less than half the average for Toronto as a whole.

Somalis in Toronto have struggled to find affordable housing for their large families, Ms. Khayre says, and the parents, who see a growing generational gap, worry about keeping their children in school and out of gangs.

But in the past decade, they have formed outreach organizations and women's centres. The first Somali restaurant has been followed by about 30 more. They have begun to produce university graduates: While the three eldest Osman offspring remember being virtually alone in their first years at York University, they now see a crowd of Somali-Canadian freshmen.

In all that time, though, the community has yet to produce a doctor. There are at least two dentists, and an older, U.S.-trained psychiatrist in nearby Whitby, but Somali Torontonians have survived without a single family physician who could speak to them in their own language and relate to their largely Muslim culture. None of the Somali doctors who arrived as refugees have been able to get their foreign credentials recognized. Often, they work as counsellors or taxi drivers.

To Deqa Farah, a community mental-health consultant, Fahima's achievement is both a symbolic triumph for her young community and a practical necessity: No matter what she does after medical school, others will have an example to follow. "It means we are here," Ms. Farah says. "We are no longer a refugee community. We are citizens."

In the Osman home in Markham, Fahima's family is fast consuming a table loaded with baked chicken, rice and homemade samosas. There are at least four conversations under way.

Her youngest sister, Shukri, who turned 6 the day before, is proudly toting her new Barbies in a shopping bag. Her brothers, Mohamed and Hamza, have set up around a plastic table in the back yard with two cousins – their father, a banker in the U.A.E., was the first brother Adam Osman put through school. Fahima's mother straightens her hijab with an easy smile, and goes hunting for forks. Except during Ramadan, when they try to break the fast together, it is rare that her nine children are all under the same roof.

Though money is always tight, it is a given in the family that everyone will go to university – not college, their father tells them sternly, but a "brand name" education.

On that subject, Fahima's parents, who can read and write only a little English, are of one mind. Zahra has been the sole breadwinner since Adam fell ill and retired from his valet job; she keeps the house and works nights making humidifiers on the Emerson factory assembly line. Flanked warmly by her daughters in the kitchen, she describes what she wishes for her children: "Just work hard and have a good life." Hodan, the second oldest, laughs. "Notice the emphasis on hard work. There is no room for laziness."

The children have complied: Hodan, 23, has a business degree from York University and plans to get her MBA. Hibo, 22, is taking statistics. Mohamed, the eldest boy, is in computer science at Ryerson University. Huwaida, 18, wants to be a teacher.

And then there is Fahima, who came first and set the family bar. Her siblings, who gave her nicknames like Party Crasher and Mood Killer, tease her mercilessly about how she pulled all-nighters studying just to "get into" high school, how she decorated her room in A-pluses for motivation, how she made them watch medical documentaries and World Vision programs.

The conversation goes something like this:

"We'd watch them for hours," Hibo says. "The worst ones were the leprosy shows. I still can't get those out of mind."

"It was to remind us to be more grateful for what we had," Fahima protests.

"She once made me watch an episode of *Law and Order* and write a report on it," sister Deqa, 13, says.

"To practise writing," Fahima explains.

They all tell of the time Fahima returned home from university having had no food and seven cups of coffee. When her mother saw her quivering hands and head, studying was banned for the rest of the day.

"You wish you could have gotten that punishment," Fahima shrugs.

She is used to the ribbing. "You see my house," she says later. "Everyone's partying. I had to put those A's in front of me, to say, 'This is my focus.'"

It has been that way since she was six years old, still living in the U.A.E., and announced to her mom she wanted to be a doctor. "God willing," her mother answered, "you will be."

But like other children of immigrants, Fahima and her siblings now have an added motivation. They are the so-called second generation – who account for one in five Canadians in their 20s and who, despite lower family incomes, language barriers and less-educated parents, are outpacing their more settled Canadians peers in the race for higher education. According to the 2001 census, members of visible minorities in their 20s born in Canada but with parents from other countries were almost twice as likely to have a university degree as third-generation-plus white Canadians. Even those who arrived in the country young had higher levels of school attendance, and a higher presence in high-skilled occupations.

They get an extra push from their working-class parents, who do not want their sacrifices to be wasted. "It's not an accident that we are here," Hodan says. "We have a prophecy to fulfill."

The Osmans arrived with some advantages: They were not burdened with the first-hand trauma of war, and they had learned some

English in school, which they perfected watching soap operas and *The Simpsons*. But there was little money. Fahima took a paper route at 11 to help with the bills, and when they got jobs as teenagers, the older children helped cover the cost of clothes and school trips for the youngest.

At home, they had to tutor each other, and at school, they had to be their own advocates, translating for their mother at parent-teacher meetings (which, Hodan observes, had certain advantages).

But Fahima and her siblings all say they felt diminished by a school system that too easily slotted black kids into lower-level courses; this, they say, is the subtle form of racism they have experienced in Canada.

"You think, okay, people don't expect much of me," Hodan says. "I am going to use that to my advantage."

Fahima cannot name a single high-school teacher who inspired her toward medicine, but she does remember a Grade 10 biology teacher announcing to the class how impossible it was to become a doctor: "Do you think I'd be here if I'd made it?" She also remembers the guidance counsellor who looked at her low mark in calculus and refused to let her take the course over, suggesting that she was setting her goals too high.

Fahima was one of only two black students taking university-track courses, keeping her marks up while working part-time at a Hallmark card store and helping out at home. She stopped saying at school that she wanted to be a doctor, and Ms. Farah, who first met Fahima at 17, remembers her unhappiness.

She had looked within her community for doctors who could advise her and found none. "She was losing her confidence," she says. "She is a genuinely kind person, but she bruises easily. She needed encouragement and she wasn't getting it in school."

But her family pushed her forward, along with close high-school friends such as Sunita Chowmik, 22, another second-generation Canadian, who is now a teacher. After graduation, the two went together to York, where Fahima could always be found in her favourite spot, among the stacks near the second-floor balcony of the university library. She made a practice of parking in the most expensive lot on campus to force herself to study past 11:30 p.m., when the attendant left and she wouldn't have to pay. Her life, except for chatting in coffee shops or going to the movies (she loves goofy comedies like *Dumb and Dumber*), was all about studying. "If I really wanted to pull an all-nighter," Ms. Chowmik says, "I'd stay with her."

That night, after the Sunday dinner at the Osmans, Fahima's brother Mohamed sends an e-mail. He is worried, he writes, that in all the funny stories, the truth did not get out – that Fahima has also been the generous big sister who helped mediate between the parents, who helped all the siblings with homework and gave them a model to follow. "I wanted," he says, "to do what she did."

In the summer before she graduated from York, Fahima went back to Somalia, and had her eyes opened. She was already planning to apply to medical school, but her backup plan was to work for an aid agency. She talked her way into an unpaid internship, split between Save the Children and CARE International. It was not a perfect experience: Looking back, she says, she spent too much time in meetings, and too little time on the ground with people.

But not even her endless viewing of World Vision programming had prepared her for what she saw – the life she could have led, had fate gone a different way. She remembers starving children wandering the streets without clothes, and the lone hospital that was missing technical things such as medical supplies and equipment, and human things like curtains between the beds.

Clearest in her mind is one conversation she had with a young woman seven months pregnant, whom she met sipping water in the sunset at a roadside café. The woman said she was hoping for a daughter, because her three other daughters had all died before they reached their first birthday. There was something about the matter-of-fact way she said it that stunned Fahima; though Somali, she was seeing their world with Canadian eyes.

"It's something normal to them, losing their children," she recalls. "They have a word for it, *iga saqeeruy*."

The woman told her how mothers were left to die when they could not produce the $40 in American money – or a necklace or bracelet in barter – for the cost of a cesarean section. Women had taken to starving themselves when they were pregnant, so that they could have easier births. She asked a doctor about it. "It's gotten to the point," he told her, "where I am delivering skeletons."

At the café, with the sun dropping in the desert, she told the woman about her plans to be a doctor. The woman leaned forward and said, "You must come back. Once people get out, they forget to come back and help us."

When Fahima got home, she worked harder than ever. "I was so motivated to get into medical school. It was a lot of sleepless nights. When you know what your life would have been like, versus how it is now, you just have to work hard." She told her family that if she didn't get in, she would keep applying until she was 55.

But of course, she did. In her second year, with one left to go, Fahima is aware of being unique. In a diverse class, with student backgrounds from around the world, she is the only African. But it has been that way at school for much of her life – and it has mostly come in handy. In a group of 128, people remember her.

It has even paid off in the operating room, where students stand for hours, their main official responsibility to hold organs out of the way of the scalpel, while the surgeons rapid-fire questions at them. "You're the target," she says. But in Fahima's case, they sometimes forget to quiz her because they are so curious about her background.

At Hamilton's McMaster University, learning is done in groups, not lectures. Fahima says she had to get over being shy to speak in front of people, but now her class is a close group, who got together on Wednesdays to watch *The Bachelor* and vote on which bride-wannabe should be next to go.

On request, Fahima enthusiastically rhymes off a list of diseases that fascinate her, and makes the kind of statement that gets her teased at home: "I really like reading about the acute abdomen." Her career goal has shifted from obstetrics to general surgery; her final decision will be based largely on what would be most useful in Africa. She plans to divide her time between practising in Canada, the country that trained her, and working in Somalia, the country that needs her badly. She will never go to the United States, she says, no matter how much money she could make (and she will graduate with $100,000 debt in student and bank loans): "I am Canadian first."

But she strongly believes she has a duty to give up movies and ice-cold Cokes and go to the desert where there is electricity only half the day, the hospitals shelves are always empty and people die daily from medical problems she could solve. She has started a student group for international medicine. Dr. Goffredo Arena, who was the resident on her surgical clerkship this spring, recalls Fahima as the first person he ever met who said she wanted to be a surgeon so she could travel to a developing country and help people.

"We're all brothers and sisters in the world," Fahima says earnestly. "We all have a duty to help each other. It was just a matter of luck that we're born privileged and not a kid starving in Africa."

Her teachers and mentors see this as one of Fahima's greatest gifts. She has not forgotten her roots. While many of her peers come from privileged, educated families, she had to find her own role models outside of her community – and she understands the importance now of being one. "She sees the world in a different way," says Dr. Samantha Nutt, the executive director of War Child Canada, who has helped to coach Fahima through medical school. "You just know she is going to accomplish great things."

The envelope that arrived that day in June and changed her life is now stored carefully in a file folder, which travels everywhere with her.

"I look at it every time I get frustrated, to remind me how much I wanted to get in."

And to remember why.

NAME THAT COUNTRY

What a difference a few decades make. Scan a sampling of names, taken alphabetically, from past graduating classes at the University of Toronto medical school. Now look at the names for this year's class, and find the new face of a changing nation.

1953

Norman Douglas Abbey, Jacob Lionel Adelberg, Philip Morton Alderman, James Edward Anderson, Robert Odillo Antoni, Harvey Lloyd Atin, Stanley Theodore Bain, Harvey Alexander Barnett, Wellington Johnston Barnett, Donald Alvin Barr, Edmond Geoffrey Beatty, Alexander Graham Bell, David Nelson Bell, Bennie Berman, William Lyle Black, Roman Bladek, Jack Donald Blanchard, Charles Balzie, Frederick Leonard Boughen, Earl Brightman, James Macburney Brisby, Joseph Norman Burkholder, Dorothy Fay Burton, Bartley Douglas Campbell, Max Marcus Carson . . .

1983

Jeffrey Paul Abrahams, Judith Ruth Abrams, Mark Accardo, Linda Marie Alison, Demo Arrizza, Mark David Atin, Jonathan Aziza, Christopher Henry Barnes, Donna Marie Battaglia, Heather A. Baxter, Valerie Anne Bayley, Natalie Baziuk, Rafik Robert Bechbache, Steven Eric Berdock, David Ben Ian Birbrager, John Robert M. Boersma, James Edward Bolton, Paul Frederick Boughen, Gerard John Bruin,

James Douglas Burrows, Paul Robert Callegari, Louis Fabrizio Canella, Roman John Chaban, David Hung Chi Chan, Neil Gerard Chang, Davy Chung Huen Cheng, Shing Sou Richard Cheng...

2003

Feisal Akbar Adatia, Anju Anand, Liane Rachel Bacal, Akshay Bagai, Vikas Kumar Bansal, Philippe Bedard, Paul James Belletrutti, Roberta Audrey Berard, Steven Jason Bernstein, Murray Jeffery Beuerlein, Michael Bezuhly, Aditya Bharatha, Daniel Michael Blumberger, Andrea Kristine Boggild, Karen Lynne Booth, Kylie Anne Booth, Jennifer Brunton, Philip Michael Buckler, Barry Robert Cayen, Patrick Cervini, Ronnie Si-Wah Chan, Martin C. Chang, Christopher Anthony Kui Yew Chong, Julie Pei-Yi Chou, Catherine Tse-Shing Chung, Doreen Eleanor Chung, Hance Alex Clarke, Blaise Clarkson, Errol Colak, Julie Anne Copeland, Simone Suzanne Cowan, Sharon Lynn Cushing, Mark Philip DaCambra, Rosemin Darani, Peter James Darby, Stephen William Daunt, Tom Deklaj, Sandra Lynn Demaries, Irfan Amir Nurmahomed Dhalla, Solange Marie Dias, David Patrick DiCiommo, Brendan Craig Dickson, Lukasz Drzymala, Amber Dawn Dudar, Jeremy Mithiran Edwards, Michael Peter Fielden, Yael Friedman, Maria Kazimiera Gibbons, Aviv Gladman, Kumudini Gnanapandithen . . .

BRAIN TRUST

The secret to the success of children of immigrants lies, in large part, in the stern words they hear at the dinner table: I gave up everything for you. You will graduate from university.

They listen. What's more, says University of Toronto sociologist Monica Boyd, at university they outpace young Canadians who by the most obvious measures – income, parents' education, language and race – grow up with the advantage.

The gap is even wider, Prof. Boyd observes, for immigrant offspring who belong to a visible minority; according to data collected by the 2001 census, people in their 20s who fall into this group are almost twice as likely to have a university degree as those whose parents were both born in Canada.

It is the same for school attendance: More than half (54 per cent) of those in their 20s with two foreign-born parents belonging to a visible minority were in school in 2001, compared with 31 per cent of their white and aboriginal peers with Canadian-born parents. Restricting the comparison to urban populations narrows the gap, but does not eliminate it.

In fact, young people with one immigrant parent and one Canadian-born parent get educated at a lower rate than those with two foreign-born parents. "People move huge distances, change cultures because they are prone to succeed," Prof. Boyd says. "Their kids come into the classroom knowing they have to succeed. They are told, 'This is your chance.'"

But there are also other factors. Immigrant families tend be more tightly knit because they arrived here knowing no one else, and often come from cultures where parents hold strict authority. Their children often benefit also from being part of a close ethnic community that tends to take a broader responsibility for the raising of families, and offsets some of the difficulties of single parents.

But not all groups are equally successful. Chinese Canadians, for instance, tend to perform better on paper than Caribbean Canadians. There is also some difference between families that arrive as selected, skilled immigrants and those who come as refugees. Refugee parents, hampered by language and suffering, may have a harder time negotiating their new society, including the school system.

One in five Canadians 20 to 29 years old are second-generation, amounting to 730,000 people, the largest count in any age group. Their attitudes are remarkably similar to people in their 20s with Canadian-born parents, according to the New Canada poll. Their age group universally ranked multiculturalism and the Charter of Rights and Freedoms as high sources of Canadian pride, but second-generation 20s ranked them the highest.

They were slightly more likely to say that people were judged on their ethnicity, not hard work, and that who you know counts in the workplace. And although 67 per cent said ethnicity was important to their identity, the number of immigrant offspring who ranked a shared ethnicity as important when looking for a spouse was only 17 per cent – and the longer they had been in Canada, the less important they considered it.

It's not yet known whether their credentials will help them overcome some of the traditional barriers that have confronted visible-minority groups, but these young Canadians have already defined themselves as hard workers: Children of immigrants are the most likely to be holding down a full-time job even while attending university full-time.

When they graduate, according the census, immigrant offspring in their 20s have a higher concentration in highly skilled occupations. About 26 per cent work in the business or financial sector, compared with 15 per cent of 20-to-29-year-olds with Canadian-born parents, and they are also slightly more likely to be in the natural or applied sciences, and equally present in health care. (They are underrepresented in primary industries such as agriculture and forestry, in part because immigrant communities are more likely to be urban.)

"They're coming out of the starting blocks with what we have always told people they need to get ahead," Prof. Boyd says. "Can they maintain it? That is the question to be answered in the future."

7

OFF THE FAST TRACK

MICHAEL VALPY

They belong to the best-educated generation Canada has ever produced, but many – especially the boys – are taking their time to get there. Or even what to major in. To their elders, some of these wayward sons and daughters look like they're messing up their futures in a competitive job market. But often, today's late bloomers are wrestling with a philosophical dilemma: How can they make a difference in the world without copying their parents' frantic lives?

FOR ALL THAT THE WORLD CAN SEE ONE evening on Spanish Banks beach, Trevor Kinsey is a man without a care. He looks, at 26, like a slightly eccentric scientist. He is rumpled and boyish. His haircut can be described as accidental. He has a sunny smile.

He is walking on his hands before an audience of fellow graduates from Vancouver's Kitsilano Secondary School, members of the Kits class of '94. "I only learned how to do this two weeks ago," he tells them.

Photo by John Lehmann

He falls over after two steps, gets up and tries again. And falls again.

Mr. Kinsey, in fact, is stressed. In three days he will marry Trish Wong, 25. And after a year of brooding about what he is doing with his life, he has decided to abandon one career path and head back to university to start another. He has a bachelor of science degree in physics from the University of British Columbia, a diploma in robotics from the B.C. Institute of Technology and a job at a UBC physics laboratory. And he has concluded that he is stagnating. He is not being creative. He is babysitting machines, he says. "I want to be constructive and help people with their lives. Since I've been studying physics and robotics, I've put all this human stuff on the back burner and I realize it's important to me."

He intends to return to UBC in September to become a high-school physics teacher.

The audience for Mr. Kinsey's handstands know this story because, in one form or another, it is their story, too. It's also a familiar story to Margaret Pederson, their counsellor at Kitsilano Secondary School for five years, who arranged for the group – friends with one another in high school – to talk about their outward-bound journeys from Grade 12.

Ms. Pederson had no inkling that just about all of them would turn out to have boarded a slow boat to wherever it is they're going – especially the boys. They're travelling along what education researchers prosaically label the "indirect path" through postsecondary education toward the world of work. They belong to the best-educated generation Canada has ever produced, but they're taking their time getting there. And the evidence, while patchy, suggests it's what Canadians in their 20s are doing in huge numbers.

Meandering. Searching. Being cautious. Deciding that they've wound up on the wrong path and changing directions. Being very, in a word, postmodern.

Many spoke in interviews about feeling overwhelmed by options, and at the same time not pressured to fit in, free to search for a future to fit their ideals. Many are confused by the message that they'll have multiple careers in their lifetimes. Many look at their work-stressed and job-drudged parents and say that isn't for them.

And a lot of them leave high school feeling lost, especially the boys. "The boys," says Ms. Pederson flatly, "don't think it through."

Ken Annandale, a former high-school principal and now a consultant to the Vancouver School Board, says that, since the 1990s, the indirect path has been "pretty consistent" and "closer to the norm than not."

Not surprisingly, this is contributing to a demographic change in the life stages young Canadians go through. Their average age to move out of their parents' home is up to 27. Fertility rates for young women are about half what their mothers' were at their age, and the average age of childbearing has climbed back to Second World War levels, when men were in military service.

Professor Lesley Andres of the University of British Columbia's department of educational studies has likely done the most thorough Canadian research into the meandering path to higher education, and she cautions that the figures don't exist – in Canada or elsewhere – to support the view that many young adults are lost and wandering. The appropriate national studies have never been done, she says.

Her own research, a 10-year look at more than 1,000 students who graduated from B.C. high schools in 1988, found that 95 per cent entered some postsecondary educational institution. About 65 per cent took the direct path to completion of a program within five years. But of those who went to university, 46 per cent of women and 61 per cent of men failed to complete a four-year bachelor's degree within five years. There are no comparable historical studies, Prof. Andres says, and no recent figures that could indicate if the indirect path is broadening.

In Europe, postsecondary education studies describe a generation living "destandardized, disordered and detraditionalized existences" where, in the words of one academic, "the notion of a 'normal biography' becomes less tenable in aiding our understanding of the courses of complex lives." In other words, if the literature is to be believed, young Europeans have abandoned life's templates and are scattered to the winds.

Young Americans? They appear rather less spontaneous. The U.S. National Education Longitudinal Study suggests those who proceed to postsecondary education are more inclined to stay in the traces and complete their certificates, diplomas or degrees from high school.

Kitsilano Secondary is a 1,200-student high school on Vancouver's west side. The neighbourhood is home to professional and well-to-do business people as well as blue-collar workers and every gradient in between. It draws students from across the city because it is a French-immersion school.

Here are some of the stories from the Class of '94:

Dustin Quezada, 26, bearded and articulate, thought he knew everything he needed to know when he graduated from Kits. Life was his oyster, and he wanted to play – to party, drink beer, go to concerts, woo girls and play hockey with the guys. Hockey is his addiction.

He didn't apply to college or university. "I wasn't ready." He worked full-time for a year as a grocery clerk and then drove across Canada with two friends. The following year he enrolled at Carleton University in Ottawa, intending to study journalism and become a hockey writer. He had fun. He had bad grades. He felt guilty about his mother and stepfather (his parents divorced when he was two) paying his tuition and living costs. His father died at the end of the year. "I am sure there are manuals out there to tell you how to deal with that, but I haven't found them."

He dropped out.

"I regret that," he says. "It would have been nice to keep going."

He came home. Most of his male friends from Kits were drifting. "None of us was really forging ahead. The girls, most of our girlfriends from high school, they all went straight into university." Why the difference? "I think women are little bit more motivated. They have to overcome" – he searches a moment for the word – "disadvantage. My ex-girlfriend figured women were better planners; they're better at time maintenance."

He recalls classmate Rachel Engler-Stringer, his date for the Kits graduation party, lecturing him and his male friends about goofing off. Ms. Engler-Stringer, 26, an academic's daughter, is one year from completing her PhD in nutrition research at the University of Saskatchewan. She writes in an e-mail: "I find it entertaining that men I graduated with said that I told them to get their shit together (probably not the language they used, but let's be honest). That is certainly something I would have said back then."

Mr. Quezada recently quit work as a valet car-parker, a job he's held since 1999, "hustling around for rich people, hoping they'd fork out money," he says with distaste. He earned a certificate in desktop publishing from BCIT. He's now halfway through a two-year journalism course at Vancouver's Langara College. He is getting good marks.

What happened? He and his guy friends, he says, started to wake up.

He wants to get married and have children. He wants to buy property outside Vancouver. He wants to buy a truck for his hockey and camping gear. "All my guy friends, we have the truck dream."

He now wishes he had taken life more seriously. His generation, he says, faces fewer jobs and more competition. "Over all I think our generation does have to work harder." He says that if he'd stayed at Carleton, he could have been on track earlier. "I told my mom recently, 'You got to kick me in the ass a few more times.'"

Alda Ngo, 26, the effervescent Canadian-born daughter of Vietnamese immigrants, grew up on Vancouver's east side and came to Kitsilano Secondary for French.

She and Mr. Kinsey became friends in Grade 9 social studies. Two years after graduation, they platonically shared an apartment until

Ms. Ngo fell in love with Sean Fulton and asked Mr. Kinsey to move out so that Mr. Fulton – her musician husband since last August – could move in.

Ms. Ngo's parents were determined she would be a doctor. "I think even before I was conceived this was the plan for me," she says. She, however, was having doubts in high school about a career in conventional medicine. She was attracted to the environmental movement and what she calls life's "moral alternative flavour." She went straight from high school to UBC, but at the end of her first year began to rebel. "I couldn't tell if I was becoming a doctor because my parents wanted me to or because I wanted to."

She moved out of her family home, the first among her friends to do so. She found a bachelor apartment in Kitsilano (when Mr. Kinsey moved in, he slept on the balcony) and supported herself with student loans and by working with Mr. Kinsey at a day centre for teenagers with disabilities.

She went to Vietnam for three months to discover her cultural roots. "My parents really objected because I was taking time off from school, and a good Vietnamese girl just doesn't do that." But the experience, she says, left her "glowing."

She returned to university for two years, dutifully aiming herself at premedical studies, but found it competitive and impersonal. She then dropped out for another term – her "little anti-establishment phase," as she called it. "It was very dramatic. I even wrote letters to my parents and told them I'm sorry but I think I've been lying to you; I don't want to be a doctor and I'm not in school this term. It was a very hard time." She went through several jobs in the restaurant industry ("I never made it to waitress"), started panicking, went back to UBC for her fourth year in biology rather than premed, and obtained her bachelor's degree.

In the end she did decide to become a licensed practitioner – of Chinese traditional medicine – and has one year left of a four-year program. "The holism of it resonates with me. It's the medicine they practise in Vietnam. I can talk to my grandma about it. I'm going to be a doctor after all."

Kevin Hunter, 26, plays hockey with Mr. Quezada three or four nights a week. He exudes confidence, talks a rapid-fire patter, has an Approach – with a capital A – to life. He arrives at a Broadway coffee shop wearing shorts and a baseball cap perched on his curly red hair.

He graduated from Kits having no idea what to do. He'd thought earlier about a career in law, but changed his mind, he says, after spending a day with a corporate lawyer. "It didn't strike me as very fulfilling. I'm a little bit pragmatic. If I think I know what I want then I go and do it. But if I don't really know then I'll hang back and think things over."

He worked for a year as a waiter. He went to Japan for four months to earn a community-college hospitality certificate working at a ski resort. One day on a train to Tokyo, he decided to study kinesiology. "My mum is in the fitness industry. It's almost like a genetic predisposition. I've been exercising in a gym my whole life."

He studied two years at Langara, transferred to the University of Victoria and spent the next four years getting a degree. His parents had retired in Victoria. He lived in a basement suite in their house. He worked part-time. He graduated, came back to Vancouver and got a job in a sports medicine and orthotics store. He's now manager. He says he learns something new on the job every day; he says it's a fit with his education.

And then he says: "Now I'm at the point of my life where I'm looking forward to nailing down specifically what it is I can see myself doing for the rest of my life. The second stage of my education."

What's wrong with his job? "The financials," he says. "I only get paid about 25 grand a year, so it's disgraceful."

He says he is considering three options: a medical degree, a master's degree in physiotherapy or some other path into academia. He says he doesn't want a job like the one his father had as a Telus manager, something that's just a job. He wants to be fulfilled. He wants to be challenged.

Peter Zerbinos's parents own the Broadway Bakery in Kitsilano. His mother Pat's spinach pies, he says, have been rated the city's best by a Vancouver newspaper.

Mr. Zerbinos, 26, big, good-looking, athletically built, had no plan after high school. But everyone he knew was taking some post-secondary education, so he enrolled in Kwantlen University College in nearby Richmond and, he emphatically says, wasted a year and a half. "It was probably the worst mistake of my life. I wasn't into it. I wasn't getting good grades. I was wasting my parents' money."

He dropped out. He went to work in the bakery, but his father Jerry declared he wouldn't have his son following in his footsteps, working from 4 a.m. to 6 in the evening. He got a unionized job packing groceries at Stong's, the local supermarket, and within a short time was earning $20 an hour. "As a 21-year-old kid, it was pretty good money. I was living at home rent-free and I had all this cash. It was a good job – and you get stuck in it so easily." He stayed at Stong's for four years.

Then two summers ago he went travelling in Europe with a group of friends and, like Mr. Quezada, woke up. "I decided I'd got to do something with my life. I can't work at Stong's forever."

He went back to community college to study human kinetics. Now, two years later with a record of good grades, he has applied to UBC to study to become a physical-education and history teacher. "I can't think of anything more I'd love to do," he says. "I'm pretty sure I'm going to get in."

Of course, some of the Class of '94 went straight like arrows. Like Ms. Engler-Stringer. And the Fassler twins, Nicos and Larissa, who rode the bus from West Vancouver with Trevor Kinsey every morning across the harbour to French immersion at Kits.

Larissa knew where she was going the moment she graduated: to Concordia University in Montreal to study art. She began having her own shows after university. She now lives in Berlin with her French husband and this year is doing further studies in London. Nicos was only slightly less decided than his sister. He went directly to university and got his bachelor's degree, but needed convincing he should be in law. He is now articling with Ontario's Ministry of the Attorney-General. He wants to do criminal litigation for the Crown.

Mr. Kinsey, thinking about his new career, says he is a tinkerer by nature.

He has an electronics lab in his and Ms. Wong's top-floor apartment and he is planning to build a device that will regulate the temperature by opening and closing windows.

His tinkering, he says, "will help me make interesting demos. Or lead a club after school hours."

Education earned

The University of British Columbia studied educational
levels achieved by the high school class of 1988.

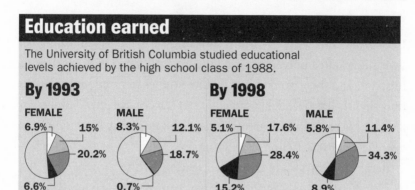

By 1993

FEMALE
6.9%   15%
20.2%
6.6%

MALE
8.3%   12.1%
18.7%
0.7%

By 1998

FEMALE
5.1%   17.6%
28.4%
15.2%

MALE
5.8%   11.4%
34.3%
8.9%

□ No post-secondary   □ Diploma   ■ Bachelors degree
■ Professional degree □ Other outcomes

SOURCE: UNIVERSITY OF BRITISH COLUMBIA   THE GLOBE AND MAIL

Parental influence

Respondents were asked who had the most influence
on their higher-education decisions, the mother or father.

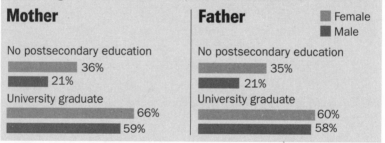

Mother

■ Female
■ Male

Father

No postsecondary education
36%
21%

No postsecondary education
35%
21%

University graduate
66%
59%

University graduate
60%
58%

SOURCE: UNIVERSITY OF BRITISH COLUMBIA   THE GLOBE AND MAIL

Marital status

Percentage of those respondents who are married
or living in a marriage-like relationship.

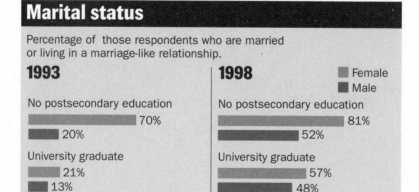

1993

1998

■ Female
■ Male

No postsecondary education
70%
20%

No postsecondary education
81%
52%

University graduate
21%
13%

University graduate
57%
48%

SOURCE: UNIVERSITY OF BRITISH COLUMBIA   THE GLOBE AND MAIL

8

OFF THE BOOKS

MICHAEL VALPY

A software developer in training, a young auto-body painter, an apprentice hotel chef – what do they have in common? They are young people in Sudbury, Ont., who realized the holy grail of the university degree was not for them and, with a little help from the government, rediscovered the nobility of the skilled trades. Some experts say Canada has succeeded a bit too well in convincing its youth of the need for post-secondary education: A nation needs its plumbers, mechanics and electricians, too.

IT'S A HARD-HAT CITY, SUDBURY, BUILT ON – and blasted out of – the hardrock of the Canadian Shield. There's a university and two community colleges here, and a newly opened medical school to keep young doctors in Northern Ontario, but the life, culture and economy of the place remain in thrall to the surrounding mines, and the road to the future for too many, if not most, of the community's young people is four hours along the Trans-Canada Highway to Toronto.

That said, the dreams and values of New Canada are as deep in Sudbury, population 155,000, as the shafts at its Inco nickel mine, as deep as in Vancouver, Toronto or Montreal. Just different, maybe . . . with a northern flavour of their own, stamped with pragmatism, rooted maybe in another kind of imagination of what life holds. Or maybe not. Canadians in their 20s, wherever they live and whatever they choose to do with their lives, have a remarkably similar vision.

This is a story of three young men, apprentices in skilled trades.

They're the products of what is turning out to be an astonishingly successful venture, the Ontario Youth Apprenticeship Program – astonishing, because skilled-trade apprenticeships these past few decades have been barely an afterthought in the nation's education ministries spending of billions of public dollars on universities and colleges in response to young Canadians' wholehearted embrace of the message that postsecondary education is the key to the good life.

But while all the surveys show Canada's newest adults to be deeply imbued with values of confidence in the future, idealism, creativity, attachment to a liberal, inclusive society and the dreams of a fulfilled life, not all of their dreams lead through a classroom.

Take Emmanuel Diaz, 21. On the dot of 11 a.m., as a visitor's car pulls up, Mr. Diaz, in white shirt and tie, is standing at the door of Aurora Microsystems Distribution Inc. at an industrial mall on Sudbury's outskirts. A brisk handshake, an introduction to Aurora president Kevin Fitzgerald, a gesture to a workspace beside the receptionist's cubicle – "This is my desk" (a framed photograph of his girlfriend of four years next to the computer monitor) – and Mr. Diaz leads his visitor into the company boardroom to talk.

He is an information technology apprentice, a computer software boffin-in-training. The first thing he did when Aurora took him on salaried staff a year ago was buy a car. "Before that my mum dropped me off and picked me up every day." The image amuses him. "'Mum, can you drive me to that business meeting I have?' It was funny at times." But not that funny, and not part of Emmanuel Diaz's self-image. The words that define Mr. Diaz are focused, determined, confident, very, very adult. And articulate.

"I've always been driven to succeed," he says, sitting at the board-room table. "I've always really had that . . . just wanting to do well for myself, force myself to figure things out and not procrastinate." Yes, he considered going to university after high school. "But I was never really fond of the idea. I guess you can say some people learn differently. I always found I never learnt very well in a classroom environment. I've always lived very well with a hands-on environment; I like to actually be in an environment, doing it, not learning it out of a book. It's great for some people" – the book-learning – "but for me it didn't do it."

Enter OYAP. Sudbury school board's OYAP coordinator Sharon Orlak identifies students like Mr. Diaz, helps them define their dreams for their futures, finds local companies that will offer them co-op placements while they're still in school – providing them with credits toward graduation – and then seamlessly morphs them into apprentices after high-school graduation, if necessary arranging wage subsidies for up to half a year through the Ontario education ministry's JobConnect program. The apprentices follow a skills-learning regimen set by industry. Their proficiency is certified by their employer and by the ministry at the end – after two or three years – and, since OYAP's inception three years ago, more than 200 students in Sudbury (a significant statistic, given Sudbury's size, says Ms. Orlak) have taken advantage of it, young Canadians who might otherwise have become dropout statistics, social and economic left-behinds.

Ms. Orlak brought Emmanuel Diaz and Aurora together, and now he dreams. Within 10 years, he plans to have his own information technology consulting business. Maybe in Vancouver, he thinks, where both he and his girlfriend have family. He may need to have an MBA to run a successful business? "I'll hire one," says Mr. Diaz.

He has no doubts – "Definitely not. No" – that he's taken the right path. He does not feel that forsaking a college or university education will leave him at a disadvantage. "I've heard the statistics, like half of people who enter university first year fail out, and you think, 'Oh jeez, is that really the right thing for me to do, or should I stick to something that's a little more solid or concrete that can get you there?' I've always believed that if you want to get somewhere and you put the effort in, you'll get there. I've had people tell me, 'If you don't go to university or college, how are you going to get a job anywhere in all this uncertainty?' I don't believe that a piece of paper can actually govern what your future is going to hold for you. If I'm going for a job, the employer might be able to look at me and say, 'He has five years experience in the industry' and he looks at someone else, and he says, 'Well, he has a degree, but he's never worked in the industry.' Now, how do you measure that? I guess it really depends on the individual who's doing the hiring."

He adds, "If it doesn't work out, I'll figure away around it. Like I've done most of the time."

He knows about the after-high-school drifters. "Yup, I know all about that. Every young person is faced with that problem. 'When high school ends, what do I want to do? What courses am I going to take? Do I really want to do this?' With the drifting, it's kind of like they're discovering what they want to do."

Mr. Diaz did his drifting, but he did it before, not after, high school ended.

He did co-op programs all the way through school, encouraged by his immigrant parents (his father, a musician, grew up in Hong Kong, his mother in Venezuela and Italy). "They had that kind of old-school work ethic." He started working at a restaurant at 13 when he thought he wanted to be a chef and later decided that was not for him. Then he did a co-op placement at a graphics design firm until he concluded that's not what he wanted to do. Then came the IT co-op and apprenticeship at Aurora, and bingo! He says, with utter conviction: "It's going to open up doors."

Philip Deredin, 21, is going to be a chef. Sitting in the empty dining room of Sudbury's Howard Johnson Plaza Hotel in the early afternoon just before his shift begins, he says: "It's all I've ever wanted to be. I love food. I absolutely love food." He watches the food shows on television like other people watch golf. Although he does that, too. "That's my other passion, sports. I'm a huge hockey, football and golf fan. Big time. Huge." He's just got cable in his apartment. He gets home from work at night, turns on the TV, and channel surfs between TSN and the food network.

Mr. Deredin started working as a dishwasher at the Howard Johnson when he was 14 – six-hour shifts, Fridays, Saturdays and Sundays – and one night soon after he started he had what he describes as an epiphanal moment. He was told to collect the dirty dishes from the main cooks, the line chefs as they're called in the business. "It was really busy, and I saw them rocking, and just knowing exactly what they were doing, putting plates together, and something kind of hit me inside. I've been here ever since."

When he was 17 and in Grade 12, the head of the hotel's food department heard about OYAP and, knowing how much Mr. Deredin wanted to be a chef, suggested he apply. Mr. Deredin spoke to Ms. Orlak whose office is in Sudbury High School where he was a student. She made the arrangements. Doors sprung open. "As soon," says Mr. Deredin, "as my boss got word that I was in the program, he moved me up to prep cook. You're not cooking at all. You're just prepping the food for that day or the next day. You peel carrots and potatoes." But no more dishwashing. He was on the road.

Nearly three years later, he's now a short-order cook – "They moved me right past salads" – and in charge of the hotel's Sunday brunch. His voice sparkles with enthusiasm as he talks about his work. "I enjoy short order. I like the speed. I like the responsibility. That's my area, and I know my area. I've been doing short order for two years, and I know it like the back of my hand. It just feels good to be able to do something so well."

He left the hotel briefly to work in another restaurant where he thought his chances of being promoted to line chef might come sooner, but he didn't like it. "Everything was written down, and you just had to read and throw in. I'm more spontaneous than just throw-it-in."

Indeed, yes. One of the defined values of Canadians in their 20s is spontaneity. And creativity. At Sunday brunch, he says, "I get to show my fancier skills doing buffets, garnishing the platters, like the way I do the tomato rows . . . it just comes to me. When I was younger, this is a long time ago, I wanted to be an architect, and architecture is a lot of designing and using your imagination. Cooking is the same way. You design a lot of different dishes, and the style goes into the plate."

No less than other young Canadians of his generation, Mr. Deredin has dreams. He dreams about one day owning his own sports bar offering truly great food. "Putting my two favourite things together [sports and cooking] would be my ultimate dream," he says. He dreams of completing his apprenticeship with a truly great chef. "I'm not knocking this place at all, but I'd like to get on my résumé a more well-known place." So he dreams of apprenticing under Prince Edward Island's Michael Smith, The Inn Chef of television's Food Network, whose program Mr. Deredin religiously watches. "He's so very good at presenting his food and talking about it, and he seems really good with people, a good communicator. I'm a pretty good communicator, that's why I'm in charge of Sunday brunch because I'm good with customers, talking to customers."

Does he feel at a disadvantage to his friends who have gone on to college and university? Mr. Deredin thinks about this for a moment. "They seem to use bigger words," he says, "and they might know how to spell a little better, and they might be better at Trivial Pursuit than I would be, because I don't go to school any more. They might know slightly more things than me, because of professors and things like that, because that's what they want to do. They're learning from these professors, whereas I've wanted to learn from chefs instead. I'm very happy with what I've chosen in my life."

Scott Gagné, too, had an epiphanal moment about his future, albeit different from Philip Deredin's. He was in jail, doing 60 days for dealing marijuana. He was 19 and he and his girlfriend had an infant son and he was still in school and, as he says, "it was taking me a little while to get through." And doing time in jail, "I realized it's not fun. Sixty days is not a lot of time, but it turned my life around. Here I was, free to do whatever I wanted, but I got stuck in there. So I chose to live a better life."

Police and young offenders courts would love him.

One of his teachers at Sudbury High School mentioned that he knew of an auto body shop – Regent Carstar Collision – that would take on a co-op student. Mr. Gagné figured out that, working at the body shop as a co-op student, he could complete the credits he needed for high-school graduation. Ms. Orlak plugged him into OYAP with a six-month wage subsidy. Today, at 21, with son James almost 3, Mr. Gagné is an apprentice auto-painter. The auto-body shop owners knew he'd been in jail. "But they thought I was a good guy, a nice guy."

He had a choice for his apprenticeship: auto-painting or collision repair. He started off as a collision-repair apprentice but that lost its appeal and – his drift – he switched to painting. "I really don't like to change panels and straighten frames and all that. Other guys like it more than doing what I do, but I just like to do what I do. I can do the bodywork, too. But I like to see the end result, the finished product, and know that it's me who did that."

He's been to a paint-company sponsored training course in Toronto. "The owners set it all up. I stayed at a hotel and everything. It was pretty nice down there." He loves being a father. His girlfriend, Kim, is completing a paramedic's program at Sudbury's Cambrian College.

With a full-time job and a three-year-old son – all at the age of 21, cemented into adult life – does he feel he's missing out on anything that maybe his friends are doing? "Most of them are in jail," replies Mr. Gagné. "But, yeah, sometimes I feel . . . like, I like to do a lot of hunting and fishing, and a lot of hunting and fishing is during the week when I'm working here, and I miss hanging out with my friends. But then again, as long as I'm here I'm staying out of trouble is the way I look at it. I make a good living. I make good money. I'd rather make legit money. The people are great to work with here. I prefer this. This is my thing."

And where does he dream of being in five or 10 years? "Here," says Mr. Gagné.

Over lunch in a Sudbury restaurant, Sharon Orlak and her superintendent, Bryan Slywchuk, allow themselves a little philosophizing. They worry about the exodus of Sudbury's young people, about them going down the road. The city's population actually fell by more than 6 per cent between 1996 and 2001, the largest urban decrease in Canada. They worry about how to keep them at home yet let them follow their aspirations to a fulfilled life. Canadians, they say, have admirably bought into the notion of the need for education after high school; the country's postsecondary education participation rate is unrivalled in the developed world. Yet the focus has become a little skewed, and the mindset that success in Canadian life is out of reach without a university degree or college diploma is not only wrong but also potentially damaging. Not every young person is suited for university or college. "Some have different talents, different dreams," says Ms. Orlak. Yet many of them are in the postsecondary institutions, reluctantly warming seats, pushed into classrooms by anxious parents, pushed there by a misconstruing of what constitutes success – or dropping out and being lost.

Meanwhile, says Mr. Slywchuk, there's a lack of awareness of Canada's need for skilled tradespersons. "The people in skilled trades are an aging workforce, a lot of them are coming up for retirement," he says. "And when that happens, who's going to do your wiring and fix your plumbing?" There are plumbers in Toronto, he muses, making $100,000 a year. And young people taking pride in making banged-up cars look beautiful again instead of sitting in jail.

9

BOXED IN

ERIN ANDERSSEN

They are service workers, single mothers, holders of McJobs – part-timers and contract employees. Their work seems pointless and the pittances they earn are often devoured by student-loan payments that seem to stretch on to eternity. They haven't given up on themselves, but the knowledge economy often seems to have given up on them, especially if they have only high-school educations. Jobs that once afforded middle-class lifestyles now won't support a family. It may not just be their youthful energy that goes to waste: As global competition squeezes the job market, these Canadians might be left behind for life.

IN ONE BOX STORE, AMONG A ROW OF BOX STORES, it is Geoff Brown's job to move boxes. Occasionally, he straightens up boxes. He returns contents to boxes. Once in a while, he endures the abuse of a customer angry at the cost of stuff inside the boxes – his favourite recollection being the old man who shouted that he worked for "robbers and thieves" over a $50 pair of slippers. But mainly the shoppers pretend not to see him, and forty hours a week, every week, as he has for the last 18 months, Geoff Brown carries boxes from one shelf to another. For this, the 27-year-old high school graduate gets the title of "operations associate." He makes $8.50 an hour. Every night, he takes a bus ride home to his one-bedroom apartment, where the closest thing he has to company is a collection of 200 DVDs, and thinks, "I'm just getting dumber and dumber."

Two stores over, Nicole Schaefer, 23, keeps the stickers and paints and needlepoint kits orderly in her aisle of crafts. She moved to Ottawa from Nova Scotia the week after her long-time boyfriend proposed one day and ran off with her step-sister the next. "I know," she says ruefully, "it sounds like a Jerry Springer show." Part-time at $7.65 an hour, she has calculated precisely how many extra shifts she needs to afford one night out with friends. She is falling behind on her mail-order course in police services; she wants to be a forensic scientist, though only, she explains, if she doesn't have to pass biology or chemistry. "It might not pan out," she says. "I might get offered a full-time job as a manager at Wal-Mart, and I'd take that." But she's already worked for Wal-Mart, just a few doors down; the best job offered her there was as a greeter in the blue apron, offering endless hellos to shoppers rushing through the automatic doors. She lasted five months.

Nicole Schaefer doesn't know Geoff Brown, though they are part of the same anonymous community inhabiting the box store streets of the nation, that soulless creation of the consumer economy. In this case, they tidy and serve under fluorescent lights in the south end of Canada's capital, but you could find them anywhere in a dozen identical malls in a dozen different cities. The people filling these slots are single parents, new immigrants, meandering young adults, part-time students who expect to escape, former students who planned their escape but did not. They are often among the lowest-paid workers in the country. Their hours are increasingly part-time, their positions easily replaced. In the knowledge economy, which so prizes skills and innovation, their role is to serve the creators.

Some are content, at least for now: Ron Taylor, 22, has been selling computers on commission at Future Shop for three months. He hopes to make a career of it. Right now, he estimates he makes about $700 in commission every week – his goal is to total $1000 – but on the day we meet he earned only $20. He shrugs it off. "Some people crack under the pressure," he says. "I'm going to the top. I want my own store some day." But others, like Mr. Brown, are miserable. Alison Nelson thought a writing degree from the University of Victoria would "mean something"; at 29, it has meant an outstanding loan of $24,000 and a part-time job stocking the shelves at Chapters for $7.65 an hour. She's lucky: Her husband, who also has a student loan, teaches at a private school. "If I was on my own, I'd be screwed."

Some Canadians in their 20s acknowledge they are wobbling on the edge, but few feel they have been permanently left behind. They talk about working their way up in their store; the high-school graduates appear not to notice the candidates with university degrees now competing for those managerial jobs. Or they insist they will eventually go back to school; except that the more years they spend outside a classroom, the harder it becomes to force themselves to return, or they can't come up with the money or don't know what to take. "I still haven't figured out what I want to do," they repeat helplessly, the mantra of their generation. But it is a far different statement coming from a 28-year-old camping out in university, than a 28-year-old with a grade-school diploma and a low-wage job pushing cardboard.

Their youthful optimism has an obvious shadow, even if they don't see it, or can't admit it. Most of them sense that the market has changed, that jobs that once afforded a middle-class lifestyle will no longer support a family, and that it takes some magical luck these days to start at the bottom and work your way up without an education on your résumé.

And while they drift, technology rushes on.

Lauren Deschenes works as a cashier at the newly renovated Loblaws, where Nicole and Jeff and the other workers in the mall often grab their lunch on break, because it's fast and cheap. In high school she took a clerical co-op, and hoped to work as a secretary with the school board. But when the cuts came, her temporary placements dried up, and the schools stopped calling. The other secretaries urged her to go back to school, but she didn't want to owe all that money. Now, she suspects it's too late; she is 28 years old and she already speaks as though her best-before-date has expired. "All the stuff I learned in high school is obsolete, and now it's out of my system."

For a few years she worked as a full-time nanny, punching the cash at Loblaws in the evenings, but she couldn't keep up the pace. She's been ringing food down the conveyor belt for five years now, long enough to make the first page of the seniority list – a feat, she says with pride, that earns notice in the staff lunchroom. She doesn't want to risk losing her place, to try for another job. "I'm not very ambitious," she sighs. "But I'm happy where I am."

Making the first page means she sometimes fills in for the head cashier. But it doesn't get her full-time hours. She usually works between 24 and 32 hours a week, for $10.50 an hour. Her parents were driving her in from Vernon each shift – a 20-minute one-way trip – but now she's moved into the city with a girlfriend, and takes the bus. She's worked for the grocery store long enough to get decent benefits and a pension, but she doesn't have much in savings. And she notices that there seem to be fewer staff doing more work even though the store has expanded; "they talk about that a lot in the lunchroom." She doesn't have a clear answer for how she will survive long-term on part-time wages. She doesn't say anything about the store's computerized, self-checkout counters, where shoppers can now do her job for themselves.

This is the risk: Eclipsed by others in the most credentialed generation ever produced in this country, and lost in a society with a widening breach between rich and poor, economists and sociologists predict that those 20s who do not get educated can expect to be left out of the new economy. Their wages will not keep up. New innovations will siphon off their jobs. Their families will be delayed because of money, not career opportunity, and if they have them too early, they may struggle to support them. The gap already shows. In the last two decades, even as 20s engaged with school and career-climbing post-poned wedding vows and baby-making, the number of young parents raising children in poverty has swelled. According to the 2001 census, young Canadians working full-time earn less today than the same age group earned 20 years ago. In every economic measure suggesting a tougher climate for 20s today, those with the least education fare worst of all. Parents without university or college are poorest. The drop in earnings hits those with only a high-school diploma hardest – and especially young men. The number of Canadians under 35 who work full-time and earn less than $20,000 a year has increased since 1981 in every educational category, but almost doubled for people with only high school. University graduates, especially those who stay current with valued degrees, will likely catch up when retiring baby boomers vacate the job market, though carrying a massive debt with them. But for those who jumped into easy-money jobs with no post-secondary education, the forecast is bleak.

Alexis Boyle doesn't need an economist to tell her this. After Grade 13, she hitchhiked with a boyfriend to Edmonton; he turned out to be a bum, she says, and so she came home to Ottawa. Her list of jobs since 18: She painted murals on tiles for a woman with a craft store; she lasted three weeks selling vacation packages over the phone before she was fired for not making quota; she sold used hardware from demolition sites, which included "slave labour shovelling bricks for $8 an hour"; she waitressed at a family diner with lots of regulars and good tips. When we meet for dinner, she has been working at Second Cup, in the mall's far end, for four days, about three shifts longer than it took to learn "it isn't a keeper." After five years in the labour force, she is earning $7 an hour, the same wage paid by her first job. She was planning to sneak out to an interview at a downtown restaurant. She gives herself 12 more months, before going back to school. She would like to take a fine arts degree, but she knows that won't pay.

"I am almost ready to sell my soul for something that has a job market," she said. "I learned enough to know I don't want to be a bottom ant."

Ms. Boyle is far from the only young worker at the box store mall to express this sentiment. Their employers may package the jobs in fancy-sounding titles and corporate mantras about career advancement, but that doesn't change the sense of their place in the hierarchy of work and the gulf between those who serve and those who get served. "It's almost like the two sides don't like each other," observes Mr. Taylor. "People see us as the lowest rung. But what's below us are those people who aren't working." At Chapters, Alison Nelson moved into the storeroom to get away from the customers; she was tired of the messy books and condescending treatment and the parents who leave their children in the kids' section while they shop next door at Winners. A Wal-Mart customer once told Nicole Schaefer that she was "at the bottom of the food chain." She just stares back at those types and says, "If I wasn't here, you wouldn't be able to buy toilet paper."

Quick comebacks aside, Ms. Schaefer is still counting on a different career, so like so many of the 20s around her, she spends little energy considering how to make service jobs better. She shows up for her shift, and as many extra ones as she can grab, and she does whatever is asked of her, and she goes home. Puffing on a cigarette on her 30-minute lunch break, she can list her objectives: "I don't want to work 50 hours a week just to make ends meet. I don't want to work a job that gets me dusty and dirty and sore. I want a job where I get respect."

She knows her dream job: dusting for fingerprints at crime scenes. But she doesn't have a clear strategy on how to attain her goals. She's reluctant to go into debt for university – every day, after all, she sees graduates working her kind of job with the burden of student loans. "I could pay $30,000 to have someone tell me how to do something," she observes. "Instead, I get paid $7 an hour to have the guy who paid

$30,000 tell me how to do it." But then, she'd probably rather not consider the long odds of becoming a forensic scientist without training in biology and chemistry.

Talking about school gives you hope, explains 28-year-old waiter Liam Nicholson, nursing a beer on a Thursday night after his shift at Kelsey's, a restaurant in the parking lot of the box store mall. "It's like they always have an option," he says, "but eventually you don't have an option."

Mr. Nicholson doesn't include himself. But by the end of the conversation, school has become his own fallback position. He's felt the weight of future prospects heavily enough to attend an information session at a local college. That's as far he went. He's been working at restaurants since he left high school, one semester short of his diploma, to try acting. He's landed bit parts in a few obscure independent films, but not enough to support himself. He lives with his sister, a single mom, and helps with her young kids, and sings at karaoke bars and imagines he might still make it as a star. After 10 years of waiting tables, he suffers from chronic pain in his feet if he stands too long, but he still goes for at least eight hours a day, without even a chair in the back for smoke breaks. "This job makes you old real fast. I've been doing it for longer than I thought I would." He lives on $12,000 a year, the whim of tips, and a dream. "I chose this life," he says. "I wish I had more but I don't." He reassures himself that he has time: "I'm a guy. I can have kids when I'm 50." If a music career doesn't work out, he says, maybe he'll marry rich, or return to school, in his 40s, for a psychology degree.

He hasn't met Jeff Canizares, obviously. Mr. Canizares is the assistant manager at the shoe store that employs Geoff Brown, but he began his formal education in psychology at Carleton University. Midway through, an academic adviser told him to refocus, so he finished up, after five years, with another major in dispute resolution. When he tried to get a job, he was told to go to law school. But he owed too much money, and his enthusiasm for school had expired.

"I'd had enough," he says, sitting in his airless office above the stockrooms in the back of the store. There are timesheets laid out on the desk in front of him, and a window facing down on the rows of shoes on display. He is 24, well-spoken and personable, and he has already given up on the career he paid almost $30,000 to learn. "Basically," he offers candidly, "I wasted four years of my life. Everybody tells you to go to school, go into debt, things will work out. That's not my experience."

When he graduated, he needed a job fast – his debts were piling up. A friend helped him get an interview at Globo Shoes in customer services. As assistant manager, he earns a salary of $28,500. In three years, he has paid down half of his student loan, met a woman he wants to marry, and thought about starting a family. He puts a positive spin on his career track: "I could be working in my field, filing paper. At the end of day, when I go home, I'm running my own business."

But he still has regrets. "Every day of my life, I realize that if I had been in an earlier generation, my life would be different. I'd be knee deep in my career right now." Even if the market opens up in his field, he says, there will be a new wave of ambitious, freshly educated university grads to leapfrog into the entry-level jobs. He expects to have kids by then and a mortgage – how he could justify a pay cut to start over again? And he's very clear: When he has a family, he will be present, not working the long hours of someone pounding out a career path. He is the son of a doctor and a nurse, and he has never forgotten the Christmas Day he opened his presents with his father over the telephone. No, he says, with a resolved practicality: "My objective is just to get out of debt – not to work in my field." He'd be better off, he says, if he hadn't gone to university at all. Except for this: One week later he lands the manager's position he'd hoped for at a neighbouring store; the company tells him his education gave him the edge.

He worked hard, and he was lucky. On the store floor below, Geoff Brown is lugging his boxes, and from his vantage point, the situation looks far different: As much as he likes his assistant manager personally, he knows that if he too had been born in an "earlier generation," men with a few letters after their names like Mr. Canizares wouldn't be clogging up his shot at a manager's post. As it stands, he sees no escape. He worries about suddenly being 40, and still moving boxes. "What do I see down the road? Poverty."

Shoving down a steak meal at Denny's, glancing often at his watch to clock his lunch break, he explains how he only took this job to escape the dirty work of flipping burgers at a fast-food joint, where he stood in front of the deep-fat fryer for up to 12 hours a day for seven bucks an hour. (He earned $10.50 for every hour over a 44-hour week.) "You'd leave at night covered in sweat, and smelling of raw meat," he says. "It was awful. That's one place I am not going back."

Globo was the first to return the call after he quit; he'd left his résumé at a dozen different retail stores. "You should see what I do. A monkey could do my job," he says, with genuine frustration. "I think about it every night. I have to get out of here. I've got to find something. But it's impossible, because nobody's going to hire without an education." He does not feel, like so many others, that he can work his way up. "You should see them over there," he waves his hand in the general direction of the store. "I think they think they're going places. But it's not going to happen."

Ask him about going to school, however, if his options are so grim, and he shakes off the question. He could pay for some of it. His mother died a few years ago, and after high school he cared for his grandmother until she passed away; they both left him a bit of money, some of which he spent on DVDs – "stupidly," he says now – and some of which he invested. But he was never much of a student, he says; his favourite classes were always gym and lunch. And he can't imagine a trade. "I'm not great with my hands." Besides, he offers, his cousin works as a plumber, and while he earns $70,000 a year, the hours are long and he "spends his day in crap." He recites all the reasons why he can't go back to school, and then mumbles his own conclusion, "but I know I need to." He wears a bright red Nike baseball hat, set too high on his head. He never smiles, not once. He checks the time, gobbles down the last few bites of food, and races back across the parking lot, back to the boxes.

THE GAP WIDENS

In the workplace facing today's 20s, the good jobs get better, the bad jobs get worse. Filling the spaces will be three types of workers, predicts Linda Duxbury, a business professor at Carleton University.

The more fortunate are the educated 20s, with strong communication skills and the confidence to sell themselves in a competition against a mass of other educated 20s. They will acquire degrees that are valued in the marketplace, they will stay current while waiting for the baby boomers to make way. More often than ever they will be women, and second-generation immigrants. They will demand flexible work hours and creative work spaces and good benefits, even a cafeteria that makes it easy to take home dinner. They watched their parents work long hours and end up downsized, and neglect their families and face divorce; their choices will attempt to be more balanced, their loyalties not so easily earned.

Less well-positioned are the young Canadians who ran off to get educated without a plan or who dropped out of the rush for credentials too early, and cannot overcome the disadvantage with a well-executed sales pitch. They may end up burdened with debt, in jobs outside their fields that pay less than they expected.

But the least lucky of all will be those who don't make the investment of postsecondary education, jumping into the work force because they are wary of the payoff from a student loan, or don't have the inclination for school, or want a paycheque first. This group has little power to negotiate better wages and conditions, and limited access to training. They will fill many of the lower-paying service industry jobs in retail and restaurants and hotels – one of the fastest growing sectors of the economy – where workers remain, as Dr. Duxbury puts it, "commodities rather than creative advantages," easily replaced by new trainees, and where the cost of living, union officials say, has outpaced earnings.

And between the first group and the last, the gulf is widening. The 2001 census found that, despite their impressive credentials, young Canadians today earn less than people their age did 20 years ago – even as highly skilled middle-aged workers saw their salaries soar.

The average earnings of a full-time university graduate between 25 and 34 in 1981 was $48,482 (in 2000 dollars); 20 years later, the same Canadian could expect to average about $3,000 less. For high-school graduates, average earnings dropped by $5,000, to about $28,000. The decline was steeper for young men.

To explain the trend, economists point to an increase in part-time work and contract jobs. Young adults have had less access to union jobs or public-service positions that offer security and better pay. According to Statistics Canada, the percentage of Canadian males between 25 and 34 who earn less than $20,000 doubled in the last two decades to 17 per cent; for women, who average lower wages overall, the same percentage has grown by just over one-third.

Of course, the job market will begin a major transition in this generation. Within a decade, the number of people retiring is expected to match newcomers to the work force, according to an October 2003 study from the Office of the Superintendent of Financial Institutions. But the people who stand to benefit the most will be university graduates, who have bided their time. New technologies like self-serve checkouts and warehouse robotics are expected to reduce the need for human capital. Expanding their hours to serve the knowledge workers, businesses will continue to increase part-time employment. For the employee, there is a social cost in varied shifts, more time spent getting to and from work, and smaller pensions at career end. Even buoyed by the optimism of youth, 20s who passed up on education worry about the future: When asked in the New Canada survey how they expect their standard of living will compare to their parents', university graduates with higher incomes were more likely to say better; low-income 20s with little schooling were more likely to predict that their living standard will be worse.

A smart education "is the ticket to the ball game," says Dr. Duxbury. "If you don't have postsecondary, you don't have skills that the economy wants, you're not going to be in a good position, even when the job market opens up."

10

DOWN BUT NOT OUT

MARGARET PHILP

In Toronto's notorious Jane-Finch corridor, two local kids grew up, got married, became a teacher and a community worker – and decided to stay to help today's neighbourhood children escape the inner-city traps that lie in wait for them. Why did they succeed where their friends from the block so often got stuck? Compared to poor people in the United States and Britain, those born at the bottom of Canada's socioeconomic ladder have a much better chance of climbing up, at least to the middle rungs. The magic word is education.

TROY FRASER LOOKS LIKE A YOUNG, BLACK, hip answer to the cardigan-clad Mr. Rogers, sitting in a rocking chair, a gaggle of small children scattered on the rug at his feet who listen with practiced crossed-legs and folded hands to the book he reads on the miracle of life in a seed. This is science class in his Grade 1 classroom, cluttered with pint-sized metal desks and children's clumsy artwork

Photo by Donald Weber

taped to the walls, where struggling immigrants from the shabby high-rises that surround the school send their children.

Mr. Fraser was one of these children two decades ago, born in a nearby hospital and raised in the Jane-Finch corridor, a north Toronto neighbourhood that has become more notorious for gangs, drugs, and guns than for the abundance of hard-scrabble immigrants and second-generation single mothers assigned to life on Canada's bottom rung. The social-housing project where he lived as a child with his single mother and older siblings is in plain view from the front door of the school where he works. Twenty years ago, when he was in Grade 1, he sat in a classroom like this one, just blocks away.

As a university graduate with a respectable salary, a man who packs his three children into a minivan, he could live anywhere. He has made it. But he stays. Mr. Fraser and his like-minded wife, Joesie Nelson, chose to raise their family here, even if that means living next door to poor neighbours who begrudge their good fortune. He deliberately chose to work in a school where white children are the lone visible minority and nearly two in three students speak a language other than English at home. "My whole drive was to work in this community," he says. "Me giving back to what has shaped me. I wanted to be a positive role model – male, black, young – for a kid. The kids need me here."

Poverty is a legacy handed down through the generations. It starts with children who tend to be sicker, earn lower grades in school, and suffer from more behavioural problems. In later years, many will repeat family history.

But not always. Poverty is not a life sentence.

Canadians have wrung their hands over a child-poverty rate that has remained as stubborn as a stain over the past two decades, at nearly one in five children. It's only in the past few years that social scientists have found that a surprising four in 10 Canadians who start life at the bottom rung rise to the top half of the income ladder.

"Being raised by low-income parents doesn't pre-ordain children to low income in adulthood," says Miles Corak, director of family and labour studies at Statistics Canada. "Canada, in a sense, is a land of opportunity."

Mr. Fraser, 25, and Ms. Nelson, 26, belong with those who seize the opportunity to climb. Among the roughly 200,000 Canadians now in their 20s who grew up poor in the 1980s – when the poverty rate never slipped below 15 per cent – they broke with tradition as teenagers in the 1990s to chase higher education.

Why them? What set them apart from neighbours, also raised by single mothers in dilapidated apartments, who became pregnant as teenagers, quit school, and now collect welfare or juggle low-wage jobs? Why were they running for election to their high-school student council when neighbours like Jen McKenzie and Maxine Cadogan were dropping out and pushing baby strollers? Was it his hard-working mother, who returned to college after her divorce in pursuit of a more lucrative job to support children on her own? Or the teacher who saw the spark and urged him to run for that council seat? What about her mother, who quit her job to care for a grandchild after her daughter gave birth in first-year university?

Or does success come down to raw talent and drive?

"That's the crucial question for policy," says Dr. Corak, who has pioneered the study of intergenerational mobility in Canada – the extent to which parents' economic fortunes are inherited by their children.

"What makes Canada different than the U.S. or the U.K.? It's got something to do with education policy and access to postsecondary education in a big way. And it's got something to do with early childhood investments and how you get those kids into a situation that they're able to choose whether they're going to have a postsecondary education or not."

Mr. Fraser is on recess duty.

Here in the Topcliff Public School playground, the demographics of the school are laid bare. Most of the faces in the crowd are shades of brown, the children of parents who hail from India, Africa, and the Caribbean. A knot of children were born to immigrants from Vietnam, China, and the Philippines. Most live in four apartment high-rises nearby that feed into the school.

Mr. Fraser sees himself in these children whose futures are still blank slates, children who are being raised in an urban jungle without the music lessons, sports teams, and summer camps of the higher classes. He understands the powerful imprint he can leave as a second-generation black immigrant from the neighbourhood standing before a classroom of poor black and Asian children who share the same history.

"Even in Grade 1," he says, "these kids know that I went to university. They know I went to York. They know that this is a place that is accessible to them. I still say, 'When you graduate from high school,' and 'When you go on to postsecondary,' so that it's not foreign to them. I want that to be something that's familiar."

University was always a prospect for Mr. Fraser. He was raised by a tireless mother who returned to college in her 40s, after her divorce, to become a nurse. He became close to a couple of teachers who, unlike the many who tended to treat all the black students like a hopeless underclass, saw a bright, ambitious young man. Aside from the teacher who encouraged him to run for student council, another enrolled him in a program that pairs high-school students from Jane-Finch with faculty at nearby York University. He would later land a scholarship at York that covered his tuition for the first few years.

He started to hang out with the strait-laced crowd in his grungy, 25-storey apartment building. It was there he met Joesie, the daughter of a struggling single mother from Jamaica, whose ambition to climb from the poverty of welfare matched his own.

She has a harder time tracing her rise. Her mother was laid-back; her father was absent. None of her teachers inspired her. But after years of skipping classes, hanging with the bad crowd, and dabbling in drugs and booze, she remembers acing a tough geography test in Grade 10. Suddenly she was basking in the realization she possessed the stuff of academic success. She became obsessed with her grades, studying into the wee hours of the night and scoring top marks.

She remembers going to a youth group in her apartment building. The group leader showed the children an article titled Trapped in Poverty, suggesting that was their lot in life. Ms. Nelson recalls thinking, "That's not going to be me."

When she found herself pregnant in her first year of university, she suddenly saw her brilliant future falling to pieces. Back at her old high school, the grapevine hummed with news that the stellar student had fallen from grace. "I'd made it that far," she says, "and was going to have to drop out and look after the child and repeat the cycle and be another poverty statistic."

But her mother would have none of it. Though she had never pushed her daughter to attend university – no one in the family had ever graduated with a degree – she was not about to watch her slip into that trap. She quit her job to care for her granddaughter.

"She knew I had the potential," Ms. Nelson says. "My mother would sacrifice anything for her kids."

She became so smitten by the academic life that her sights are set on studying for a PhD, although for now she is consumed with her job as a community-development worker. Like her husband, she works in their old neighbourhood.

A handful of young women sit on lawn chairs in the backyard of a row of Jane-Finch townhouses, keeping an eye on their children who run back and forth from the kitchens to the playground. In the basketball court next to the playground, dozens of tall, strapping young men in baggy trousers are oblivious to the kids, their eyes only on the ball, dribbling and shooting baskets.

Jen McKenzie, 23, suffers the late-afternoon heat. Seven months pregnant with her third child, she leans back in her chair to ease the weight of the bump under her red T-shirt and tucks into a cheese sandwich.

She collects welfare and has never worked. By the time she was a teenager, she was spending far more time with boys than books. "Boys and sex were my drugs," she says simply.

In Grade 9, she became pregnant. Since her daughter Tymika was born eight years ago, she has returned to school a few times to try to finish her high-school diploma. It never lasts long. "Every time I try to go to school, I get pregnant," says the blunt Ms. McKenzie, whose children are fathered by different men. "I was supposed to go to school this year, but I got pregnant with this one." She patted her belly.

Her Jamaican-born mother raised the family without a father, sometimes collecting welfare, other times working odd jobs in a store, a hotel, an old-age home. Ms. McKenzie still lives with her in the same subsidized apartment.

Her mother, who now collects social assistance, would like her to leave, finish school, find a husband, get a house with a white picket fence. While she resents the pressure, Ms. McKenzie confesses that she aspires to leave the neighbourhood that has trapped her mother. "She always says she wants to get out," she says of her mother, "but she's not going anywhere." It is as if leaving Jane-Finch is a life's ambition on its own – a notch on the barometer of success, like a university degree or a lucrative job.

"When I get a good job," Ms. McKenzie says dreamily, "I'm out of here. I've been here for 23 years, and I don't need to stay here for the next 23. I don't want that for my kids."

Unlike her childhood friend Jen, Maxine Cadogan returned to high school a few years after her teenage pregnancy, dragging a baby, a stroller, and a two-year-old toddler on the bus every morning for two years. "I was tired of staying at home," says the 25-year-old. "I was tired of waking up in the morning with nothing to do. I mean I was raising my kids, of course. But I wanted more for myself. I noticed every time my mom was coming home, me and her would argue. She was tired of seeing me around the house. I wasn't doing nothing with myself."

Her mother, an immigrant from Barbados whose husband left when his daughter was six years old, had worked a handful of jobs at a time, often as a hotel chambermaid and a nursing assistant. She was seldom home to watch her two sons and wild daughter. They lived across the street from a school, but her mother insisted Ms. Cadogan commute to one outside the confines of Jane-Finch to avoid unsavoury influences. It didn't work.

"I grew up in the 'hood. Of course I got into trouble," says Ms. Cadogan, a striking woman with enormous brown eyes and meticulously manicured nails. "I hung out with the wrong crowd. Basically it was boys. I wasn't into drugs."

By Grade 10, she was pregnant with her elder son, Trayvon, 9, whose name is tattooed down her left arm. Her mother was "heartbroken," long fearing that her daughter would slip into the neighbourhood contagion of teenage pregnancy and poverty. "It hurt her because she wanted me to go to school and get an education and do better," she says. "It put me in a big setback."

A second son, Demar, arrived two years later. Ms. Cadogan now lives several blocks outside the projects in the basement of a house that her mother bought with savings from years of working night and day.

Ms. Cadogan graduated from high school three years ago and landed a job as a receptionist at a medical clinic. She quit a few months ago and has started to upgrade her marks at a local high school; she wants to apply to college to study nursing.

"Eventually, I want to go on to better. I don't want to stay here forever," she says. "There's so much more out there for me, so why should I stay at this level?"

It was not until Mr. Fraser and his wife reached university, outside the confines of their neighbourhood, that they realized how poor they were. Growing up, they had few possessions. But neither did anyone else.

Now that they are close to being middle-class parents, they are lavishing toys and clothes on their three children – Brianne and her two-year-old twin brothers, Brayden and Jayden – that they themselves were blissfully unaware of as children. Their daughter tears along the street on a Barbie bicycle and a scooter that are the envy of her poor friends. Some of the children are so jealous that they refuse to play with her. Their parents accuse Mr. Fraser and Ms. Nelson – whose salaries are far from lucrative and whose student loans are the size of a mortgage – of being rich and no longer belonging.

But a nagging sense that their affluence is a passing phase – a fleeting stroke of luck that could turn sour in an instant – pushes Ms. Nelson to buy her daughter all that her heart desires while she can.

"I always live with this fear of what happens if we lose it all. I wasn't born with money, so I know what it's like not to have it."

MOVING UP

Who remains at the bottom and who rises? What pushes Troy Fraser and Joesie Nelson on to a university campus when most of their high-school classmates have barely graduated?

Statistics Canada's Miles Corak spent several years trying to peg a number to the likelihood that children raised in poverty will themselves be poor as adults. He and a colleague studied 400,000 tax files, comparing fathers' incomes in the late 1970s and early 1980s with those of their children more than a decade later.

They discovered that only some of the parents' socioeconomic disadvantage is passed down to the children. A young man raised at the bottom 10 per cent of Canadian incomes stands less than a one-in-six chance of remaining there, and one-in-17 odds of reaching the very top of the ladder.

"What we're saying is that more than a quarter of people who start out at the bottom won't get higher than the [middle]," Dr. Corak says.

The other part of the story is that a lot go beyond that. They found Canada to be more a land of equal opportunity than either the United

States or Britain, where child poverty is close to the same level as in Canada but children born to poor fathers have twice the chance of remaining poor. A college or university degree has become the ticket to a fatter paycheque in Canada.

The research uncovered a few other distinctions. The children of fathers who collected employment insurance tended to have lower incomes as adults than those whose fathers never relied on that form of assistance. So did children from poorer neighbourhoods. But children whose fathers collected income from investments – even those at the bottom with little to invest – reported an average of $3,000 more in yearly income.

"You don't have to have a lot," Dr. Corak says. "It could even be interest from a savings account. But broadly, it signals that you're thinking ahead."

SOURCE: STATISTICS CANADA

THE GLOBE AND MAIL

PART III

NEW FRONTIERS

11

OUR TOWN, THEIR TOWN

ERIN ANDERSSEN

The meatpacking plant near Brooks, Alta., employs workers from all over the world, especially Africa. In a few short years, the town has gone from white-bread trading post to one of Canada's most youthful, diverse rural places. But there are two racial solitudes in this boomtown, locked in an uneasy embrace.

"THERE'S TOO MANY NIGGERS HERE," Cliff James says. "I avoid them."

At the Brooks Hotel Bar, a singer is crooning country tunes while couples two-step on a small dance floor, and Mr. James is drinking whisky with his friend Pete Thiessen. It is a white crowd, with few exceptions, and the waitresses show a lot of belly as they go by balancing pints of beer. Mr. James, 21 and baby-faced, is a rancher's son; he spent the day branding 650 head of cattle. Mr. Thiessen, 23, is a beefy guy in a muscle shirt who works at a feedlot outside Brooks, a nondescript Alberta town in a rough patch of prairie almost 200 kilometres

Photo by John Lehmann

southeast of Calgary. They tip back their cowboy hats to talk at a round table in the corner.

"I'm not racist or anything," Mr. Thiessen begins. "But the black guys are causing a lot of trouble, date rapes and muggings. I've heard it from people who've heard it from the cops."

Neither of them knows much about the Africans who have arrived in Brooks in large numbers in recent years to work the assembly line at the meatpacking plant. Mr. James doesn't think all of them are trouble-makers; it is the mass of their presence in his "little town" that disturbs him most. When pushed on it, he even says he could accept his sister marrying a black guy, "if he was nice." But, he declares more than once, she wouldn't.

Mr. Thiessen takes a harder line: "They don't belong here. They don't want to adapt to our ways." He refuses to be shaken from his crime-rampage theory, which police say is untrue. "If they published everything that went on in this town, people would be moving out."

A different kind of conversation flows the next night, on the other side of town, with beer cans piling up in Lonny Finkbeiner's living room. One of Mr. Finkbeiner's friends describes him as an oil-patch redneck who cuts the sleeves off his shirts, and the laid-back 29-year-old endorses the label. He owns several guns, all reluctantly registered under the federal gun-control law, and he didn't get past high school.

But he and his two roommates, who are both drillers on the patch, can't be stereotyped so easily. They speak pragmatically about how multiculturalism works and where it falls down, and about the sudden, dramatic diversity that has come to a white-bread place like Brooks.

Mr. Finkbeiner says people "just don't know what to say" to the newcomers. While he personally wouldn't marry a black woman, he likes the fact that his seven-year-old son has a school friend from a different culture. But Stan Tumoth, 32, suggests their new black neighbours share the uneasiness. "Their minds are made up that they're going to be persecuted."

"In all fairness," remarks Shane McLaren, 29, "if there was a white guy on the street I didn't know, I wouldn't go up and say hello."

Mr. McLaren read about the Sudanese in *National Geographic* because he wanted to know more about the people flooding to town. He is one of the few non-official people in Brooks who speaks knowledgeably about the war and famine the newcomers fled, and the cheques they send home to help their starving families. "I was blown away by all the shit they went through," he says. "They're just trying to make a better life. It opened my eyes."

But not his heart – at least not enough to follow up with the beautiful African woman he met at a bar one night. He tossed her number out the next day, worried what people might think, and now he's kicking himself. "I've been looking for her every time we go out."

In their distinct ways, these five guys sum up the state of race relations in Brooks, where fear feeds rumour, rumour feeds fear and even tolerant minds seem paralyzed. In a few short years, the meatpacking workers have turned this prairie town into one of the most multicultural spots in the nation.

This is not a typical Canadian tale of friendly dinners and happy cross-cultural weddings. But neither is it just about rednecks and cowboys. Brooks's problems lie more in misunderstanding than in malice, but the openness so loudly espoused by the nation's next generation is being tested in a town where half the residents are under 30. In Brooks, a black woman with a stalled car can still count on a white man to run home for his booster cables. But nobody talks about the night when authorities had to quietly douse three burning crosses.

In early May, with the occasional hail still falling on the people of Brooks, the syrupy-sweet perfume of manure wafts through the air. It's a mild stink, and your nose adjusts. But in the summer, residents say, with barbecue season causing a run on steaks and a hot wind blowing from the northwest, the slaughterhouse stench smacks you in the face. The spin, here in beef country, is that it's "the smell of money." In Brooks, to mixed reviews, it is also the smell of change.

Five kilometres up the Trans-Canada Highway toward Calgary, under 14 acres of steel roof, 2,500 people work two shifts carving up a million carcasses a year, one in every three cows slaughtered in the nation. Lakeside Packers, expanded under new American owners in the late 1990s, is now one of the most modern meat-processing plants in North America, and it's meant a lot of new jobs. Brooks, a trading-post kind of town for ranchers and oil crews, didn't have the people to fill them.

Lakeside boasts a no-layoff policy, and even when the mad-cow scare closed the U.S. border, a work-share agreement with the federal government forestalled pink slips. There's no experience required, so long as you pass the on-site physical, and the wage is decent: Lakeside employees start at $11.35 per hour (35 cents more for the night shift); after 15 months, it can jump to $16 an hour. The trick is lasting 15 months. It is tough, joint-buckling work, either in the heat of the kill floor hacking off 60-pound heads of cattle, or standing for hours on the processing side, slicing future hamburgers off the slabs that swing by on conveyor belts. It's not hard to find a Lakeside employee who can't make a fist with his knife hand any more.

In an oil-rich province full of easier offerings for its homegrown labour force, that has meant two main types of workers at Lakeside – young Newfoundlanders forced west to find their fortunes and new immigrants who hear about the jobs through the grapevine, often with families to support and not enough English to take opportunities elsewhere.

There are more than 30 different dialects spoken among the swinging carcasses on the Lakeside plant floor, and the signs are often printed in four languages. Chatter on the line centres on sports and small talk. "You have to be careful," one former employee says. "Your joke can be someone else's frustration."

Muslim employees kneel at break time on prayer mats in the locker room. The cafeteria, which serves hot dogs and French fries, is self-segregated by table. Arabs, Africans and Central Americans all tend to keep to their own, with some of the younger workers meeting in the middle. But at the company picnic, the baseball teams are mixed up randomly.

About 40 per cent of the workers at Lakeside were born in a country other than Canada. And because of them, Brooks is bucking national trends: It is young when most rural places are aging fast; booming, when so many small towns are withering; and diverse, in a country where 94 per cent of immigrants who arrived in the past decade flocked to cities.

Alberta has the third-highest proportion of both members of visible minorities and foreign-born residents of all the provinces, after Ontario and British Columbia. The Global Immigration Friendship Centre, the main immigrant-aid group in Brooks, estimates that more than one-fifth of the 12,000 people now living in town were born outside Canada. The largest and most organized group is composed of about 1,200 Sudanese.

It is a rerun of history, with the newcomers recast. Not since 1931 has Canada had so many foreign-born citizens within its borders, and before the Second World War, most of them arrived first on the Prairies, to build the railway and settle the land around fledgling towns like Brooks, first surveyed with nine residents in 1907. Back then, though, they came from England, Scotland or the Ukraine, not refugee camps in Ghana. They came to be farmers and ranchers; the latest wave of newcomers to Brooks comes to carve the meat raised by those earlier immigrants' descendants.

It takes five minutes to see this isn't your ordinary prairie town – when you spot the mother in the hijab driving though the grocery-store parking lot with an Indian pop song blaring, or the young African men on their way home, or Sam's Oriental Market on Second

Street West, where the owner is Cambodian and the shelves are loaded with exotic samplings labelled in Arabic.

But the locals lament that their town is getting too big too fast, and doesn't feel safe any more; the newcomers complain that it is too small (translation: small-minded) and doesn't feel friendly. The two groups pretend to ignore one another, eyeballing each other warily across an imaginary fence.

They were not coached to be optimistic. Before Lakeside expanded, a U.S. expert on meatpacking towns spoke at a community meeting, warning of crime and ghettoes. As James Nesbitt, editor of the Brooks Bulletin, describes it, "it was a little bit of scare mongering." But it's true that the housing shortage is dire and the crime rate did spike, though the RCMP says it is declining. More importantly, the people of Brooks suddenly found their town inhabited by new arrivals who had never experienced snow and car insurance, who spoke English, if at all, with thick accents they couldn't understand. Any place would react with culture shock – big cities such as Toronto and Vancouver also went through tense periods when their complexions changed radically a decade or two ago.

There has been kindness in Brooks – gifts of furniture, volunteers who teach English and offer rides to appointments, one anonymous donation of $900 to bring a man's son over from Nairobi – and although it is rare, there has even been romance. The tension is subtle, folded into a live-and-let-live sentiment that doesn't extend a hand in either friendship or hostility.

"Don't matter to me none," offers a self-proclaimed cowboy named Don. "There are more assholes in Brooks than moved to Brooks." Don jokes that he is diversified because he likes Snoop Dog and Eminem.

"Like any society, you find good and bad people," observes Aleer Joi, 27, a Sudanese employed at Lakeside. "If you turned it around and took these white guys home to my country, you'd get the same thing."

Staff Sergeant Ray Noble, who runs the local RCMP detachment, says there is a core of people working hard to build links, in community groups and churches (the Roman Catholic mass includes an occasional African choir). "Of course, we have the ones who live up to the redneck title," he says. "But they don't get much of an audience." The largest group "are people who look at it with trepidation and fear. They'd like to see everything work out, but they don't want to personally take any risks."

Rumour rushes in to fill the vacuum: The Sudanese refugees don't have to pay taxes for three years, the immigrants are driving up the crime rate, Lakeside recruits in prisons overseas. None of them are true. Sudanese in Brooks grumble about the tax dollars sliced off their pay along with everyone else. The crime rate, still high but dropping, is the result of a young, transient and mostly white population, Staff Sgt. Noble says – the African or Arabic names that turn up in the court pages of the Brooks Bulletin stand out, but there are few.

And far from coming from foreign prisons, among the people trimming fat and pulling bone at Lakeside are doctors, lawyers, pharmacists and engineers, university students midway through degrees interrupted by war.

Then there were the two young women, home late for curfew, who told their parents they had been chased around town by a group of black guys; only when their parents took the complaint to the police did they admit to making it up. "But of course," Staff Sgt. Noble says, "the rumours spread through town: 'We've got to do something about the guys chasing our women.' Every story spins into four or five permutations."

Which explains why the police hushed it up when the three crosses were set on fire one night last fall, one in front of the town hall, one at the fire hall and one in an empty lot. The police figured it was a couple of drunks, and since no specific individual was targeted, left it at that. The RCMP didn't even put out a press release. No need to risk starting something.

•

In an old storefront near downtown Brooks, the members of the All Nations Harvest Church sing their opening hymn to African drums and electronic keyboard. A projector flashes the words on the wall: "Jesus is the light of the world. *Yesu hawa kaawat ad-dunia*." There are about 35 people at the service, of many backgrounds; a world map hangs on the wall. An Asian woman sits in the back row, and there are several women in traditional African dress. A prayer is made for help with "pains in the body from working at Lakeside."

Burnabas Thucnar sits near the front with his son Kama, 20, presented with applause to the congregation – Kama arrived in Brooks only a few days ago, retrieved in person from Sudan by his father, who had not seen him for 19 years.

On the drums is a Liberian named Edward Fully, and since the pastor is away, he gives the sermon. "We have come a mighty long way," he announces to the gathering. He tells the story of Isaac, whose cattle were dying and whose wells were dry in the promised land, who almost gave up and left. "But he decided to stay and things started to change." Eventually, he prospered so much the Philistines envied him.

It is, for Mr. Fully and many of his fellow Africans, the story of their arrival in Brooks, and of how they would like it to end. But when he speaks of it, a few nights later, in the small townhouse where he and his wife, Mawa, are raising their three children, there is little optimism in his voice. The Fullys first arrived in St. John's from a refugee camp in Ghana, forced out of Liberia because of war. They came to Brooks for the wages at Lakeside; his wife still works there, trimming fat on the day shift, but Mr. Fully is taking nursing courses and now mows lawns for the town.

It was different in Newfoundland, he says – strangers brought meals to their house, and one woman gave the family a lift home in a downpour. They would soak her car seats, he told her. "But she said, 'These are material things. You guys are important.' You don't find that here. Even if you say hello, they just pass you by."

The Fullys have been in Brooks for three years, but they have yet to make real friends with anyone. Mr. Fully, who worked for the Red Cross in Ghana, has perfect English, but at their daughter's soccer game, they sit off to the side from the other parents. Sometimes they join them, but Mawa says she can tell people feel uncomfortable, and it can be just too much work.

The hardest thing, Mr. Fully says, is the awkward smiles – as if he doesn't notice when people cross the street to avoid him. "They don't want to show they don't like immigrants. They want to pretend. But the body language doesn't match. They smile, but inside it is different."

Veronica Lissa, a Sudanese who moved here from Seattle with her young daughter, gives the same assessment of Brooks. Like Mr. Fully, her English is excellent. If you ask for help, she says, people here will give it – a man she didn't know once drove home for cables to boost her car. But as a group, she says, they walk the streets with blinders on. "Any change in your community, you approach with caution. Here they just try to block it out."

She often waits longer than she should at store counters. "Finally, you say, 'Excuse me, are you open for business?' It's like you don't exist." At school, her daughter punched a boy who called her "blackie" during a basketball game; now she wants to go back to Seattle. "I told her, 'We're going to change those people's attitudes. We're going to teach them.'"

Such complaints are not universal, at least not openly. Chan Ray, 21, a Cambodian who moved here as a teenager and now works out on the oil patch, shrugs off questions about race. The cowboys "just wear their pants a bit tighter than I do," he jokes. And at a pizzeria, Nassrullah Cheema, a Pakistani Muslim, offers: "I have never had anyone tell me I should go back home to my country. I don't have problems with the people here."

But at Sam's Oriental Market, some customers will quietly express reservations. A Muslim teenager tells how his classmates call him a "terrorist," but when pushed for more details, he nervously insists that they are only joking.

The owner, Sam Chum, describes all the nationalities that line up here after pay days at Lakeside, and talks of expanding. In the manner of all wise businessmen, he has only praise for his customers' town. He points cheerfully to a regular, a middle-aged white man with a handlebar mustache who has come in for a jug of water, and urges me to talk to him.

In the parking lot, the man says he stops here only because it is on his way home. There are "too many different cultures" in Brooks, he says. "If I didn't have so many years on my pension, I'd be gone." And he drives off, without giving a name.

On a Friday night in May, the social options for Brooks's young and single are limited. There's one aging movie theatre, the bowling alley is closed except for group reservations, and the Brooks Bandits have packed their pucks away for the summer.

Brooks offers many routes to Jesus (but no mosque), and at the Victory Church of Brooks on the edge of town, you could take in a 30-minute sermon weighing the discipleship of Peter against the idolatry of Britney Spears. The people in theirs 20s there, all white, will passionately debate how they should get to pray in class, if their teacher gets to wear a turban.

It's a different crowd, though still mostly white, at the Oxford Hotel, a dark, dingy place that everyone in town calls the Zoo. At least it is on a Wednesday afternoon, when the main game is to throw coins at the strippers sliding around on the dance floor. On weekends, they have a band, and the place is filled with young locals dumping cash on cocktails.

Among them, monitoring his slurring, slopping friends, is Errol Sturgeon, 23, home for the summer from studying nursing in Hamilton. "Anxiety is contagious," he observes when asked for his assessment of race relations in town. He says people who have been away are easier with the "new scene" – he plays pickup soccer with a few guys from Sudan – but he's still careful.

"It becomes very awkward once you get a black guy and white guy in a room. You don't know how to act. You never know if you're going to say hello and he's going to snap, if he's one of the black guys who's been harassed by white guys. Even though I have nothing against him, I don't know what he thinks of me."

What is striking is how the uneasiness stymies even the young adults most open to change – on both sides. The wary circling seems based on fear, either of experiencing racism or of being perceived as racist.

"It's like when you come close, they don't want to be near you," says Kongolo Kebwe, who just turned 30, and is originally from the Congo. "After a few years, it becomes normal. Before, I tried to understand it. Now, I don't see it."

"By the time we've evolved enough," says Larissa Stone, a 20-year-old from Brooks, "it will be too late – because they will have been hurt."

The New Canada survey found that rural people in their 20s expressed a similar openness to diversity as urban 20s. They were slightly less comfortable hearing different languages on the street – but then, they experience it less. Other studies have suggested that an urban-rural gap on ethnic tolerance can be explained in large part by education level: Where you live matters less than what you've learned.

But in a small town like Brooks, Mr. Sturgeon and Ms. Stone explain, there are fewer mixing opportunities. There's no university to facilitate it, and the young Sudanese tend to save their money, not going to restaurants but spending their free time learning English instead. People party with the friends they have known from high school and plan their eventual escape from town.

It will be better, Ms. Stone suggests, for the next group, growing up together.

But that doesn't mean she feels comfortable with the split she sees now. "I worry that because they put up with it from some people," she says, "that they will think I am the same."

Consider Ezzie's, she says, the infamous hip-hop club across town, with the metal detector at the door and the bouncers linked by headsets. Its clientele is about as mixed as you get in Brooks. It has a reputation for fights, but usually, customers and staff say, it's just a stupid scuffle between two drunks of the same race – a few years ago, police pepper-sprayed a rowdy crowd watching two white guys pummel each other outside.

Cowboy hats may be replaced by backward baseball caps, but there is an invisible line drawn, and the black clientele hangs out in a corner, by the DJ booth and the shooter bar. On the dance floor, there is the odd mixed couple. Often, the black guys dance alone, their eyes closed.

Ms. Stone remembers how she used to chat with the Sudanese women about clothes in the washroom, but that doesn't happen any more. The mood has turned frosty. "I think they've put up a wall," she says. "The ones that still walk around [the nightclub], I think they're new to Brooks, they haven't experienced being treated like shit."

At Ezzie's tonight, Ms. Stone grabs a black guy walking by and hauls him out under the disco lights. She might have danced with him anyway, but she also knows she is being photographed. His name is Motie Shekata, a 22-year-old Ethiopian, who works at Lakeside.

"I don't like it here," he says, standing outside later. The women, he says, can be friendly, but for the most part people look right through him. "If you say hi to them, they are strangers to people. Their minds are closed."

Under twinkling icicle lights and a stuffed version of the Elks Community Hall's namesake, the Sudanese of Brooks are having a party as if the world outside – with all its uneasiness – doesn't exist. A group of women worked all night cooking bucketfuls of traditional Sudanese food, and now the buffet table has been emptied. A few community leaders give political speeches, updating the audience on the situation in Sudan, and celebrating the May anniversary of the birth of the Sudanese people's liberation movement. (The community is itself occasionally divided by politics – Christians outnumber Muslims, forming a majority they don't hold back home.)

Then, in black-and-white costumes, a group of young men and women step out in front of the large hall and perform a flirting, taunting tribal dance – a love song, traditionally performed at weddings. One man videotapes it so it can be distributed to parents who want to teach their culture to children with few memories of Sudan. This gathering stands in contrast to the boisterous town party two weeks later, the Brooks Rodeo, where a mostly white crowd will watch mutton busting and steer wrestling.

There are several hundred people at the hall, and this is one reason why so many of the discussions about race in Brooks centre on the Sudanese: While other nationalities have kept a low profile, the Sudanese are organized. The weekend before, with some funding from the town, they officially opened their own community drop-in centre.

"Personal contact is not working here," says the head of the Sudanese-Canadian Association of Brooks, 30-year-old Atek Monydhar. "What we understand in Canada is that if you don't unite yourselves, no one will listen to you."

You could count the white people in the room on your fingers. The pastor of All Nations Harvest Church, Dean Southern, has brought his family, but along with many of the younger families, they leave before the disco ball and dry ice come out for dancing.

There are a few young white women hanging out with Sudanese guys, including two who are a few months from having babies with their boyfriends. But just about the only white man present, sitting quietly at one of the long tables, is blond, blue-eyed Cameron Segaert. He comes from Saskatchewan, works in the boiler room at Lakeside, and has fallen in love with Nyaibol Deng, 25. She sits beside him in a fancy evening dress. They met one night at a laundromat where Ms.

Deng was unhappily doing her roommate's laundry, and between the wash and dry loads, Mr. Segaert struck up a conversation, and offered to drive her home. "I'm from Saskatchewan," he assured her. "You've got nothing to worry about."

She was surprised. Most white guys, she says, were too intimidated even to say hello. When he phoned repeatedly, she finally gave in and said yes to a date. Last Christmas, he took her home to meet his parents. They moved in together a week ago.

At first, Mr. Segaert says, some of the Sudanese guys were jealous. Ms. Deng was asked why she had to date a white guy. "There aren't many single Sudanese women," he explains. "But I used to work in the patch, so I don't scare easily."

At a wedding in Medicine Hat, Ms. Deng says, some of Mr. Segaert's friends weren't that friendly. "But some people from my country aren't friendly either. So it didn't hurt my feelings."

They get looks when they go out, and Mr. Segaert notices that he gets treated differently when he is by himself. "But it is unspoken."

In a back room before services at All Nation, two boys stand on a chair, playing basketball on an old arcade game. Their names are Mayar Mayen and John Curlew, both 5, best friends, and fond of teasing the girls in the kindergarten playground – as if it were the most natural thing in the world that a Sudanese boy might become friends with a truck driver's son in a small town on the prairies.

In a few years, the children of Ms. Deng and Mr. Segaert might be on that playground. They are the promise of the place Brooks could be, in time – the place that, in its heart, it wants to be.

12

CITY LIGHTS

ERIN ANDERSSEN

In the past generation, this has become the most urbanized nation in the world, with 80 per cent of Canadians living in cities. But what kind of cities? It's a question that will define the 21st century, and many active people in their 20s have a clear answer – smart cities are creative metropolises where people in technical and artistic fields can mingle and meet a wide variety of others. They see plenty of potential in a young city like Calgary, a place that 'satisfies your split personality.'

THE ELEVATOR AT CRITICAL MASS IS WALLED with navy marker board and scrawled with company-sanctioned graffiti, like a bathroom stall without the phone numbers. Pens are supplied. Staffers passing between floors have drawn bars of musical notes and random doodles, conversing anonymously in quippy slang. "Make it hip," one writer entreats in blue fluorescent ink. In white pen, above a green spaceship, someone answers: "Things are hip on the mother ship."

When clients visit, the elevator walls are wiped down and an e-mail goes out advising self-censorship. But the rest of the Critical Mass workspace on the south side of downtown Calgary is one chic advertisement for creativity, the kind of place never imagined by the factory workers who once made glass in this gutted brick warehouse still known as the Pilkington Building. This is the décor of the new economy: silver-faced fridges and fancy faucets in the kitchenettes, soft lights floating in the shape of waves over the workspaces, central oases of bean-bag chairs and pillows. There are only four offices among more than 200 employees. On a Friday afternoon, three guys have booked a viewing room to watch the Tour de France. In the basement, certainly a grim spot in days of old, there are now treadmills, a game of table soccer, a sink and dryer for the subsidized hairdresser who shows up three days a week; next door, in what staff call the "bistro," the 21st-century workers sit under mood lighting in high-backed leather chairs, eating bowls of Asian noodles with chopsticks.

All these trappings to grease the human machinery: Critical Mass, an enterprising Canadian new media company that designs award-winning Web sites for Fortune 500 companies like Mercedes-Benz and Dell, is in the brain business.

A chat with a few staffers doesn't happen in a boardroom; it happens in the middle of the design floor, in a round room bordered with glass windows, where string curtains of plastic circles hang from the doors, a stereo sound mixer for the resident DJs sits in the corner, and the lights are paper lanterns. Skeleton lollypops are scattered on the table, left over from Halloween. The average age at Critical Mass falls under 30. These three are a typical sample: Karen Chu, 25, a slim Chinese-Canadian, with highlights in her hair, Simone Zahradka, 24, a laid-back blonde in an athletic shirt, and Carl Lukasewich, 28, with a tattoo of a bamboo branch twisting up his right forearm and a white T-shirt that shows a werewolf hoisting a thermos of blood. "I'd cover up my tattoos if a client was coming," he volunteers.

The bamboo branch says it all, really. When you ask this trio of young designers what they like about Critical Mass, they will list the perks. When they work late, which can be often, their managers bring dinner; on Labour Day weekend, the company supplied a masseuse. But what they focus on is the variety in their environment. This is where fresh thought originates, they say: in places where techies mingle with designers, every kind of music blasts from the work stations, and tattoos are incidental. "Being open to new ideas," recites Ms. Chu, "is the only way to bring better ideas." There is, of course, a conformity to the non-conformity: It's assumed that anyone in a suit and tie must be headed for a job interview. But Ms. Zahradka says that "people are looking deeper, they question things here." They know their work can be the best, compared, as Mr. Lukasewich suggests, to a general sense among Calgarians and Canadians "that we're not good enough." And they are not reticent about considering a future move, to another city, another country: They have an articulated sense of their value.

"You realize that everything you are going to contribute to the world is within you," says Ms. Zahradka, "so your package moves with you wherever you are."

"We work for the Web," says Ms. Chu. "And the Web teaches us that you can be anywhere."

This, then, is why place matters. Educated and set loose into a global economy fuelled by human innovation, talented Canadians in their 20s expect to be on the move. Companies have a tenuous hold on their loyalties, and their sense of Canada is not tied to physical borders. They see opportunity not only in Vancouver and Toronto, but in London, New York and Barcelona. A young architect in Calgary named Kevin Offin explains: "I'm committed to myself, and not to anything else. I just want to be mobile. I want the feeling of discovering something new."

And ultimately, it will be the cities that decide the contest for their skills. The most successful will become larger, democratic versions of workplaces like Critical Mass; weaving designers with techies, artists with corporate execs, while preserving their individual characters. They will offer parks and bike paths (the treadmills in the basement) and a spirit of inclusion (the busting down of the office walls). In these urban centres, software developers rub shoulders with abstract painters who bump into medical researchers, swapping electrical bursts of random creativity. Canadian cities have traditionally fared well on the mixing part and the quality-of-life meter, not as well on the innovative spark. But Calgary is still considered, by the skilled young adults walking its downtown streets, and by some of the leading urban experts looking from outside, as a place of huge potential – a city of entrepreneurs dripping in talent, with a growing brew of cultures, and the mountains, always, carving the horizon.

For a short moment in history, it was supposed that the Internet age would disperse humanity; instead, innovation has thrived where people cluster. Canada has become a nation of urbanites – more so than any other country in the world. While rural places grey, cities host 80 per cent of the population, and young people especially. According to the 2001 census, 50 per cent of Canadians now live in the four largest urban regions: Ontario's Golden Horseshoe around Toronto, Montreal, British Columbia's Lower Mainland, and the Calgary-Edmonton corridor. But these cities are competing with more than each other for the best workers; this recruiting game plays on a global field.

The clear advantage of a smart city has stoked debate over how to create one. In recent years particularly, the discussion has shifted away from the idea of a great city being built in industrial parks with tax incentives to woo marquee businesses. Now the municipal leaders speak of creating an environment that draws people rather than firms – especially the kind of young, talented workers chased by the knowledge industry. A leading voice in this discussion has been Richard Florida, a Carnegie Mellon University economist in Pittsburgh. His

book "The Rise of the Creative Class" shaped an economic argument
for tolerant, diverse cities with a vibrant cultural and artistic sensibility
– building on the case city guru Jane Jacobs made in the 1970s about
the vitality of a multi-layered urban scene. Creative people, Dr. Florida
argues, seek out places that offer a variety of opportunities for inspiration, at work and at play. In his model, places like Austin, Texas, with
its vibrant musical scene and respected university, have seen economic innovation – research, software development, high-tech companies – thrive; cities like Miami, with a service-industry economy
wrapped around tourism, face a greater challenge.

In conversations with creative young Calgarians, Dr. Florida's ideas
resonate, even if, as in most cases, they haven't heard of him. The kind
of environments they seek for work are similar to the places where
they want to live: It's no coincidence that one 25-year-old's concept of
a healthy city, where an artist would feel free to chalk a mural on the
sidewalk, sounds so much like the doodling elevators at Critical Mass.
Simone Zahradka speaks of how "creative people feed off diversity," of
the sense that in Calgary she can be "the next big thing to make the city
more than it already is." Keir Stuhlmiller, a graduate architect, reports
that the African presence on the street where she lives makes her feel
as "though something is right" in her community. Veer Gidwaney, the
VP of business development for his own software company, says: "I
don't ski – I'm not an outdoors type, but I still talk about how great it
is to have the mountains nearby . . . When work is done on Friday, it
should not be a stretch to figure out what you want to do." They share
a similar sense of place, and that is not something you happen upon
by accident or force. It is a choice you make, wisely.

In a swank restaurant on Stephen Avenue, four Calgarians – the kind
of engaged, enterprising citizens any place would covet – have come
together to talk about their hopes for the city.

There's Amanda Affonso, a financial business analyst with a
pipeline company, born in Montreal to East Indian parents, and

Suzanne Boss, who calls herself an Inspiration Catalyst in an e-mail, which means she works as a development consultant for organizations and manages a grassroots arts company. They are both 27, and openly lament the difficulty of balancing their careers with the families they'd like some day. "Here's criteria number one for me [in a partner]: Do you have something outside your engineering job – just cause there are so many engineers in this city – that you care passionately about," says Ms. Boss. "Yeah," sighs Ms. Affonso, "drinking beer and watching the football game."

The two guys at the table have broader hobbies than the Stampeders and beer. Chima Nkemdirim, 32, is a corporate lawyer who returned to Calgary in his late 20s after living in Ottawa and Toronto; his parents emigrated to Canada from Africa. Joel Tennison is a 26-year-old from Edmonton, and the only married one in the group; he's just gone back to law school after working as a marketing manager for a software company for four years.

It's easy to get them talking about what they like about Calgary. They see it as a place where merit prevails, where young people can run the business when they might be filing papers somewhere else. In Calgary, says Mr. Tennison, you can get in to see the head of the bank. Mr. Nkemdirim suggests that in the other cities where he's lived, people spend more time asking about your parents and what school you attended. The others at the table nod in agreement: "Here, if you can make them money, they don't care."

They cite the example of a 28-year-old entrepreneur named Drew Railton, who raised $7-million for a new city theatre, opened it in 32 weeks, and now sits as the chairman of the board. Calgary's future is open to influence: A visiting friend of Mr. Nkemdirim once observed that the city "looks like it was just uncrated." Adds Mr. Tennison, sounding remarkably like Simone Zahradka at Critical Mass: "I like the fact that we can be engaged in the struggle to bring the city around to something new." They approve of the "maverick" sensibility of the place, seeing the advantage in a community that doesn't, as Mr. Tennison says, "always fall in line."

Even the Stampede, which plays such a big part in Calgary's continuing image as a conservative cowtown, finds a niche in their vision for the city. "It's not every place," points out Ms. Affonso, "where you get the majority of the population dressing up and looking ridiculous." Someone notes the highly successful Ismaili breakfast during the stampede, or as Mr. Nkemdirim describes it, "all these brown people making pancakes wearing cowboy hats." Maybe, suggests Ms. Boss, if it wasn't the only thing outsiders knew about Calgary . . . "but I've learned to embrace it." The Stampede, she decides, works as one element of the city's character, when you also count the extreme mountain bikers, the stay-at-home moms, the grassroots artists, the oil and gas engineers, the techies, all building a place together at the foot of the Rockies.

At its best, she says, "Calgary satisfies your split personality." Mr. Tennison loves her assessment: "That's an awesome way to characterize a city."

These four are familiar with Richard Florida and his research; three of them, Ms. Affonso excepted, even attended a conference he held in Memphis, a city that gets his lowest ranking on the creative scale. Calgary, on the other hand, does exceptionally well. In a study with University of Toronto professor Meric Gertler, Dr. Florida ran his calculations on Canadian cities, comparing the number of university graduates (the talent), the proportion of high-tech companies (the tech-pole), foreign-born citizens (the mosaic) and full-time artists (the bohemians): the theory being that cities with the highest mix of these groups are best placed in the new economy. Using 2001 census data, Calgary ranks fifth overall in Canada, after the larger cities. But among North American urban centres of its size, Calgary places second to Austin, the model city of the Florida theory.

It may be no surprise that the city scores so well in the first two categories: Calgary, according to the census, grew faster than any other metropolitan area in the country between 1996 and 2001, attracting a mass of young, often skilled residents from British Columbia, the prairies and further east. Its economy has been buoyed by oil and gas development; it has an entrepreneurial spirit that spawns new companies.

But in a province with a reputation for homogeneity, Calgary has also attracted its fair share of immigrants. One in five city residents are foreign-born and, more significantly, Calgary's share of visible-minority citizens (which doesn't count aboriginal Canadians) is almost the same – the fourth highest proportion in the country, and growing at a slightly faster rate than Toronto or Vancouver. Calgary's share of "bohemians," remarkably, is only a few points lower than Montreal's, though its composition differs: As Dr. Gertler found, Calgary slants toward musicians, artists, interior designers; Toronto, Vancouver and Montreal are more weighted with producers, actors, fashion designers.

So Calgary, our quartet in the restaurant agree, has a pool of people that can make it an international city – along with its deep labour market, clean air and green spaces, and the recreational options afforded by the mountains. But some parts look better on paper, they say.

On the matter of the city's public relations message, they share an embarrassment – reflected by many other downtown 20s in Calgary – with Premier Ralph Klein and his hard-line opposition to same-sex marriage; they cite this, along with Calgary city council's 12-year refusal – reversed only in 2003 – to proclaim gay pride week, as positions that sustain the city's image as unreceptive to difference. (And indeed, urban research has suggested a link between creative cities and visible gay communities, as a first test for tolerance.)

The city is also a victim of urban sprawl and a lengthening commute, as every young resident in search of a downtown culture will tell you. It is a place, Mr. Tennison says, where too many people live in boxes: "Out of the box in the suburbs, into a box that's a garage, into the box that's a car, downtown, into the box that's underground parking, into an elevator up to your box in the sky. This is not healthy." The downtown, one 20s lawyer complains, is often "rolling with tumbleweeds" by 7 p.m., especially in the winter.

Young artists, says Ms. Boss, are only now starting to realize they could build a career in Calgary, but despite their reported numbers, they remain a largely unheralded, underground group. The four are regular patrons of the city's offerings: Among them, they have attended the symphony, the ballet and a Calgary Flames games in the last year, though they are more regular participants in the informal street scene, going to dinner after 9 p.m., visiting galleries, listening to local music at nightspots. They clearly seek to live in a city with an artistic vibe. No one would say Calgary comes close to matching Austin on this measure – the discussion around art in the city often seems forced – but they point to the number of grassroots theatre companies as untapped potential, and the nightlife on 17th Avenue.

The mix "is hugely important," says Ms. Affonso. She gives her own work as an example: She jumped into finance with an arts degree, and works in teams with engineers. "What I bring to the group is a new way of thinking – they think within the box and I connect the dots. And they would say that if you asked them."

"A life well lived has different parts," concludes Mr. Tennison. "You get that from bumping into people who aren't like you."

On a Friday night, sipping cocktails at a martini bar where the waitresses wear slinky evening gowns, Kevin Offin leans back on a mod-shaped couch, and ponders the question of cities. He is the kind of guy who "gets queasy when he can't see downtown." Calgary, he suggests, has pockets of real culture but lacks a web to link it together. You can, with initiative, go clubbing until 5 a.m. but he jokes that his efforts to order a beer at 8 a.m. have routinely failed. The city, he says, is working to create a downtown presence – one he shows off in visits to a trendy jazz lounge and a couple of smoky nightclubs on 17th Avenue. "The more urban amenities I have around me, the more alive I feel."

But a city is not built solely around citizens like Kevin Offin.

A few blocks away, on another weekend night, in a small rented house in a newly trendy neighbourhood called Mission, another group of Calgarians, equally important to the urban blend, are having a potluck of curry and vegetarian lasagna and homemade custard. There's a math teacher working on a comic book, a potter who's brought her four-month-old son, the members of the Old Trout Puppet Workshop. Hosting with her sister Kristin, an art therapist, is Jill Boettger, who has just had her first book accepted by a publisher – a novel in poem called "Heartland." Though she sometimes feels her hometown is "formula trendy," with its suburban preoccupation extended into the urban core, Ms. Boettger returned to Calgary from Vancouver with a vision of the life she wanted – she was "aching to get back to the prairies and mountains" and wanted to be close to her family, in a community of "kind-hearted people." The martini clubs aren't for her; she'd rather go to a coffee shop to hear one guy on acoustic guitar. She works part-time as a writing teacher at Mount Royal College; eschewing the "old tidy roles," she is emphatically against "a corporate job with a gold watch at the end." But she worries about paying the bills. She wants to be able to stay downtown, to afford a life that inspires her, maybe start a family. But there's not much money in poetry, and her boyfriend, Stephen Pearce, is a puppeteer. He says that diverse populations help performers too, and not just by filling the street: "Artists are not very good at talking about art with other artists."

But neither can fail to see the high-end condos and luxury renovation jobs popping up around them as urban life gets hip. It's an old story; when artists and immigrants make a neighbourhood desirable, the prices go up, and it takes some careful planning not to push out the residents who led the renaissance in the first place. Ms. Boettger admits she feels resentful: "Here you build a sense of space, you help give it personality, and yet the work you do isn't valued enough to help you live there." Either you're relegated to the "scungier areas," she says, "or heaven forbid, to cookie-cutter suburbia." Two of the members of the Old Trouts are already living in vans parked outside the group's studio – a third member lives inside – and the troupe is pondering its long-term viability. Ms. Boettger and some of her friends have even talked about buying a house collectively. "There's this whole idea that artists thrive on struggle, that they like to live in vans," she says. "It's as if their whole legacy is to make places cozy and just move on." This is not, she insists, the role they want.

A few hours earlier on that Saturday afternoon, in a new community called Garrison Woods, built on the grounds of a defunct military base on the edge of downtown, Adam Legge and Shannon Ryland have delayed their stroller shopping to offer a tour. He's an urban development consultant, she's an IT business analyst; they are expecting their first child in April. They live in a renovated military home, on a street, as they readily point out, with front porches and sidewalks. They like the community because it has made an effort to place people before cars – the narrow streets slow traffic – and it has concentrated on mixed housing – a seniors residence, condos above new storefronts, houses that look distinct from each other, and affordable housing.

They have strong thoughts on this last part – many young Calgarians, in fact, raise the high costs of downtown apartments as enforcing a bland space. They do not want their child growing up in a community where everyone comes from the same place in life – by nationality, occupation or income. Mr. Legge, who volunteers for an affordable housing program, says that deliberately mingling different socio-economic groups is as essential as putting artists and techies together. "Go down 17th Avenue, you'll pass everyone from panhandlers to skateboarders to people with million-dollar homes," he says. "It creates a better reflection of what life is like. It makes us more balanced." What's more, it allows for spontaneous interactions between groups that might not otherwise connect – the whole premise around vibrant cities. It says that the guy who serves coffee at the shop on the downtown corner – and isn't forced to live on the outskirts – has something to offer.

"A city," says Mr. Legge, "must be about more than moving traffic." It must make a place for everyone.

LETTING DIVERSITY DEVELOP NATURALLY

Betsy Donald likes to tell the story of the day she was reading to her daughter in the children's section of the Public Library in Kingston, Ont., and a Lebanese woman began asking her to translate book titles. Soon her husband joined them, explaining how they had recently arrived in Canada, and sharing stories about life in Lebanon that had nothing to do with terrorism. "I just came away very enriched by this everyday social interaction," says Dr. Donald, an assistant professor in geography at Queen's University. "And that happened because I met someone in a public place. And not because I paid $10 to go to a festival and eat some cool Lebanese food."

Dr. Donald studies cities, and she warns against simplifying the route to urban vitality down to funky nightclubs and eclectic restaurants, what she calls the "Hey-we-have-a-gay-district-we-must-be-cool" mentality. What's more important is creating public policy and social inclusion that allows diversity to develop naturally – and build the kind of cities that attract innovative, skilled workers from around the world. Cities, she says, need to avoid the consumer approach to culture: the kind that says, "Oh, we love to live in Little Italy because it is so diverse and cool. But the reality is everybody is wearing black and drinking lattes."

In the current test for the smart city, following the statistical calculation devised by Richard Florida where cities with the most university graduates, foreign-born citizens, high tech companies, and artists prevail, major Canadian cities perform better in some categories than others. Considering all North American cities with more than a million people, Toronto has the most foreign-born residents per capita (based on 1996 census data) and Vancouver comes second. For their blends of artists, Vancouver and Toronto place third and fourth, respectively, behind only Los Angeles and New York. They fall well out of the top 10, however, with talent and tech; the former may reflect an education system that produces more college graduates, suggests Meric Gertler, who co-wrote the study, while the latter suggests the need for a stronger climate of innovation.

But Canadian centres have certain advantages in the global competition, says Dr. Gertler, a professor at the University of Toronto. The largest are less expensive than other international cities their size, both for businesses and residents. They are building a highly educated population. They have the reputation of being safe, clean and welcoming to newcomers. "Our cities are viewed as beacons of opportunity. That is a huge advantage."

At the same time, he points out that cities could do a better job integrating immigrants into the workforce, starting with a recognition of foreign credentials. The major centres have public transportation systems that don't compete with those in continental Europe. Their public places have declined under budget cuts. And there is evidence they are becoming more polarized with housing costs – that the same artists and immigrants who foster a neighbourhood revival risk being forced out when property values soar.

Canada's cities are a true social experiment on how to equitably and authentically mix a diverse population in one space. Dr. Donald relates the comments of a young restaurant owner who insisted he can find better Chinese food in Toronto than in Hong Kong – a fact he credits to the fusion of cultural influences mingling on the city's streets. Says Dr. Donald: "We are building something new."

13

THE TIME OF CROSSING OVER

ALANNA MITCHELL

As a proud young native man gives a convocation speech at what is about to become the First Nations University of Canada, the radio crackles with a reminder of his community's demons: the trial of three white men for the rape of a 12-year-old aboriginal girl. But as the native population of Saskatchewan booms and more of its youth attain higher education, people here eagerly await 'the flip' – an imminent tipping point that could see native people take a leading role in shaping the Canada of the future.

Wednesday

Damon Badger-Heit, 23, has spent all night riding a bus across the Great Plains, his people's ancient homeland, working on the valedictory speech he is to give in two days time at his university's convocation ceremony.

He's nervous. Sitting here on a park bench in the blistering May sun of downtown Regina, his sleek black ponytail hanging down his back, eyes ringed with the shadows of fatigue, he's a little spooked about speaking on behalf of a whole graduating class of aboriginal students. At first, in honour of the august occasion, he felt obliged to sound stuffy and learned. But now he's thinking he should just speak from his heart.

"We all went there for the same reasons: to improve our lives, to improve ourselves, to improve the communities around us," he says, pulling heavily on a sweaty bottle of lemonade Snapple.

But Mr. Badger-Heit is speaking for more than the 118 members of his graduating class. As he prepares to take on the world – he's considering a master's degree in fine art, perhaps teaching drama on his reserve or travelling to other countries to teach English – he represents the hopes his aboriginal forebears had for their people when the Europeans started arriving and demanding to share this rich land.

The sharing has not been as they dreamed. Not even close. After Europeans arrived, Canada's First Nations were "systematically dispossessed of their lands and livelihood, their cultures and languages, and their social and political institutions," the 1996 Report of the Royal Commission on Aboriginal Peoples has documented. They lost not just the trappings of their society, but life itself. Before Europeans arrived, in about 1500, the aboriginal population of what would eventually be Canada was roughly 500,000, according to the commission's research. By 1871, right after Canada became a country, the aboriginal population had plummeted to just over 100,000. It would not regain the half-million mark until the 1980s. Today, it is not quite a million.

And those who survived have made up a Third-World-style native underclass in Canada with measurably poorer health, housing, water, education and income than the majority of Canadians; a life expectancy that, after years of dramatic improvements, is still five to seven years shorter; and a rate of incarceration that runs roughly six times that of the general population.

But apart from carrying the weight of the crushed hopes of the past, Mr. Badger-Heit represents his own generation, too, struggling to learn and earn its way into an aboriginal middle class; to invent itself – it's a tricky game – as both fiercely aboriginal and proudly Canadian.

And he represents the future, a Saskatchewan that is heading toward being more aboriginal than not for the first time since the Europeans arrived all those generations ago.

It could be decades before what many aboriginals here call "the flip" – five or six of them, maybe, depending on birth rates and the pace of white flight and the province's success in attracting and retaining other cultures. But already, a critical mass of Saskatchewan identifies itself as aboriginal – 13.5 per cent, against 3.3 per cent of Canada as a whole, according to Statistics Canada's 2001 census. More significantly, fully a quarter of Saskatchewan's children are aboriginal. That birth rate is slowing down a little, but Statistics Canada estimates it is still roughly double that of Canada as a whole.

As the flip approaches, the potential is for the province's levers of power to be shared with or possibly controlled by aboriginals, along with the good jobs and the assets and the resources. And not just on reserves, but far past that into the broader community. In fact, many of the wise elders of Saskatchewan – both native and not – take the view that the very prosperity of this beleaguered Prairie province with its droughts, pests and vanishing family farms rests in the hands of this new generation of aboriginals.

There will be implications for all of Canada in this. There will be a joyous stretching of definitions; a painful sharing of wealth; a gradual chipping away of stereotypes, hatred and bigotry. Once one of the provinces is run by aboriginals, what is to stop aboriginal men and women from holding the highest offices in the land?

This is the hopeful scenario, the one that peeks its merry face around the obduracy of Saskatchewan's past. But there is another possible future. Even if Saskatchewan's aboriginal population reaches the half-way point and beyond, it may be that power will remain the enclave of non-aboriginals, that the scars of colonization will not fade so quickly on one side or the other. Or that prosperity, if it comes to aboriginals in Saskatchewan, will remain there, unable to make its way to aboriginals in other parts of Canada's south.

All this rests on the pole-straight shoulders of Damon Badger-Heit as he sits here drinking deeply from his Snapple. And if this new dream of peace and mutual prosperity between aboriginals and non-aboriginals across Canada fails to take wing?

"Things will carry on," Mr. Badger-Heit says. "There will still be love and kids and everything. But I think it'd be pretty chaotic."

A refrain is humming through Regina on this same sunny day. It is an old and a hellishly common one that sums up the obstacles that dreamers like Mr. Badger-Heit still face. This time the refrain is being carried by the local CBC radio affiliate on its cycle of news programs: "Closing arguments are expected to begin this morning at a sexual-assault trial in Melfort," the announcer tells listeners at 8 a.m. "Three Tisdale men stand accused of assaulting a 12-year-old aboriginal girl. Dean Edmondson is the first to go on trial. The CBC's Dan Kerslake reports ..."

The trial has transfixed the province; stiffened the stereotypes; angered the native community and stirred the terrible ghosts of historic injustice. The 12-year-old, not yet 90 pounds or 5 feet tall, had a fight with her mother, walked 11 kilometres to the bar in a nearby town in the farming heartland of the province, took a ride in a truck with three white men and woke up hours later, her tender vagina torn and bleed-ing, cuts and bruises on her back and legs, unable to walk properly, stinking of alcohol. A dominant issue at trial is whether the girl looked old enough to pass for 14, when she could legally consent to have sex.

The testimony has been heart-rending, including evidence that the girl drank enough liquor to pass out and then awakened in kalei-doscopic snatches to find one man holding her down while another tried to remove her underwear. The men testified in court that each tried in turn to have intercourse with her, but each was too drunk to maintain an erection. Most difficult of all is that DNA found on the girl's underwear was that of her own father, possibly from an earlier incident. The girl has testified that her father did not have sex with her, but was physically abusive to her and her mother.

Citizens of Saskatchewan, both native and not, have been paying close attention to this case. They paid attention at the beginning when the three accused men were released from custody without bail. They noticed the troubling stories about the girl's life on the reserve. The question that keeps coming up is whether the case would be played out differently in the public arena if the skin colours were reversed. It's the quintessential test of systemic racial prejudice: If the 12-year-old girl had been white and her accused attackers three drunk native men, would the men have been released from jail without bail into the bosom of their community?

This is the context in which Mr. Badger-Heit holds onto hope. He knows about the larger forces of his society, the shocking cases that have gone before, the terrible problems within some aboriginal families. His own father was killed on the streets of Saskatoon some years back. He is not denying. Not shutting his eyes. There's probably anger inside him somewhere. But he is capable of honouring what has gone before as history, as being the best that could have been done then, and moving on despite it.

Thursday

The symbol of the will to move from desperation to middle class is the Saskatchewan Indian Federated College, which is affiliated with the University of Regina. It opened here in 1976 with nine students after the more prestigious University of Saskatchewan in Saskatoon refused to have anything to do with it. Now it has about 2,000 students spread over several campuses and is launching a raft of graduate programs.

Today, the day before Mr. Badger-Heit's convocation address, crews of workers are laying underground watering equipment and plenty of sod, trying to get the site spruced up. As usual, the fabled Saskatchewan weather is not co-operating: fearsome winds whip the topsoil across the empty fields toward Manitoba, except for the grains that cake inside damp eyes and noses, embed themselves in pores.

Mr. Badger-Heit will give the final convocation address of the Saskatchewan Indian Federated College. In a few weeks, the college will be reborn as the First Nations University of Canada, to reflect its growing academic ambition in this country. And it will inaugurate its new building, which is beyond dispute the centrepiece of the University of Regina campus. Designed by internationally famous architect Douglas Cardinal, who is aboriginal, it is a sinuous, organic structure that eventually will be anchored by two soaring glass tepees, one inside and another at the outer entrance.

This building is visible from the Trans-Canada Highway that runs around the perimeter of this capital city of Saskatchewan and from the main north-south route through town. It is a beacon of postsecondary education – and of the native place in it. The native community itself raised $30-million privately and through government to construct it.

It is a far cry from when Wes Stevenson, the elegant acting president of the SIFC, started at the University in Regina in 1973. He was a tall kid from the reserve who ended up at university because he loved to play basketball. His first day on campus, a counsellor took him aside, looked him in the eye and said: "Your kind never make it here." He meant it kindly. He didn't want Mr. Stevenson to get his hopes up. Now the college is the driving force behind young aboriginals, mostly women, getting university degrees in Saskatchewan. The number is still achingly small: For all of Saskatchewan, just 460 aboriginals in their 20s who were out of school held a degree in 2001, when Statistics Canada did its census count, compared with 9,445 non-aboriginals. But the increase is huge from 1996: 78 per cent for aboriginals in the first half of their 20s and 65 per cent for those in the second half, says Andrew Siggner, StatsCan's dean of aboriginal data.

Education means jobs; jobs mean money and good houses and better schools for their children and social influence. It's a return to the aboriginals' centuries-old dream of respect, sharing wealth, living in harmony.

In Saskatchewan, just 42 per cent of aboriginals 15 and older were employed – with an average annual income of $15,994 – when the 2001 census was taken, compared with 66 per cent of non-aboriginals who earned an average $26,914. However, while the gaps are still wide, they have narrowed in recent years. Today, slowly, aboriginals are joining the white-collar economy of the province, says Bill Asikinack, one of the most influential professors at SIFC and a man with a deep faith in the future. "The lazy Indian, the drunken Indian, the welfare Indian, those ideas are going out the window," he says, boxes of his books lining his brand-new office walls, a hammer and nails lying on his desk, the remnants of putting together bookcases and hanging pictures.

As for the First Nations University of Canada, he sees it growing, too, turning out smart graduates eager to take on the world; a generation that, for the first time, will have the same choices as those available to their non-aboriginal peers. They will not necessarily use their talents on the reserve, either. "It's not going to be just a minor drip, drip," Mr. Asikinack said. "In a little while, it will be a major explosion."

"Jury deliberations are in their second day at a sexual-assault trial in Melfort," the CBC radio announcer tells Regina at noon. "The trial involves allegations of sexual assault by three men on a 12-year-old girl. As Dan Kerslake reports, the jury asked another question of clarification this morning . . ."

Friday

Mr. Badger-Heit's mother, Mary Heit, 51, is telling a story over lunch just hours before the convocation. It's a love story. She grew up as one of seven Roman Catholic children in an isolated German-Canadian farming family in Saskatchewan, and never had anything to do with aboriginal Canadians. Then she went to university and fell in love with Jacob Badger, the native way of life and the ideal of racial equality. His Cree people were isolated, too, on the reserve at Mistawasis near Saskatoon; five families living in five adjacent houses.

Their fathers were against the marriage, but it went ahead. Damon was 2 when it ended and 10 when his dad, an alcoholic who by then was living on the streets of Saskatoon, was killed. The other Badgers of Mistawasis pitched in to help Ms. Heit keep Damon's native roots alive.

Ms. Heit raised her son alone, teaching at SIFC, a linguist by education, holding both professionally and personally to the dream that aboriginal Canadians could have equal opportunity in her country. A few years ago, she fell in love again – again with a Cree man, an academic who taught social work at SIFC. Now she is stepmother to the three children Sid Fiddler, 51, had with his first wife, a German-Canadian physician.

Damon is the first of the grandchildren to graduate from university, she says, close to tears. "We were going to change the world," she says, brushing the tears away. "And I guess it's happening."

She turns to her mother, Kay Heit, 78, sitting across the table. The elder Mrs. Heit lives in a seniors' home in Unity now, but she wasn't about to have an aboriginal grandson and not know about his culture. Once her husband had died, she opened herself up to native culture, insisted on experiencing native sweats and other spiritual rituals. She got to know her grandson's native relatives.

The other day, she tells the table, she had a get-together with some old acquaintances who were going on about all the good-for-nothing Indians who were ruining Saskatchewan. It was an hour of torture, she says. They were just so ignorant. Finally, she piped up: "Listen here, I've got a son-in-law who's an Indian and who's educated." She's still trying to puzzle out why people she knows would feel free to express such bigotry.

Rachel Fiddler, 21, Damon's stepsister, has just finished her first year at the University of Saskatchewan in Saskatoon and she has seen the prejudice firsthand, she says. Some of her fellow students don't know she is proudly native. They let things slip. She is eager for the day when aboriginals are routinely elected to office: mayors, city councillors, MPs. She believes hers is the generation that will do it, born in what she calls a time of "crossing over." They are emotionally healthy, educated, secure, without the previous generations' scars of residential schools, abuse and addiction. They are helping to change attitudes. That's the way she sees it. "I think people realize that Indian people are people, not some kind of infestation," she says, her eyes narrowing.

Her brother Derek Fiddler, 16, rail-thin and intense, is the youngest at the table. He has been listening silently to all the talk. When it turns to residential schools ("We were inmates in a maximum-security institution," his father Sid Fiddler remarks), the passion overtakes him. The last residential school was closed in 1986, the year he was born, he says, voice dripping with disgust. Like his father, he is convinced that native Canadians are fated for better. That they are no longer going to be second-class citizens in their own country. "It's more or less a matter of when it's going to happen," he says. "Not if."

Just as the family rises from lunch, the jury reaches a verdict. "A 26-year-old man has been found guilty of sexually assaulting a 12-year-old girl near Tisdale," the CBC announcer says. "Dean Edmondson is first of three men to go to trial charged with the crime. The court was told that Edmondson and his two friends got the girl drunk and then sexually assaulted her on a country road. The CBC's Dan Kerslake has this report ..."

Friday evening, convocation

In native culture, just as blame is collective, so is credit. The honour of one is the honour of all. So a convocation of 118 aboriginal students from all over the province – and even from other parts of Canada – is an event like no other. More than 700 people have assembled at the Delta Hotel, to bear witness, video cameras in hand.

It is one of the fanciest hotels in Regina, and the splendid rooms sport the names of a European culture from far away: Raphael, Lombardy, Tuscany, Umbria. The tables are covered with white linen. Each is lit by the romantic light of a candle. Many of the women are wearing backless gowns, high-heeled sandals, dangling earrings. Mr. Badger-Heit and some of the other men are in bold native patterns. Each graduate is wearing the sky-blue robe that only representatives of the Indian college are allowed to wear.

A little girl dressed in a sleeveless pink linen dress can hardly stand the excitement. She slides over to a table laden with desserts to try to snag a piece of chocolate cake. Her grandmother intervenes just in time.

A few older people get up to the microphone to remind the revellers that just a generation ago, aboriginals were overtly consigned to "paraprofessions," allowed to be handmaids to the white people who held the real jobs in teaching, engineering and law. Tonight, some of the students are getting master's degrees. And there will be more. Demography is on the natives' side this time, they say. Their numbers are growing in Saskatchewan. They are eager to take their place front and centre in the labour force. The "flip" is coming.

Then it's time for the valedictorian. Mr. Badger-Heit walks up to the podium. His mother yells, "Go, baby!" He is ramrod straight. When he starts to speak, everyone in the room falls silent. He is speaking to his ancestors, to his peers, to the people of the future. And on behalf of them. His people have stumbled and endured but they are bound to prevail, he says. They have to keep going, keep dreaming.

Then he turns to just one person in the crowd – his mother – who is perhaps the biggest dreamer there. He picks up his black electric guitar and starts singing a tribute to her, to the power of a dream. It is a Phil Ochs song about having to get things done before he's gone.

Tears are streaming down his mother's face. Then her clear voice rises with his and they sing the gentle song of endurance together.

Epilogue

The summer is ending. The Saskatchewan Indian Federated College has been reborn. Now it is the First Nations University of Canada. A hopeful new crop of students has started classes. But that uncomfortable refrain won't go away. Dean Edmondson's sentence has finally been passed down. He has been handed a two-year conditional sentence for sexually assaulting the 12-year-old girl. It's an unusually light sentence. The Crown attorney had asked for four years in jail.

That means Mr. Edmondson will be confined to his home for two years and electrically monitored. But he will be able to work. He has also been ordered to do 200 hours of community service, undergo alcohol and sex-offender counselling, and pay a fine of $500.

The judge in the case explained his reasoning this way: The 12-year-old had been sexually abused before she ran into Mr. Edmondson and his friends and might have been showing "unpredictable sexual behaviour." By extension, that might mean she was a willing participant or even the aggressor in the assault, he said.

The other two men who tried to rape the child were acquitted in a trial in July.

14

ON THE STREET WHERE WE LIVE

KEN WIWA

Toronto's Bloor Street is a one-stop United Nations where anywhere between 80 to 135 languages are spoken, an unfolding narrative of what it means to be a new Canadian in the 21st century. A variety store run by a former Burmese liberation soldier sits next to Somali roti shops, Bangladeshi curry houses and Portuguese churrascos. 'In a new city,' as a local poet wrote, 'there are ghosts of old cities. There are lies and re-creations.'

THERE IS A SCHOOL OF THOUGHT THAT if you want to see what it means to be Canadian, all you have to do is walk up and down Bloor Street in Toronto. There are, depending who you talk to, anything from 80 to 135 languages spoken on the street. It has a United Nations of cultures, a collection of fugitive pieces, historical ironies and exotic hybrids. Eritrean, Italian and Ethiopian restaurants stand side by side, there is an Indo-Japanese sari shop and the oldest mosque in Canada is in a converted Anglican church in a Ukrainian neighbourhood.

Photo by Fred Lum

Bloor Street is a long billboard to tolerance, a panoramic route to the mythology of a Canada for all.

This notion of Canada as multiculture was constructed on the idea of the ethnic mosaic. But is the new Canada still a mosaic – or a melting pot where new generations of Canadians are being integrated into a nascent idea of the country? How have the children of immigrants negotiated the spaces between their roots and their identity as Canadians?

I walk up and down Bloor, talking to these Canadians, to see how they are living out the myths of multiculturalism.

To walk east along Bloor is to trace the narrative of an old story unfolding with new characters. The distance from the tough neighbourhoods around Lansdowne Street in the west, to the institutional ghetto of downtown Toronto near Yonge Street, is a measure of the range of what it means to be a new Canadian in the 21st century.

Any journey on Bloor Street still begins on another continent, and this one starts in Seoul, South Korea, where a fiercely proud Torontonian was born 21 years ago. Ryan Cha was 10 years old when his family immigrated to Canada. These days, between studying hotel management, Mr. Cha runs Webfusion, an Internet café at Bloor and Dundas Street West.

It's something of a surprise to find a Korean business at this juncture of the street. Koreatown is concentrated further east, where almost every other store between Christie and Bathurst is an Internet café – the new variety stores of Toronto. The block is a facsimile of the most technologically advanced culture in the world.

"I hang out there once in a while. Personally I don't like it too much," Mr. Cha says in the small reception area looking out onto a Greek restaurant on the north side of Bloor. He speaks with the conviction of a young man who knows his mind. "There's too many Internet cafés," he says, explaining what led to him locate his business away from the home comforts of Koreatown. "If you go to those cafés all their windows are written in Korean, so it makes it difficult for the non-Korean to understand what the operating system is all about."

He looked instead at the cheap rents – and close proximity to a high school – at Dundas and Bloor, and decided to reach out to a market beyond Toronto's 80,000 Koreans. "Koreans are welcome to come here, obviously, but I am trying to look for as large a market as possible, not only one certain market."

The dynamics that created Toronto's Koreatown are much the same as those behind immigrant ghettoes the world over. Language is the first. "The reason why a lot of people stick with the Korean community is that people that just came from Korea, they can't speak English very well, so they don't know how to do business," Mr. Cha says.

And without collateral to get bank loans, immigrant communities turn inwards. Credit unions and churches often provide financing, networks and markets. Some Korean businesses are still financed by a family-based loan scheme known as Geh.

Geh was "very popular in the pioneering days of Korea immigration into North America but with growing affluence amongst second-generation children, [there is] little need for it now," says a community member who doesn't want his name used, Koreans being generally unwilling to talk about the scheme. But I gather it is still popular in the newer Korean churches, centring on small groups, usually no more than 10 people, often born in the same district in Korea.

The scheme's tight bonds seem a reflection of the intimacy of Koreatown. But that intimacy also contributed to Mr. Cha's decision to expand his horizons beyond its saturated markets.

"What happens with Korean communities is it's so small," he explains. "If you have a Korean friend, I probably know one of them or know his parents or my parents know his parents. See, what happens is as soon as one person hears that the business is doing well, they put another one right beside it. When Koreans come here they don't be creative or try to create new ideas, they stick to what they know or what Korean culture in Toronto knows. The stereotype is that Koreans own all the convenience stores, smoke shops, dry cleaning, laundromats, Internet cafés, Coffee Time, etcetera. Slowly by slowly it's changing. I wouldn't complain if we had a huge community just like the Chinese community. They can afford to compete with one another. We can't. Next thing you know a competitor goes bankrupt and that's when they learn."

Mr. Cha clearly lives a second-generation dilemma: While his immigrant identity roots him, Canada has pulled him to other parts of Bloor Street.

"I'm proud to be Korean but I'm proud to be Canadian as well," he says, outlining the neighbourhoods of his bicultural personality. "I am bilingual; I speak both Korean and English. At home I speak generally Korean because they [my parents] have trouble with English, but with my friends and my older brother I speak English."

After listening to him manoeuvre his way around the congested and contested side streets of his identity – like his anglicized name and his views on interethnic marriage ("I'm actually very open-minded about it but my parents would kill me"), I decide to test his loyalty: Which country would he support if Korea went head to head with Canada in his favourite sport? "I would, er, I would cheer for Korea," he offers hesitantly, "but I will still be cheering if any of those teams lose." He adds, laughing: "We won't be seeing anything like that because we're not very good at hockey."

And if the two countries went to war, I ask tactlessly? "Oh man, that's not good," he says, grimacing at the prospect. "In that case I think I would go back to my Korean culture. There's a difference between the government and the actual land of the country. I think the Canadian government is doing a great job but if they go to war against Korea I might change my perspective on the whole war. It depends on the circumstance. If I think Korea deserved it in some way, I'd just say 'Yeah, we deserved it.'"

I leave Ryan Cha to ponder a dilemma that may be unthinkable for second-generation Canadians raised on the national mythology of peacekeeping and safe havens. I head east, crossing Lansdowne into the stretch of Bloor leading to Ossington. This is Canada's waterfront, the place where many new immigrants land and literally set up shop in anticipation of fast-tracking the next generation into the mainstream Canada. I pass a variety store run by a former Burmese liberation soldier, Bangladeshi curry houses, Somali roti shops and Portuguese churrascos until I come across a sign featuring a shield in the red and white check of Croatia's national colours. The Croatian Credit Union is open but the atmosphere inside gives off a sense it has seen busier days.

Joe Vinski, the general manager of the credit union, gives me a brief tour around 30 years of Croatian immigration that confirms my initial impression. "There used to be a Croatian restaurant on Bloor but the owner died and it was taken over by Somalis," he says. I gather that the Croatian community around Bloor has largely dispersed to Mississauga and the church behind the credit union had been up for sale.

Further east, between Ossington and Christie, is a strip that confirms Toronto's reputation as a space where peoples from countries in conflict can live side by side. It is here that I run into Daniel Michael, a sociology student at York University, his long limbs casually draped over a stool in Sawa, an Eritrean restaurant. An Ethiopian restaurant is next door.

What is it like living side by side with Ethiopians in Toronto when there had been a war on back home? "We know that the war is basically politics," Mr. Michael shrugs. "It's the politicians in Eritrea who have a problem with the politicians in Ethiopia, we don't let that get between us. We feel that we are one people regardless of whether we are from Ethiopia or Eritrea."

I can't decide whether this is youthful optimism talking, or whether he is toeing the Canadian party line of tolerance. It is not as if distance had lent him a sanitized perspective of the war, because he had almost been caught up in it in 1998, when he was 17.

Mr. Michael, now 21, was born in California and spent most of his life divided between Windsor and Las Vegas. He had just finished a year of high school in the land of his parents. "The war started the day I left Eritrea," he recalls. "I was on a plane going from Frankfurt to Toronto and there was a CNN newsbreak saying the war had just started, and my mom and dad went crazy and they just wanted to know if my plane got off right."

It was his first – and so far only – experience of the place he insists is home. "My identity as in my nationality is Eritrean, I have citizenship there and that's what I tell everybody." But as ever, it is Canada that has afforded him the space to be Eritrean. "Because of the multicultural population here, I just feel like another Canadian," he explains. "Being Canadian ultimately just means you're from somewhere else and you've made Canada your home and that's the case for most people here."

Can a country continue to happily accommodate citizens who also see themselves as foreigners? And isn't Mr. Michael's retention of his Eritrean identity a rejection of Canada's aspirations to build a colourblind society? "Even if we did lose our identity there would still be racial barriers because in their eyes we're different," Mr. Michael insists. "If you look at America where they denounce where they're from and they still have racism there, then it's not going to change. I think it's going to be there no matter what. The idea is to celebrate the differences, work together."

I imagine that Mr. Michael's split identity could be bound up in the communal experiences of the 10,000 Eritreans living in Canada. Although they are part of one of the earliest diasporas from Africa, they are dispersed around Toronto and have not had the economic impact or concentration of the Korean community. "The community had been suspended between Canada and Eritrea," Amanuel Melles, a leader in the community, later tells me. Much of Eritreans' capital was sent back to Africa to support first the 30-year liberation struggle against Ethiopia and then independence, he says.

"The community does not have a lot of social asset," Mr. Melles explains, "but the children are growing and there is a growing interest in taking part in civic life in Toronto."

But even as young Eritreans embrace Canada, the old country still makes demands on them. A group of 120 Eritrean professionals around Canada were instrumental, Mr. Melles says, in getting the Canadian International Development Agency to approve a $3-million aid package in April to help alleviate the drought in Eritrea.

Back at Sawa, Mr. Michael outlines his vision of the future for young Eritreans in Canada. "We're going to play a big part in the development of our countries," both Eritrea and Canada, he says. "We've had more opportunities than our parents did, that will be the focus for it in the near future."

I leave Sawa and double back on myself to make a mental note of the range of cultures between Ossington and Christie. It confirms poet Dionne Brand's simple evocation of these streets: "Selam Restaurant, Jeonghhysa Buddhist Temple, Oneda's Market, West Indian and Latin America Foods, Afro Sound, Lalibela Ethiopian Cuisine, Longo's Vegetable and Fruits, Astoria Athens Restaurant, Coffee Time, Star Falafel, Vince Gasparos Meats, Africa Wings Travel, PCI House-Internet Cafe, Kholsa Travel, Greek Credit Union, Menalon, Asmaria Restaurant and Bar, Sawa, Wing Po Variety, Ramon Humeres – Dentist, Universal Beauty Supply."

"In a new city," Brand wrote in the same piece, "there are ghosts of old cities. There are lies and re-creations."

Mi Linda Managua is one of those recreations. I have never been to Nicaragua but the modest furniture, the mud-red colour of the walls and the giant television at the back of the restaurant feel authentic.

"I see myself as 100-per-cent Nicaraguan," says Liza-Maria Peneda-Lopez, a 20-year-old waitress at her sister's restaurant, who came to

Canada at the age of four. She learned English from television and at school, but she also grew up speaking and writing perfect Spanish. "You know what the funny thing is that people come in here and say, 'Oh my gawd your accent. You have a perfect Nicaraguan accent,'" she says in a perfectly breathless and treacly North American falsetto.

"Once you cross from Nicaragua to Costa Rica," she continues, "there's such a big difference in accent and they're both Spanish languages. But our accent is so typical – like the way we use the words and the way we use, like, sayings. Like, I can tell you a joke and whatever, and all that would be, like, really funny, because people would come here and say, like, 'I just came from there and you know it's amazing.'"

As I leave Ms. Peneda-Lopez in her memories of Nicaragua and cross back into North America, I begin to wonder about the dialogue between Canada and the countries its immigrants come from. The bargain of multiculturalism is that the newcomer gets to keep his or her culture – but what is the relationship between this culture and Canada? When does the old country or culture lose its influence and the immigrant begin to speak Canadian? Or is "Canadian" the sum of its immigrant voices?

When you walk Bloor Street you get a palpable sense of its panorama, of the bright colours at one end bleeding and eventually blending into the downtown core. The juncture of Bloor and Spadina marks a kind of watershed, a boundary between new Canada and old Canada. The kaleidoscope of colour gives way to the sober buildings of the University of Toronto.

On the southwest corner of Bloor and Spadina is the a sleek glass building, a $10-million renovation of the Jewish Community Centre (JCC) that will house an Internet centre, a franchise of the ubiquitous Second Cup, and facilities for a theatre, fitness room, rooftop parties, and a Jewish daycare centre. On a grass verge opposite the JCC, I sit discussing the renovation with 24-year-old Adam Marrus, who came to Canada from England as a four-year-old and has spent his life since then in the neighbourhood.

"I've been coming to JCC for years," he says. "I went to nursery school here, my mother, aunts and uncles have been coming for years. It's like a second home to me." The renovation is happening at an "exciting time," he says, concurring with the suggestion that the JCC's reinvention is a reflection of the shifting preoccupations within the Jewish community. "Some people see it as a cultural centre and others see it as an athletic centre."

Skittish about whether he is religious ("That's rather a personal question"), Mr. Marrus nevertheless protests that he doesn't see himself as only one thing or only another. "As events arise my Judaism may come to the forefront. In other cases I feel proud to be Canadian. I don't feel I have to choose."

Again, two masters – this time the religious and the secular. And again, I wonder whether the rallying cry of peace, order and good government is enough to hold all these stories together. What will be the thread that knits all these masters?

I get my answer as I come to the end of Bloor Street, where I run into a strident voice and advocate for a brand new Canada in the guise of an Indian-Canadian who spent the first twenty years of his life pretending he was German.

Rahul Raj grew up in Kitchener, Ont., which he cheerfully informs me has the largest Oktoberfest outside Germany. It wasn't until he arrived at university in Toronto as a 21-year-old in 1997 that Mr. Raj began to discover himself. "I had to make a choice: Hang out with the visible minority or the majority," he recalls. The decision was made when he discovered there were other East Indians who had grown up under the same conditions as him, giving him a new perspective on the community.

He even started to date from his own culture. "I'd never have dreamed of marrying an Indian girl as a child, it was too complicated.

I associated Indians with recent immigrants who held on to old beliefs. I considered myself hybrid, but when I moved to Toronto I found that there were cool Indian girls that were hybrid."

Mr. Raj used to market Procter & Gamble products for a living, but he had an epiphany of sorts when he visited India. Watching his grandmother giving alms to beggars inspired him to start thinking of ways to hitch a social vision to his commercial skills. He gave up the day job and set up Mealexchange, an innovative project for students on 36 campuses to donate their unused meal points to charity. Paradoxically, this reacquaintance with his long-lost self triggered Mr. Raj's evangelical belief in Canada. He sees it as a country with a social vision, one that practises capitalism with a human face.

"The culture of most countries is like a brand," he enthuses, his marketing background coming to the fore. "A brand has core values that are common to most users but the Canadian brand is not 'affiliated'" – not yet something that ties everyone together, he contends.

Mr. Raj is a Leader for Change Fellow at the Maytree Foundation at Bloor and Avenue Road, an intersection that appears to be entirely old Canada, anchored as it is by the Royal Ontario Museum and expensive boutiques. The Maytree is a charity that works to better integrate immigrants into Canada, and the Leaders for Change programme is an initiative that identifies leaders and leading organizations that have the capacity to make change and advance the common good.

"With immigrant families you sacrifice not for Canada but for family, so I took this concept and turned it on its head," he says, explaining his pitch for branding Canada as a country where sacrifices are made for the common good. "Would a Canadian have made this decision? I don't know. I'm taking Indian values and applying them to a Canadian reality. I feel I am representative of this fusion, I am looking to apply best practices from our ancestors to the problems of today.

"At the periphery you have poverty," he says, pointing down Bloor Street. "At the core you have institutions. What brings them together? You have to find a way to connect those with a will and ideas with those with the money."

I leave Mr. Raj to the task of remaking Canada in his fused image and head back onto Bloor. I've come to the end of a beginning and it occurs to me that perhaps the story for this generation of Canadians has barely started.

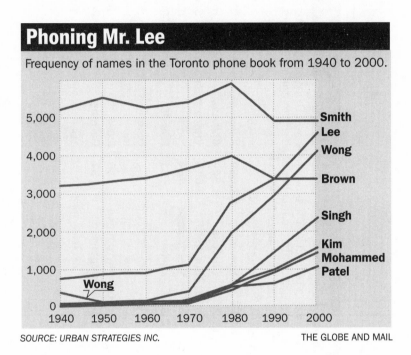

Phoning Mr. Lee

Frequency of names in the Toronto phone book from 1940 to 2000.

SOURCE: URBAN STRATEGIES INC.   THE GLOBE AND MAIL

Toronto's libraries of the world

Toronto's public libraries reflect the makeup of immigrant communities on Bloor Street, from Runnymede in the west to Yorkville in the downtown core. Here are the number of library materials – books, periodicals, videos and CDs – lent in 2002, in the top five languages for each branch.

RUNNYMEDE		BLOOR GLADSTONE		PALMERSTON		SPADINA		YORKVILLE	
Russian	20,023	Chinese	40,067	Korean	13,969	Hungarian	2,543	Chinese	1,056
Polish	3,970	Vietnamese	11,202	Chinese	4,844	Chinese	2,236	Hindi	737
Ukrainian	2,509	Spanish	8,575	Spanish	2,015	Vietnamese	470	Spanish	377
German	1,234	Portuguese	7,545	Vietnamese	454	Hindi	359	Italian	250
Lithuanian	482	Tamil	2,359	Italian	81	Russian	191	Russian	192
Others in the top 10 list		Others in the top 10 list		Others in the top 10 list		Others in the top 10 list		Others in the top 10 list	
Hindi	209	Urdu	1,460	Portuguese	58	Farsi	52	Urdu	145
Farsi	98	Gujarati	514	Japanese	37	German	37	Polish	122

SOURCE: TORONTO PUBLIC LIBRARY, PARKDALE BRANCH   THE GLOBE AND MAIL

15

REWRITING OUR STORIES
ALISON GZOWSKI

Canada's character is not just found in its cities and towns, its schools and workplaces. It is most colourfully expressed in the arts and culture that have blossomed here, especially in the past three decades. Thanks to that bloom, the new technologies that followed, and the keen interest in first books in international publishing circles in recent years, today's new authors seem to spring on the scene fully formed. But how much do they share with the Atwoods and Richlers that went before them? Four of the country's most prominent writers under 30 get together to talk about their work: How Canadian is Canadian literature now?

OF ALL THE ELEMENTS OF CANADIAN CULTURE, literature may be the most definitive. Canadians are voracious readers of their own writers – from the founding "CanLit" boom featuring Margaret Atwood and Mordecai Richler to, more recently, Barbara Gowdy, Rohinton Mistry and Yann Martel – and Canadian writing tops bestseller lists and wins awards internationally. How is the next generation carrying on this legacy and how is their work affected by such factors as Canada's racial diversity, media saturation and changing values?

As part of the New Canada project on Canadians in their 20s, *The Globe and Mail* assembled a panel of four of the country's most prominent authors under 30, who all published their first books in the past couple of years. Naturally enough, they were already acquainted with each other, but their opinions were anything but uniform. Alison Gzowski moderated the discussion, conducted by both conversation and e-mail.

ALISON GZOWSKI: Would you place yourselves in the "CanLit" lineage? Is there something Canadian about your writing you could address?

SHEILA HETI (*The Middle Stories*, 2001): I don't think so, personally. It would only make sense if you only read Canadian writers. You're influenced by whatever you read in your most vulnerable moments. For me, in high school that was Kafka; writing *The Middle Stories* it was Jane Bowles; and last year it was Emmanuel Bové. The only Canadian that directly influenced me was Barbara Gowdy – I had no idea before reading *Falling Angels* at 16 that Canadian writing could be fresh and sexy and modern.

LEE HENDERSON (*The Broken Record Technique*, 2002): Unfortunately the way Canadian literature was taught during my formative high-school years left a long-lasting scar on my palate. How many times can a kid in the 1990s read Man vs. Nature stories, where for example a man trudges home through waist-high snow only to open the rickety cabin door and find his wife screwing another man, and then, without alerting the lovers to his presence, goes back out into the cold, cold weather and commits suicide just by standing outside? This might be a great story but its relevance to my life felt very distant indeed – so I hated it, loathed it to the point of an indelible memory laced with resentment. Other than Michael Ondaatje's *The Collected Works of Billy the Kid*, the literary predecessors for what I wanted to accomplish didn't seem to exist in Canada, not on my radar at least. Although there are Canadian writers I admire like crazy.

MS. HETI: But who knows why one thing and not another changes the way you think and see? If you read writers from various different countries there's no reason why your writing should be particularly Canadian.

EMILY SCHULTZ (*Black Coffee Night*, 2002): Well, except that I think that we have a lot of Canadian geography in our writing.

MR. HENDERSON: I think Canadians put a lot of context and kind of profound meaning in their landscape and in their geography.

MS. GZOWSKI: But is it different than the way that, say, Richler's novels are all set in one place, Munro in one place, even Nino Ricci's are in a certain area . . . Is there a different thing that you guys are doing?

KEVIN CHONG (*Baroque-a-Nova*, 2001): Actually, Mordecai Richler is an interesting case in point. I think he once said something to the effect that, well, he was writing in London at that time and he decided to write about Montreal because it seemed like this exotic place compared to a place like London, which has been written about so many times. I wrote my first novel when I was in grad school in New York, and I remember just walking in the street and feeling as though I was in a Woody Allen movie or in *Goodfellas* – it was always *Goodfellas* in my mind. But Vancouver, back home, was sort of less described, for me. There was more fresh ground, I thought.

MR. HENDERSON: For me, if I'm writing about Vancouver or Saskatoon, it's because of a deep-seated hatred for the places. I have no romantic feelings about it. I've hated almost every place that I've lived, and I hate Vancouver – I hate everything about it. So that comes out in the writing. I think western Canada is embarrassing in a lot of ways, and that's something I want to address, even subliminally.

MR. CHONG: "We write about this world because this is where our scores are settled." That's what I heard somebody say once.

MS. HETI: I don't think you feel an obligation to write about

Vancouver in order to make Canada a place that exists in literature, though?

ALL: Oh, God, no. Definitely not.

MS. HETI: I don't set my stories in any particular place. It doesn't matter if a certain street I see in my mind does not exist, because the reader will be making up their own street anyway.

MS. GZOWSKI: Do you see different themes between your generation and older ones?

MS. HETI: I don't think it's even really quite fair to say the older generation has these themes. What does Michael Ondaatje have to do with Mordecai Richler? Why do they have more to do with each other than, you know, Emily has to do with Mordecai Richler?

MR. HENDERSON: We might have something new to say about Canada's obsession with historical novels. Personally I find the genre to be almost entirely pretentious. And so I am currently writing a historical novel, as punishment maybe for future crimes. I hope in some way my historical novel will address the issue that many writers of historical novels fail at: "How the hell does this have anything at all to do with what's going on right now?"

MR. CHONG: I think we all have some sort of thing that we want *not* to be writing. Being a Chinese-Canadian, I've really been loathe to write any books that might have a cover with bamboo lettering on it. That was something I've always been afraid of.

MS. SCHULTZ: I don't want to feel compelled to write an epic novel. I love the elegant slim volume. I really don't want to feel pressured to write a big book.

MS. HETI: Really, everyone knows shorter is better, except publishers, book buyers and critics.

MS. SCHULTZ: Don't you think, though, that our literature is changed by social mores? We grew up in a different time, certainly, than our parents did, and we converse, probably, differently, and conduct ourselves differently than they may have. Certainly my parents would have studied Henry Miller, but today we have nationally syndicated columnists like Dan Savage coming up with terms like "pegging." I don't plan to use that word in my fiction, but I do describe the act. These are our ordinary lives. These kinds of words are in our lexicon. Apparently, it's important to my generation to know – before entering a committed relationship – whether their partners are into certain sexual acts. Since most fiction is about human relationships in some way, how we meet one another's standards plays into the writing, even if we aren't writing specifically about a sex act.

MS. HETI: I'm not right now so interested in what differentiates now from 20 years ago but more what's sort of remained the same between now and 20 years ago and 100 years ago and so on. The details change, but people don't.

MR. HENDERSON: I don't know if I necessarily agree. When you see a book come out today by someone who's 25 and it reads like an Alice Munro book, you don't think, "Oh, this is very contemporary," you think, "Aw, jeez, this person is living inside the very heavy shadow of Alice Munro's great career." You feel like it's almost reactionary or afraid to speak of its own temporality or something. I want to react to what I see as the structure of the world today. Just the stuff that you can use as metaphor in writing, like the Internet or television, these things have dramatic effects on people's fiction writing.

MS. GZOWSKI: Is there anything you guys feel you can't write about? Are any topics off-limits?

MS. SCHULTZ: I'm not sure we have that many taboos anymore.

MS. HETI: I don't know. A certain kind of sincerity, perhaps.

MS. SCHULTZ: Maybe taboo has more to do with tone than with actual subject matter.

MR. HENDERSON: I don't really like quotation marks. I don't think I'll ever use them. . . . And I also don't really like brand names very much. Except for Chrysler. I like certain words, so maybe I'd put Chrysler in a story.

MS. HETI: A writer might find that when they go into the street, all they notice are ads, and for them the fulcrum point of the whole culture is a Calvin Klein billboard. Why shouldn't such a person include brand names in their writing? But it has to be a conscious choice. Too many writers are sloppy about brand names. They haven't considered why they should be put in or why not, and this is foolish, because brand names are tremendously potent. Lee's stories take place in a universe like our own, except things that happen slowly in our world happen quickly in Lee's, and the reverse. If he had a character talking on a Nokia phone, it would create this nice little release and we'd be comforted by Nokia's familiar face. But if you want to unsettle – which is the best way of making a reader vulnerable and therefore open to the world you're presenting – you don't put in Nokia.

MR. HENDERSON: The temptation to use brand names is almost unbearable, for the reasons Sheila outlined, but also because the word Nokia is so gorgeous. Many expensive people sit around for many days trying to think of a brand name that is going to be just so lush and deliquescent that people will want to let it rest on their tongues as often as possible. Nokia. Amazing how great that word is, especially because it had no meaning until its owners granted it one.

MR. CHONG: Don Delillo's original title for *White Noise* was *Panasonic*.

MS. HETI: Wow. That's super.

MR. CHONG: I think brand names tend to date a story 10, 15 years after they're written, but after some point, they become period details. I mean, Joyce used commercial jingles in *Ulysses*.

MS. GZOWSKI: Do you feel any obligation to get involved in writers' politics? I was thinking of PEN and the Writers' Trust – a lot of writers in Canada have been very active politically.

MS. HETI: I don't get involved in writers' organizations.

MS. GZOWSKI: Would you?

MR. HENDERSON: How do you get involved in them?

MS. HETI: I don't know. I think you have to pay dues, yearly dues.

MR. HENDERSON: I'd like to help pick the Nobel Prize winner.

MR. CHONG: That'd be great. You'd have to be Swedish.

MR. HENDERSON: Politics is a dastardly game. I don't want anything to do with it.

MR. CHONG: You sure picked the wrong profession for that.
Writing's all about the politics.

MS. GZOWSKI: Do you write at all self-consciously – we're talking
about identity politics now – as women, or Kevin as a Chinese-
Canadian, or Lee as a straight white guy?

MR. CHONG: I definitely don't think it should be the main concern.
I know for some writers it is.

MR. HENDERSON: Well, this maybe draws us back to that whole
conversation about generational differences. There was definitely
something going on in the seventies and such where feminism became
an incredibly important thing for a certain kind of writer to speak
about. And that's cool, but it dates the work – you read some of even
Atwood's early stuff and it feels like seventies writing.

MS. HETI: You're not very easily going to create a fictional character or a fictional world if you're holding on so tightly to yourself and
your own identity.

MR. CHONG: I think there's ideology in a lot of novels. Dostoevsky,
he writes about positivism, and with Turgenev there's nihilism, and
with Tolstoy there's the whole idea of being Christian. And somehow
I think they've survived because those ideologies have just been set in
a human sort of story. Some writers like to deal with the big issues of
their day. At the same time, the human condition will always be the
biggest issue, and sometimes the ideology works because it's sub-
servient to writing about consciousness and how we think and how
we live, and how the world feels and smells.

MS. HETI: But being a Chinese-Canadian is not an ideology, or
being a woman is not an ideology. We all have our ideas about the
world – of course that's going to get into our fiction – but being a
woman is not an idea about the world.

MR. CHONG: Feminism is an ideology, and I would say there's
the whole idea about critiquing media – the media reality, I think, is

a big theme that a lot of writers are dealing with – or the whole story of the blurred distinction between private consciousness and public consciousness. And dealing with ethnic identity is an ideology, starting with writers like Maxine Hong Kingston, because some people believe that you're not allowed to assert your ethnic identity because it's too "otherly."

MS. GZOWSKI: I want to know about the question of regionalism, because here we have two writers based in Toronto and two in Vancouver. Are there not young writers in smaller towns across the country that are as prominent as you guys?

MS. HETI: Only in Canada would a newspaper feel obliged to ask, "Why are most of the prominent writers living in the major cultural centres?"

MS. GZOWSKI: Is your attitude towards publishing different because publishing has become so different? I mean, electronically, people are more independent, they can publish on a desktop printer or on the Web.

MS. HETI: I think most of us have had some experience with zines, or publishing on the Web, and it does change the way you see regular publishing. Mostly, I think it makes one comfortable with the idea of a small audience. I think I would be very frightened if my book was a massive bestseller. If it's small, if the book only exists in the heads of several hundred people, it still feels familiar, it still is what it was when I made it. When I read a favourite book, there are certain people I want to share it with, but not everyone in the world, because a book that is loved is a delicate thing; anything that is loved feels fragile, and you only want it in the gentlest hands. I think people who make zines experience these sensations – they can manifest themselves as superiority or cliquishness or hostility, but they don't have to.

MS. SCHULTZ: I agree with Sheila. People have been asking me why I only print 100 copies of my Pocket Canon chapbook series, and whether I would ever get them professionally printed rather than hand-folding and hand-cutting every one. I've received more pleasure from making the Pocket Canon than I have from the publishing my own book – no disrespect to my publisher.

MS. GZOWSKI: Could you guys ever see leaving Canada and not coming back?

MS. HETI: No, my family's here. I would feel bad about leaving them.

MS. SCHULTZ: Yes. I see Canada as a very big country that's very small. I'd like to leave, mostly because I'm hungry for experience.

MR. CHONG: I wrote my first novel in grad school in New York. My second's been hard for me to write in Vancouver. Too much e-mail and dog-walking. I did a residency in Spain this February and appreciated the time away.

MR. HENDERSON: I'm cool where I am. I work in the turret in the top of an old heritage home, and I overlook the whole city from this turret kind of point of view. I have sort of a Quasimodo lifestyle right now.

MS. GZOWSKI: Do you feel like you're part of a community?

MR. HENDERSON: I like my community. There's a difference between, you know, living in a city or place and becoming a part of its shape and how it creates itself. I'm finding lately that having a book published is leverage to enjoy being part of my community here. Like, I have friends with this record shop, and we put on little events, kind of semi-literary events, and they go really well.

MS. SCHULTZ: I find it interesting, though, that you would say that you use your book as leverage.

MR. HENDERSON: I was much too shy to approach people to do this kind of thing before.

MS. SCHULTZ: Now it's like you're legitimate?

MR. HENDERSON: Yeah, in the eyes of myself.... Don't you think you use being a writer as leverage?

MS. SCHULTZ: I think it's unfortunate, though, don't you? I mean, I think that it's unfortunate that we start to view people differently once they have something like a book.

MS. HETI: Well, you and I became friends before all this.

MS. SCHULTZ: We did.

MS. HETI: We're pure of heart!

MR. CHONG: Lee's a friend of convenience.

MR. HENDERSON: It's very mercenary over here. I only hang out with Kevin for what I can get from him. He uses his book as leverage to hang out with me all the time. I'm like, "I don't want to hang out with you today, Kevin." He's like, "But I wrote *Baroque-a-Nova!*"

MS. GZOWSKI: What's the number one thing you'd like to see change in Canadian literature in your lifetime?

MR. CHONG: I feel as though there's still some lingering insecurity about our literature, and I hope in the next several decades we won't care about what Canadian literature is, we'll just have a sense of it. But maybe that's just part of being Canadian.

MS. HETI: I think it would be nice if the schools taught more interesting writers. I certainly didn't read anybody interesting in school. I think that makes for a culture of readers who aren't very open and aren't very excited by literature.

MS. SCHULTZ: I think we need a lot more poetry readers. And I think it's unfortunate how little we're read in the U.S.

MS. GZOWSKI: Why does it matter to you to be read in the U.S.?

MS. SCHULTZ: Well, why shouldn't we? We buy a lot of American books.

MS. HETI: They don't need to read us.

MR. HENDERSON: They're better writers than we are.

MS. GZOWSKI: They're better writers, did you say?

MR. HENDERSON: Yeah.

MS. HETI: American writing may not be better than Canadian writing, but it is generally bigger. Bigger ideas, bigger heart, bigger ambition, and so on. Canadian writing tends to be more timid. The first time I went to London, England, all of a sudden Canada made so much more sense. I hadn't before realized quite how restrained we are, and that our politeness is a way of holding other people at a distance. I think these traits make for art that is quieter, a little more afraid of the world, a little receding into the shadows. We have one tenth of the people. There's a provincial attitude. You're afraid of what your neighbour might say. You equivocate. You muddle the language, pretty it up. American literature is more like Americans – spontaneous, vain, flag-in-the-moon. The results are more exciting.

MR. CHONG: You know, many of my favourite writers are American, and until recently I might have agreed with you. But American literature can be so pompous and, because so many American novelists are Don Delillo-heads, still recovering from *Moby-Dick*, it results in big, baggy, monster novels that try to cram in every big theme ever stumbled on.

MS. HETI: Lee may be a big David Foster Wallace fan, but I much prefer the strange, evocative simplicity of Paula Fox, Paul Bowles, Flannery O'Connor and Henry James. American writing was much better 50, 100 years ago, before America became a superpower. That country's writing has become oppressive and domineering.

MR. CHONG: Kazuo Ishiguro states it really well in an Atlantic interview: "A writer describing what it's like to grow up in a particular neighbourhood of New York automatically gains a kind of global significance simply by virtue of American culture's current dominance in the world. The trouble is that you can get a certain inward-looking society. You can start to feel that you don't have to look further."

MS. HETI: If you're living in a superpower you must feel like the world has either just begun or is ending. You feel you ought to write a work which takes in everything. Whereas here we know it's just another day. We can deal with one thing at a time. We know there'll be a future and that there's a past. If you're a writer in the States right now I think the burden of the present is overwhelming.

MS. SCHULTZ: Funny, I would say that might be why so much Canadian writing avoids themes entirely. Or plot, or character development, or style . . . I just can't imagine why any Canadian wouldn't want to be read in the U.S. I would like to think that the ego of Canadian literature is becoming secure enough to travel – not just internationally, but also to knock next door. I should say that I am both Canadian and American, and hold citizenship in both countries.

MS. HETI: I just don't think that it matters if it's an American who's reading your book or, like, a German who's reading your book.

MR. HENDERSON: I'd really like it if a Canadian would read my book. I just want to start with a Canadian. If I can convince a Canadian to read my book then I might move on, but right now that's a challenge enough.

MR. CHONG: That should be our goal for Canada Day: Make a Canadian read our books. Just one.

The Writers

Kevin Chong is the author of *Baroque-a-Nova*, a novel (Penguin Canada, 2001), which has also appeared in France and the United States. Born in Hong Kong, 1975, and raised in Vancouver, where he presently lives, he attended the University of British Columbia and received an MFA at Columbia University.

Lee Henderson wrote *The Broken Record Technique* (Penguin Canada, 2002), which recently won the Danuta Gleed Award for a debut collection of short stories. He was born in 1974 in Saskatoon and was raised there and in Calgary before moving in 1994 to Vancouver, where he lives with his wife and a small rabbit.

Sheila Heti was born in Toronto in 1976. Her collection *The Middle Stories* was published by Anansi in Canada in 2001, by McSweeney's in the U.S. and in translation in Germany, France, Holland and Spain. She runs Trampoline Hall Lectures at the Cameron House in Toronto.

Emily Schultz was born and raised in Wallaceburg, Ont. (pop. 11,500), with her American parents, and now lives in Toronto. She is the editor of *Broken Pencil* magazine and of the fiction anthology *Outskirts: Women Writing from Small Places*. She is the author of *Black Coffee Night*, a short-story collection published by Insomniac Press in November, 2002. She turned 29 in March 2004.

PART IV

THE CANADIAN WAY

16

THE RULES OF ENGAGEMENT

MICHAEL VALPY

Canadians in their 20s largely don't vote, and they certainly don't join political parties. But look closer – for instance at this small circle of friends in Montreal. They have little faith in traditional institutions and media, but many of them are passionately concerned about the state of the world and what they can do to change it – in their own lives, and for one another.

GENEVA GUERIN, AS A LITTLE GIRL, organized neighbourhood children for talent shows. She organized them for garage sales. She organized them for scavenger hunts. She organized them for roller-skating lessons. "Always she was organizing something, from the moment she was able," says her mother, University of Victoria philosophy professor Susan Turner.

Today Geneva Guerin is 25 and has only just finished full-time classes at Montreal's Concordia University; she graduated with a bachelor's degree in communications. She has successfully raised $25,000

189

Photo by Christine Muschi

to finance a sustainable-development project for the university. She has created a company, Sustainability Solutions Group, to move the project from feasibility study to implementation and to offer consulting advice to other institutions.

She was a member of the federal government's youth advisory delegation to the 2002 United Nations summit on sustainable development. In 2003, as a member of the Sierra Youth Coalition, a non-government environmental organization, she organized a group of environmental activists from across Canada to cycle to Mexico to protest against World Trade Organization negotiations in Cancun.

She spends three days a week at meetings at the university and the other four at her company. She spends her nights on telephone conference calls. She gives speeches. She writes: She's working on a 350-page book, and a documentary film, on the Concordia project. "Every second I'm awake, it's go, go, go. It's never been this insane," Ms. Guerin says. Standing at the door of her small apartment near Concordia in downtown Montreal, she touches a hand to her cheek and declares, "I look sick." She looks tired.

When political scientists examine the political activities of Canada's newest adults and proclaim their alarm at the health of Canadian democracy, they do and they don't have Ms. Guerin in mind. They see a generation registering the smallest voter participation rate for its age group the country has ever known: Just 21 per cent of Canadians in their 20s cast ballots in the 2000 federal election, resulting, over all, in the lowest electoral turnout in Canada's history. The cohort's absence from the polls, the academics say, foreshadows its voting behaviour as it ages.

They see a generation which has virtually no membership in political parties, a generation that believes more strongly than any other demographic group in Canada that advocacy organizations – like Ms. Guerin's Sierra Youth Coalition – are more able than political parties to effect political change.

They see a generation that, because of political illiteracy or political alienation, or both, increasingly finds the traditional institutions of Canadian democracy irrelevant to their concerns and their daily lives. And a generation disengaging from other forms of civic engagement as well.

The phenomenon is showing up in other Western countries. Moreover, it didn't just happen in Canada with this fresh generation of adults. The last time voter turnout for a federal election hit traditional levels was in 1983. Canadians in their 20s have merely made a disquieting trend more pronounced.

Behind this generation's civic conduct lies a more subtle and layered story, one found in snapshots of Ms. Guerin and her Montreal friends, with some of their seeming contradictions in a postmodern world.

Ms. Guerin is not civilly disengaged. And she votes. But?

But after her experience with the UN summit delegation, she has vowed she won't again be part of any government-sanctioned political activity. It was a sham, she says. "I tried that as an experiment to make sure I hated working within the system, and it was awful. That's not my ball."

Ms. Guerin has multiple identities; she belongs to a generation of "ands." She is an activist and a jock. And a community volunteer. And a young woman in search of nurturing her spiritual and emotional health, as well as someone with limited financial means needing a roommate to share the rent. All of which has led to the acquisition of a rather paradoxical circle of friends.

She met Adrienne Moohk, 23, when she volunteered at Frigo Vert, a non-profit store providing low-cost, organic, non-genetically-modified vegan food at prices poor people can afford. Ms. Moohk – it is a name she has assumed – is a paid employee at Frigo Vert, a former Calgary street kid who left an unhappy broken home at age 14. She spent a year sleeping on friends' sofas and in empty buildings, sometimes literally on the streets, until she qualified for child welfare. It was a time, she says, of feeling alone and scared, which led her to become an outreach worker to other homeless and at-risk teenagers, many of them young natives. She also organized fundraising events for community groups trying to provide housing and services.

This won her a $50,000 scholarship from a national bank to be used for four years of postsecondary education (to qualify, she had to first graduate from high school, which she did) and the offer of a summer and part-time teller's job. Two years later Ms. Moohk moved to Montreal because she wanted to attend Concordia. She has a year to go to complete her degree.

She brought her compassion for lonely, alienated and homeless young people with her, organizing street gatherings and "renegade tunnel parties" – dances under bridges and in other empty public spaces – without, as a matter of principle, obtaining municipal permits. The police usually closed them down. She organized an "emergency February party" in winter for people who felt sad. She brings lost and lonely people into her home, a huge space above a row of shops in east-end Montreal where she lives communally with six other young people.

She is civilly engaged.

But she does not vote.

She rejects governments as oppressive undemocratic instruments of the rich and powerful and the capitalist patriarchy.

Ms. Moohk, a small, engaging woman – a gamine – who wears her brightly dyed hair in dreadlocks, labels herself a feminist without hesitation. She sees no contradiction in the fact that until recently she worked for an Internet pornography company, and she plans to return to the job soon. She could earn $12 an hour just sitting in front of a live camera in her underwear, and an extra 25 cents a minute from paying viewers if she took off all her clothes and simulated masturbation. "You can fake a lot of things. It's pretty funny." The extras usually amounted to an additional $30 a shift.

"I don't think it was a huge jump for me . . . it's pretty easy to get paid for masturbating," she says at home over tea. "I think what's hard about it is that there's such a stigma, because people tell you you're so objectified, you're so commodified; that's really hard. I don't think pornography is necessarily more degrading to women than flipping hamburgers. I think capitalist labour is exploitative, and I think you're exploited doing pornography just as you're exploited in a restaurant, but you're probably making more money. It sucks that the industry is large-scale men-owned, but so is capitalism. And I don't think sex is a bad thing. Sex is a great thing. People should get really comfortable with sex. Pornography is not in itself a bad thing."

Ms. Moohk is both poetic and passionate, talking about the quality of life she aspires to live. Her words tumble out.

"If you don't have a community, you can't survive. So as a matter of survival, you have to care for other people. I think that's where my passion comes from. Because if I don't change things, my life is going to look too much like my mother's life. If I don't take care of people, people aren't going to take care of me, and I need that care. I want to feel inspired all the time, I want to feel creative all the time. I want to feel open and honest. I want to feel caring and cared for. I want to feel challenged. I want to feel I have the strength to take risks. . . . I guess I don't ever want to feel numb. I think a lot of people are walking around dead."

She admits being discouraged. She tries so hard, so often, to build better, caring communities. She talks about "embracing" the pain of people who are lonely and numb. Nothing seems to change, she says. She talks a lot to Ms. Guerin about where she's going in her life.

She asks not to be photographed with Ms. Guerin and her other friends.

Ms. Guerin met Sascha McLeod, 29, playing university soccer. Ms. McLeod is a project development manager for a Montreal-based corporate Internet service provider, Open Face, and a close friend of the company's co-owner, Tan Soamboonsrup, also 29.

Mr. Soamboonsrup has an SUV, and used to drive the two women to their soccer games, until Ms. Guerin gave up playing because of lack of time, while she railed at him about the environmental unacceptability of his car. "She accepts rides with us, and I get an earful from her every time I drive her to soccer," he says, laughing.

When she wasn't lecturing about the car, she was forcefully presenting other views. Ms. McLeod recalls one heated discussion having to do with Nigeria, another about Ms. Guerin's declaration that nation-states and international borders should be dissolved, leaving local communities to govern themselves. The three developed an affection for one another. They began warmly anticipating their soccer-ride debates. Mr. Soamboonsrup did Internet research on his SUV and presented information to Ms. Guerin showing his six-cylinder model consumed less fuel than several non-SUVs.

Ms. McLeod often turned to the Internet for information on other subjects Ms. Guerin raised. "It made me go home and research what she was saying. And Tan would get excited, he'd say, 'We're going to be driving with Geneva, so let's talk about this.'"

They are not, they make clear, on the same page of the political hymnbook as Ms. Guerin. "Geneva is *out there*," says Ms. McLeod. "I see someone who maybe hasn't been exposed to the full spectrum of what working is about," says Mr. Soamboonsrup.

And they are not active politically. Yet . . .

They talk about the irrelevancy and pettiness of much of Canadian politics. They don't like the one-sided domination of government by the Liberals. The opposition parties don't feel real, Mr. Soamboonsrup says. "They're just there to banter," Ms. McLeod says. She talks of getting angry one night watching TV news: "Five minutes on a story about someone calling someone else a moron. That drove me nuts."

They understand the political role of activists like Ms. Guerin in creating public awareness of environmental issues. They think, though, that change happens only incrementally. They say they may become

politically engaged later on, when their Internet business is more estab-
lished, larger, more successful, perhaps giving them more influence in
the community. Adrienne Moohk wouldn't like to hear that.

Beatrice Parsons, 22, falls closer to Ms. Guerin on the political
spectrum. She came a year ago to Montreal from Saskatoon to learn
French, decided to stay and needed a roommate. So, at the time, did
Ms. Guerin. They found each other through a mutual acquaintance.

Ms. Parsons, soft-spoken, of Cree descent, can be called a silent
activist. "I've never been outspoken about anything. I've always been
a quiet kid." She enrolled in Concordia, met people Ms. Guerin knew,
started going to protest marches. "I feel optimistic after them, except
when I walk home along Ste.-Catherine Street and realize what a consuming society we are."

She already had an interest in environmental and consumer issues.
She furnished her bedroom with cast-off furniture left at curbsides. She
followed Ms. Guerin's example and stopped using toilet paper. "I was
really enthusiastic about it. It was another thing I could cut back on in
my life. My mum said, 'Well, don't forget to wash your hands.'" Ms.
Parsons laughs, a sound like water in a brook. "Yes, Mum, thanks for
reminding me."

Her only major purchase has been a computer. It is her doorway
into the Internet for environmental information, especially information on unacceptable food. "It makes life more meaningful and easy to
cope with to make decisions, to take action: composting, being less of
a consumer, buying foods that don't wind up in the garbage."

She votes. She gets political information off the Internet although
she's started to watch television news with Ms. Guerin.

Both of them have suffered severe allergies. Ms. Parsons has passed
on her naturopathic remedies. "She is doing way more for me than I
am doing for her," Ms. Guerin says.

Lately, Geneva Guerin has been thinking that the anxiety disorder she has suffered most of her life is linked to her strong sense of

dissonance in the world. She says it is time to separate herself from the dissonance. She was going to begin studies at McGill law school. Instead she decided to keep going south, after the World Trade Organization protests in Mexico, and spend a year in South America not being political.

One less Canadian voter in her 20s if an election is called within the next 12 months. But she'll be back.

17

DINNER DANCE

MICHAEL VALPY

The Muracas are an energetic and accomplished family that bridges the gap between ancient Europe and the Canada of tomorrow. Those two forces often pull in opposite directions, as the dynamic young women at the table know better than anyone. But they've been promised equality since birth.

THE TWO-STOREY HOUSE IS AN ARCHITECTURAL blend of Mediterranean airiness and stoic Ontario brick, something only Italian-Canadian builders can achieve. From Nicoletta Muraca's kitchen come smells of ricotta cannelloni, oven-roasted chicken and lamb cooked with red peppers. It is nearly 8 o'clock on an early summer's evening. The house rings with laughter and conversation, a dozen people talking at once. Pastry hors d'oeuvre are being passed around. Franco Muraca is filling wineglasses. Bowls of salad and platters for meat and vegetables are ready on the serving counter. The table is set.

"Since Eve ate apples," Byron wrote, "much depends on dinner," and for many families, the evening meal is about more than just food. It's a parliament, the common terrain of younger and older generations, of men and women, where narratives from the outside world are judged against the family's values and traditions, and the rules set for its own security and nurture.

A family successful by any yardstick has assembled at the home Franco Muraca built 13 years ago in Toronto's suburban North York. The sound of Muracas together describes them: love, intimacy and pleasure in each other's company so concrete they can almost be touched. Theirs is a family that values and maintains many of its Italian traditions – and fits the Canadian immigrant template to a T. The Canadian-born children and their partners, all in their 20s, have moved almost en masse into the professional world.

Tonight, they are sitting down to dinner, and to share their thoughts on the one group that most strikingly defines the newest generation of Canadian adults: young women. There are four members of this group at the table.

Maria Muraca is 28, four days away from marriage and has just begun a residency in family medicine.

Her cousin, Giulia Muraca, is 21 and co-ordinator of a medical research project at Toronto's University Health Network.

Trish Muraca, 28 and married to Giulia's older brother, Carmine, is a chartered accountant and senior financial analyst with a telecommunications company. She, like Maria and Giulia, is the daughter of Italian immigrants.

Genny Pires, 27, has been dating Maria's brother, Giuseppe, for four years and teaches at a Montessori school. Her parents came to Canada from Portugal.

Nothing has put a more distinct imprint on the generation of Canadians in their 20s than the attainments, values and attitudes of its women. Successful, pragmatic, confident and secure in the sense of their equality, they are stepping into a culture that in so many ways seems made for them.

They are surpassing young men in educational accomplishment. They make up 57 per cent of university students. They are responsible for more than 78 per cent of the increase in university enrolment from 1997 to 2001. They are the majority in all fields of study, except engineering, mathematics and applied and physical sciences, but even in these disciplines, they are gaining on men.

In a Canadian generation marked by values of acceptance of diversity, social justice and adaptability to a complex world, young women are in the vanguard. More than any other demographic group, they identify the Charter of Rights and Freedoms as a symbol of their pride in Canada, and theirs is the only group in which a majority opposes capital punishment. They're striking as well in their approval of same-sex marriages.

The New Canada survey shows women in their 20s to be most acutely aware of, and most strongly opposed to, racism and discrimination. They are the strongest advocates of government programs to care for children and the elderly, for social housing and for state intervention to ameliorate income disparity.

They are the daughters of feminism, even if their mothers didn't call themselves feminists. They assume they will not face disadvantage because of their gender, either in the workplace or in a relationship. And if they do, they won't put up with it. They also reveal themselves in the CRIC-*Globe* poll to be the most highly stressed group in Canadian society. They may be shaping the adult world they are entering, which carries its own tensions, but they're also women on the threshold of both their careers and of raising families of their own.

As the meal begins, the young women talk about what it's like to be them. They talk about how they were raised, about their relationships with the men in their lives, about their work, their society, about how they will become mothers and what it is like to belong to two cultures – southern European and Canadian.

With them at the table are parents: Nicoletta, 51, and Franco, 58, are Giulia's mother and father, and Franco's widowed brother Mike, 60, is Maria's father. And there are young men: Giulia's brothers Carmine, 29, who went into business with his father rather than remain in university, and Sergio, 28, a medical student with a master's degree in science; and Maria's brother Giuseppe, 27, an environmental consultant with a master's degree in environmental studies, as well as Maria's fiancé, Angelo Tsebelis, 28, a child of Greek immigrants who has a master's degree in business administration and co-owns a restaurant with his brother.

The dynamics of the conversation are fascinating. This is a family skilled at debate. Gibes slice through the air with affectionate but surgical deftness. Points are made with economical precision. The topic may be the young women but the young men have the most to say. They sometimes answer questions put to their sisters. They, unlike their sisters, sometimes make such comments as: "I can speak for the family in saying . . ." Under these male pronouncements, the women slide sharp, pointed comments of their own. "It is cultural," Giuseppe says, laughing. Maybe. There's a lot about it that's universally male.

Maria, crisply assertive but soft-spoken, raises her voice only once – to argue with her father over the tradition that children, male and female, live at home until they marry. "You were independent enough to leave a country," she tells Mike, "and come to a completely new one, and get a job on your own, with hardly anything, and we're not allowed to live in an apartment by ourselves."

"Twenty-eight," she mutters with heavy irony, "is not old enough to make your own decisions."

Every one of them, it turns out, still lives at home – except Carmine and Trish, who left when they got married a year ago. Giulia says softly that she doesn't intend to wait that long. "I have a completely different opinion than everybody else."

"I can't hear you, Giulia," her father, Franco, says lovingly, having heard very well what she said.

Franco and Mike Muraca came to Canada from Calabria in the 1960s, and married two other young immigrants, Nicoletta Mancini and Rosarina Palma. The brothers were artisans who began as brick-layers and within a few years created their own successful companies. Mike has a heating and air-conditioning business; Franco is a specialty flooring contractor. The two couples (Rosarina died nearly 10 years ago of ovarian cancer) had children for whom, as Carmine put it, "they dreamed up the world." In Mike's words: "We wanted to change ourselves. We saw people who could change to whatever they want.

They changed themselves through their sons and daughters, and raised those daughters to see the same unlimited opportunities as their sons saw. "It was easy to do," says Mike, choosing his words carefully, "because it was rewarding. It made our families stronger."

Maria recalls being told by her parents from the age of 10 or 11 that she was going to be a doctor. Her brother Giuseppe interjects: "There was an attempt at equality. The reality is, and . . . I'll get shot at this table for this [a chorus of laughter] . . . we were expected to have advanced careers, whatever that would mean, but the expectation was also that, when there was something needed around the house, when there was help needed, my sister was expected to do it, that was part of her duty. It created that balance. And I see her today, and I think she thinks that's a great thing and, you know, at the same time she's got a university degree, she's got her career . . ."

Maria cuts him off. "We were equally encouraged to pursue our dreams," she says flatly.

"They're equal," their father says.

But, interestingly, it is a theme the young Muraca men keep return-ing to through dinner. Yes, their sisters were raised equally to pursue their dreams. Yes, they have their degrees and their careers. But, yes, there is the cultural expectation that they will be "maternal figures" [quiet female voices ask, "What about *paternal* figures?"] and will choose to be at home with their children. Although, Carmine acknowledges, times have changed and the values of the larger Canadian society are encroaching. "We're not *expecting*, we as men, we are *asking* . . . and I think we're evolving to being part of a team." Maria gestures around the dinner table. "We clear the plates," she points out. Giulia asks quietly: "Have you seen any man get up and help?"

Nannies are discussed briefly, and not with enthusiasm. The impression is clear that the next generation of Muracas is not likely to be nannied. Women in business are compared to women in professions. Mike says: "If you really want to be a CEO, a woman has to be single. You cannot have a child every year, every two years . . ."

Trish, the woman in business, says: "If she's a CEO of a company without children, people look at her and say, 'Wow, what's wrong with her, why doesn't she have any children?' The assumption is that, if a woman had been married, she wouldn't have that life, but if a man is married, he'd still have that life." Finally, Maria the doctor addresses the issue. "I feel torn between succeeding at my profession and my role as mother," she says, admitting that she foresees problems. She is asked if she wants her children to have the same at-home parenting she had. "Probably . . . probably," she replies. In fact, the more Maria and Trish talk about their career plans, the more clear it is that they have carefully planned their futures with motherhood in mind. Rather than rejecting their mothers' stay-at-home lives, they are tailoring them to suit their needs.

Trish says she became a chartered accountant in part because it offered the chance to scale down her work week, to work at home and perhaps run a business from there. "But I also see that you need to be assertive and aggressive in what it is you want [when integrating family and career], because you're never going to have anything handed to you on a silver platter."

Maria chose family medicine because the residency is relatively short, two years compared with five in other specialties – she plans to have children within five years. Also, she can work in a clinic with colleagues to share the load. "So I can take a year off and know that the rest of the doctors will be responsible for my patients and it won't be left to me to find a locum."

"Women plan," Genny says. "Women micro-plan," Trish says. And men? A chorus of female voices say they don't really plan at all. They can handle life only one day at a time and don't really care if something that should happen doesn't.

Then again, Maria and Angelo have talked about sharing family responsibilities, about both taking time off from work. She wouldn't have married him, she says, if his values were different. "Our parents," he says, "wouldn't have had the conversations that Maria and I have had."

When they're on the job, the Muraca women do not see enough gender discrimination to make it a significant issue. But sociologists say they may still be too young to have experienced it. The world looks too rosy. Women don't start smacking into glass ceilings until they're in their 30s. Still, according to the CRIC-*Globe* poll, twentysomething women are much more likely than their male counterparts to see men being given promotion advantages and people being judged on the basis of race and ethnicity.

Giulia works in a medical research office staffed, as she says, by "young energetic women" who are more likely to face discrimination because of their age rather than their gender. They see gender bias when they attend conferences in the United States, while the men at home are overly helpful. "But we sometimes have difficulty being taken seriously because we're young," she says.

Trish sees the workplace in the midst of great change. "I'm looking at my organization and it's headed up by a male CEO and a lot of the vice-presidents are male. I think it's still dominated by the old boys' club, and I think they still have a lot to improve in their mentality. But it's filtering down – in a good way – because of the people they're hiring, the people they're putting in place to lead divisions or departments, the subordinates like myself, they're strong females. And I'm saying it's a matter of time."

Maria doesn't see gender as an issue on the job. "It's the quality of decision-making that counts," she says, and Genny, the Montessori teacher, nods.

Stress?

Trish suggests surveys report higher levels of stress for young women because young men won't admit to it. "They think it's a sign of weakness." Then she ticks off the events of her life over the past 10 months: "Getting married, moving out of my parents' house, being on my own for the first time of my life – I'd never cooked, I'd never cleaned – and dealing with my career at the same time."

The meal draws to a close. Over dessert – superb pastries from a nearby Italian bakery – the gathering is polled on same-sex marriage. Should it be legalized? The young men say they're struggling with the concept. The parents are quiet. The young women are decisive: Yes, they approve, so long as there's no negative impact on children of homosexual families.

It's a good word – decisive – to describe the newest generation of Canadian adult women. Decisive, certain of what they want in their lives and in Canadian society, these are themes threaded through polling surveys as well as in academic research done by sociologists such as Bonnie Erickson and Sandy Welsh at the University of Toronto and the University of Alberta's Graham Lowe.

They have found Canadian women in their 20s won't accept the status quo for its own sake, either in jobs or in relationships that don't satisfy their values or their quality of life. They're significantly more prepared to leave marriages they think don't work than young men are, even when children are involved. "They're the ones who are driving up the divorce rate," Prof. Erickson says. And a study Prof. Lowe co-wrote for the Canadian Policy Research Networks says they are significantly less happy in the workplace than young men and less inclined to stay with an employer who doesn't treat them right.

It's an age of well-educated, forthright young women. Women like those at the family dinner.

The meal ends. Franco stands up to help the women clear the plates from the table. "My father always does. He wasn't pretending," Giulia says later. "Now if Carmine had, it would have been worth an Oscar."

Good nights are said. Angelo and Maria drive off to look at the apartment that, in a few days, will be their first home away from their parents' home.

WOMEN OF DISTINCTION

How special are young Canadian women? Very special, as illustrated by these findings from two national surveys, broken down by age and gender.

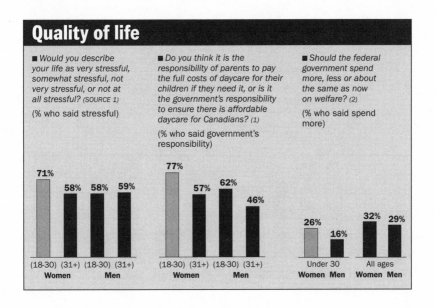

Quality of life

■ *Would you describe your life as very stressful, somewhat stressful, not very stressful, or not at all stressful? (SOURCE 1)*

(% who said stressful)

■ *Do you think it is the responsibility of parents to pay the full costs of daycare for their children if they need it, or is it the government's responsibility to ensure there is affordable daycare for Canadians? (1)*

(% who said government's responsibility)

■ *Should the federal government spend more, less or about the same as now on welfare? (2)*

(% who said spend more)

	71%	58%	58%	59%
(18-30)	(31+)	(18-30)	(31+)
Women		Men	

	77%	57%	62%	46%
(18-30)	(31+)	(18-30)	(31+)
Women		Men	

	26%	16%	32%	29%
Under 30		All ages	
Women	Men	Women	Men

Crime and punishment

■ *Which is the best way to deal with young offenders who commit violent crime: give them tougher sentences or spend more to rehabilitate them? (2)*

(% who said rehabilitate)

■ *Do you favour or oppose the death penalty for persons convicted of murder? (2)*

(% who said oppose)

■ *Only the police and the military should be allowed to have a gun? (2)*

(% who said strongly agree)

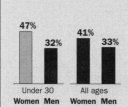

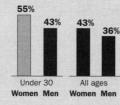

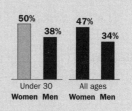

Sexual tolerance

■ *Would you feel very comfortable, comfortable, uncomfortable or very uncomfortable if a close member of your family, such as your brother or sister, or one of your children, said he or she were gay? (1)*

(% who said they would be very comfortable or comfortable)

■ *Gays and lesbians should be allowed to get married (2)*

(% who said they strongly agree)

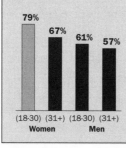

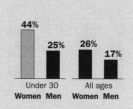

National identity

■ Please tell me whether each of these makes you feel proud to be a Canadian. Use a scale of 0-10, where 0 means it does not make you feel proud at all, and 10 means it makes you feel very proud. *(1)*

(% giving scores of 8, 9 or 10)

| Having two official languages, English and French. | That Canadian airports took in planes diverted on Sept. 11, 2001. | That Canada decided not to participate in the war on Iraq. |

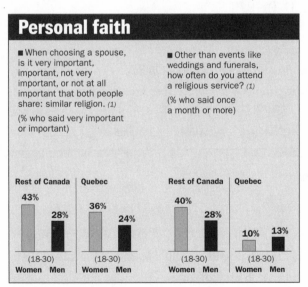

57% / 37%
(18-30)
Women Men

70% / 53%
(18-30)
Women Men

67% / 53%
(18-30)
Women Men

Personal faith

■ When choosing a spouse, is it very important, important, not very important, or not at all important that both people share: similar religion. *(1)*

(% who said very important or important)

■ Other than events like weddings and funerals, how often do you attend a religious service? *(1)*

(% who said once a month or more)

| Rest of Canada | Quebec | Rest of Canada | Quebec |

43% / 28%
(18-30)
Women Men

36% / 24%
(18-30)
Women Men

40% / 28%
(18-30)
Women Men

10% / 13%
(18-30)
Women Men

SOURCES:
1. THE CRIC-GLOBE AND MAIL SURVEY ON "THE NEW CANADA."
2. 2000 CANADA ELECTION STUDY (CONDUCTED BY McGILL UNIVERSITY, UNIVERSITY OF MONTREAL & UNIVERSITY OF TORONTO)

THE LANGUAGE OF CONFIDENCE

INGRID PERITZ

The same way young women take the achievements of feminism for granted, the young generation of Québécois are casually confident in the gains their parents made protecting French language and culture. They work in global business and high-tech, they cheerfully switch between French and English, and they aren't bitter about the past or threatened by "the ethnic vote." As for independence? No thanks, they say – they've already got it.

THERE OUGHT TO BE A SIGN ON THE electronic glass doors at Newtrade Technologies in Old Montreal. Warning: Young staffers inside will smash stereotypes and induce anxiety in aging Quebec separatists.

Behold the cast of characters in this dizzying Quebec generation. Frédéric and Benoît, the two francophone business partners in their 20s, spend their days schmoozing with Seattle and jetting to London and Las Vegas. They're self-made and self-confident and regard

Photo by Mackenzie Stroh

Quebec independence as a relic of their parents' past. Chinda, the Laotian-born receptionist – part of the "ethnic vote" blamed by ex-premier Jacques Parizeau for the separatists' defeat – in fact voted yes in the 1995 referendum, and insists on being served in stores in French. Then there's Scott, born in Ottawa and reared on bigoted views of French Canadians. Today Scott has a francophone girlfriend and works enthusiastically for Frédéric and Benoît, his two Québécois bosses.

This small slice of Montreal life offers an eye-opening glimpse of Quebec's under-30 crowd. In their own way, these 20s are rebels: rebels against their parents' generation, and their parents' old beliefs – the ones that kept Canada on the edge of its seat for three decades.

Benoît Jolin picks up the phone in his office. "*Oui?*" He switches to English. "I'll be there in a minute."

Mr. Jolin, 27, and Frédéric Lalonde, 29, run Newtrade Technologies, a high-tech company that develops software for the tourism industry. Last fall, after only five years in operation, the company was snapped up by the U.S. on-line travel giant Expedia. Newtrade's offices buzz with young computer programmers in jeans who look like they could be somewhere in Silicon Valley – except, of course, that the common language is French, and when Mr. Jolin takes a cigarette break in the company cafeteria, he puffs on Gauloises.

Both Mr. Lalonde and Mr. Jolin are the children of sovereigntists. As boys, they heard about how their parents were forced to speak English to get served in Montreal stores, the kind of unfairness that justifiably enraged francophones of that generation. To Mr. Lalonde, such reports are like lore out of the tales of King Arthur. "I've never been told 'Sorry, we don't speak frog,' which is what my parents said happened to them," Mr. Lalonde says. "I was never stigmatized, so none of that stuff is remotely part of my reality."

Mr. Jolin grew up attending church every Sunday and was schooled by priests at a traditional Catholic school in Quebec City. Part of the mythology of his youth was that Quebeckers were a little people, unsuited for the cut-and-thrust world of business – in the words he remembers, "*né pour un petit pain*," or born for a bread roll. "I'd hear it from teachers and grandfathers or aunts and uncles: It's okay to under-achieve," Mr. Jolin recalls. "It was part of the Catholic education; God will forgive you if you were meant to be small and not disturb anybody else. It's fine not to make waves, attract attention or be overly successful. It just left me infuriated. Up in arms. That's exactly what distinguishes the old Quebec generation from the new one. With us, we can be whatever we want to be, and the sky's the limit."

Anyone who set foot in a movie theatre in Quebec in 2003 will have the eerie sense they already know Mr. Jolin and Mr. Lalonde. That's because the two are real-life versions of Sébastien, one of the central characters in the acclaimed film *Les Invasions Barbares* by renowned Quebec director Denys Arcand. The movie is about a ter-minally ill Quebec college professor and his baby-boomer friends, and the generational divide between them and their children. The character who embodies the new Quebec is Sébastien, the dying man's son. He's a smooth, jet-setting capitalist based in London, constantly speaking into his cellphone in English.

When Mr. Lalonde and Mr. Jolin went to *Les Invasions Barbares* and saw Sébastien, they were bowled over. It was as if they were watch-ing themselves.

Much like Sébastien, they have a view of the world in which Quebeckers compete with New Yorkers, Londoners or anyone else. In this view, the purpose of a separate Quebec is far from obvious.

Don't call these two men federalists, however. Like most Quebeckers their age, they think the sovereigntist/federalist labels are meaningless. They're not turning their backs on their culture, either. To Mr. Jolin, to cease defending the French language would be a tragedy. "To abandon this fight [to preserve French] is like blowing up those Buddha statues in Afghanistan," he says, referring to two statues dynamited in March of 2001 by the Taliban. "But instead of making it a fight between anglophones and francophones, we should use two languages to be a microcosm for what's best about our country – something the United States doesn't have. What we're doing here is teaming up two cultures, French and English, so that Quebec products can be known around the world."

Mr. Lalonde and Mr. Jolin are the products of pitched battles waged before they were born. They're reminiscent of young women who've benefited from the struggles of their feminist elders and take their freedoms for granted. Mr. Lalonde and Mr. Jolin were born around the same time as Bill 101, Quebec's famous French Language Charter. The two grew up under the law's protective cover, unburdened by many of the insecurities of their parents' generation. "We didn't inherit the psychology of being colonized by the British," says Mr. Lalonde, his company's chief technology officer. "All that happened before us."

Around these stylishly renovated offices, software engineers from all over the world use French as the common language of work. Among the bilingual, which is most of them, conversations free-flow between English and French like a jazz duet.

At 10 a.m. one typical day, Mr. Jolin is conducting a conference call with Expedia staff in Tampa and Atlanta; everyone around the conference table in Montreal listens and throws in comments in English about "connectivity," "configurations" and "strategic value." The call ends, the Americans hang up, and the men and women in Montreal turn to one another. "*Et puis?*" someone says. Without missing a beat, as if everyone decides simultaneously to switch channels to another station, they all join in a rapid-fire conversation in French.

Sitting at the heart of the ebb-and-flow at Newtrade is the resident keeper of the separatist flame – Chinda Phommarinh, the cheerful, multilingual receptionist. Ms. Phommarinh was raised in a traditional Laotian family in Montreal and did what any self-respecting rebellious youngster does: she dyed her hair blond and got her tongue pierced.

She also adopted the ways of Quebec youth. Growing up in Quebec since she was three, she saw reports on television of massive pro-Bill 101 rallies. She got the message: French mattered.

Like nearly all immigrants, Ms. Phommarinh was already required to attend French school, where her classmates were Cambodian, Haitian and Italian and her best friend was Portuguese. French was the obvious language among the friends. Still, those street protests over language affected her. "I said to myself, if this is making news on TV, it means that the Québécois take it to heart. I realized, I have to make an effort."

When Ms. Phommarinh – still sporting the tongue stud, but back to her natural black hair – answers the phone at Newtrade with her Québécois-inflected accent, it's impossible for a caller to know she's not from the province's heartland. The 26-year-old is the living incarnation of Bill 101's most unassailable success, the conversion of immigrant children into functional French-speakers through the education system. Ms. Phommarinh insists, when she shops downtown, on being served in French. "I want to change the clichés that immigrants didn't want to speak French. I grew up here. For me, Quebec is as French as Ontario is English."

As old-stock francophones like Mr. Lalonde and Mr. Jolin lose their nationalist ardour, new Quebeckers like Ms. Phommarinh might be separatism's best hope. She voted yes in the 1995 referendum on sovereignty. "I'm not 100-per-cent Québécoise. I have my culture from Laos, I'm not *pure laine*," Ms. Phommarinh says. "But I grew up here and it's what shaped me. I'm not as attached to Canada as to Quebec, because this is where I grew up."

Standing by Ms. Phommarinh's desk with his laptop is Scott Martin, 32, one of Newtrade's program managers. Mr. Martin was raised in Ottawa with what he acknowledges was a narrow-minded view of French Canadians. "I really didn't have any idea about the entrepreneurship going on, or anything that could change the world that was coming out of Quebec," he says.

His narrow view came clattering down two years ago. He landed a job with Mr. Jolin and Mr. Lalonde and, armed with 10 years of French immersion, moved to Montreal. He now has a francophone girlfriend and he made francophone friends. Mr. Martin discovered one of those underreported facts, that Montreal is a de facto bilingual city. Finally, reporting to work every day at Newtrade, Mr. Martin cleared his final hurdle over the wall between the solitudes.

"What we're doing here is groundbreaking," he says. "The fact I work for a company run by two young guys from Quebec, who sold their company to Expedia, a mass conglomerate from the U.S. – that's pretty amazing."

19

AMERICAN WITH AN "EH"

MICHAEL VALPY

The reported 250,000 Canadians in New York City are the poster children for the perennial stories of the 'brain drain,' our national myth of gifted children led away by the Pied Piper of American money and advancement. But the legend ignores one important fact – that many of today's prodigal sons and daughters have every intention of bringing their new knowledge and skill back to their home and native land. Though their mailing addresses end in USA, their values and ideals, the lifestyles they aspire to, are proudly stamped Made in Canada.

IT IS ONE OF THOSE MIDTOWN MANHATTAN trattorias perfect for a drizzling November day, dark-wood cozy, alluringly aromatic, deafeningly noisy and bouncing with talk, waiters in long white aprons moving at frenetic speed among the crowded tables – Tre Colori on West 45th Street, halfway between Sixth Avenue and Times Square.

Over the shrimp-pasta special, Axel Bernabe, wearing a well-cut blue suit, the knot of his tasteful tie slightly loosened, is telling an archetypal Canadian anecdote. He has just turned 30 and been called to the bars of New York State and Ontario in the same two-week period. At each ceremony, a judge gave a speech . . . and that's pretty much where the similarity ended.

"It was the tone. So different," says Mr. Bernabe, laughing.

"In Canada, the speech was about the idea of Canadian society, and about the obligations we have toward that society as lawyers, obligations to ensure the dissemination of notions of social respect and equality, the good things that are quintessentially Canadian. We were encouraged to participate in our society, running for office and volunteering for charitable organizations. And we all came away feeling 'Great, let's get at it.'" The stress being on the organic collectiveness of Canadian life? "Absolutely. It was the overarching theme."

And in New York?

"In New York, the judge's speech started with a Bible reference. Then there was a long exposition about how to be a better lawyer, about learning from the people who have done this for 20 years – and do pro bono work, as one of the pragmatic tasks you engage in. But no attempt to tie you into a greater project."

It is one of the reasons Axel Bernabe of Ottawa, practising corporate law in New York for just over a year with a firm that recruited him from McGill University, is certain he will be coming back to Canada.

There are reportedly 250,000 Canadians living and working in New York City, a quarter of a million stories, eh? in the naked city. The ones like Mr. Bernabe in the first decade of adulthood are the potential cream of Canada's future, and the faces behind the dreary reports of Canada's brain-drain – super-talented young lawyers, investment bankers, artists, scientists and other professionals, lured out of Canada by money and the opportunity to hone skills and strut talents on a stage far larger than their home and native land supposedly can ever offer them. Except what the statistics don't show – but the anecdotal evidence increasingly suggests – is that a huge chunk of this newest cohort of young Canadians gone south has little intention, unlike most of their predecessors, of staying there. They may be swept away by the energy of a place like New York, they may love being in one of the world's great cities, they may love their jobs and the skills they are learning – but they want very much to export those skills back home.

Why? Because they are acutely aware of a gulf between Canadian and American values that they don't want to cross. Likely more so than their peers who have stayed home, they have thought a great deal about what Canada means. They are not anti-American so much as they are comfortably, consciously, proudly and profoundly Canadian.

They talk readily in interviews about the cultural ethos of American survival versus a Canadian ethos of aspiring to a more holistic and fulfilled life, a life bonded to community, family ties, recreation and always the beauty and space of the land. They are ambitious, energetic, but they want to smell the roses.

Some express surprise at the degree to which they find Americans deferential to authority. "That's supposed to be reserved for Canadians," says Mr. Bernabe. They find alien a class structure more rigid than at home. They are uncomfortable with what they describe as the prism of race through which so many Americans interpret their society. They find that their American peers tend to have greater difficulty dealing with life's complexities. They tell jokes about how Manhattanites reacted to the great power blackout of summer 2003.

They are not adherents of big government and an interventionist state, but, when they talk of Canada, they talk about a place where public services work. They also talk about Canada as a place where there's more space in their lives to nurture idealism and creativity – whether this is in comparison to life in New York in particular or America in general, they acknowledge, may be a moot point. Still, Sean Brown, 27, an investment banker with JP Morgan Chase, points out: "If you're from somewhere else in the States and want to do banking, New York is it. Like, you can't go home. I can go home and do exactly the same thing." Although where they do have doubts about returning to Canada – as architect Jessica Strauss, 27, explains one evening in the panelled

library of Manhattan's Cornell University Club on East 44th Street –
they are doubts focused on whether they indeed will find outlets for
the idealism and intellectual challenges they're preparing themselves
for in New York.

In sum, these young New-Yorker Canadians sound precisely like
their peers at home. They sound precisely like they've just walked out
of the pages of pollster Michael Adams's 2003 book, *Fire and Ice: The
United States, Canada and the Myth of Converging Values*. They're all
there, Mr. Bernabe and the rest, plotted on Mr. Adams's "socio-cultural
maps" in the book's appendices.

Mr. Adams's Toronto-based Environics firm carried out extensive
values surveys of Canadians and Americans in 1992, 1996, and 2000.
The findings are quite startling. As the two countries' economies grow
ever closer together, the two societies' dominant values – especially
for Americans and Canadians in their 20s – head in the opposite
direction.

Environics found the values of the youngest cohort of Canadian
adults clustered around personal creativity, spontaneity, personal
control of their lives and rejection of authority, adaptability to com-
plexity, ecological concerns, global consciousness, religion à la carte,
interest in the mysterious and what Mr. Adams calls "flexible gender
identity." The values for Americans in their 20s were clustered around
financial security, ostentatious consumption, living virtually, more
power for business, confidence in big business, active government, civic
apathy, acceptance of violence, everyday rage, sexual permissiveness,
fatalism, sexism and a penchant for risk.

Here are four stories of young Canadians discovering the meaning
of their cultural inheritance and identity in the Big Apple.

Jessica Strauss grew up in Ottawa and came to New York as a teenager
in 1992 when her diplomat father, Howard, was posted to Canada's
mission at the United Nations. She graduated from high school and
went to Cornell University in nearby Ithaca to study architecture. She

stayed on after her family's return to Ottawa and subsequent move to
Nigeria where her father now is Canada's high commissioner.

She is, she acknowledges sheepishly, losing some of her accent,
what linguists call the Canadian raising, where the diphthongs – like
our famous "outs" and "abouts" – are sounded up near the roof of the
mouth. Ms. Strauss's diphthongs are falling. "So I need to go back,"
she says, wryly. "But I've kept my 'eh.' In high school, whenever I said
'eh,' my girlfriend would say 'B.'"

Ms. Strauss graduated from Cornell in 1999. What she calls "a fairly
elaborate job search" in Canada and the U.S. led her back to Manhattan.
She's passed the New York State licensing exams for architecture and
will soon apply for comparable professional status in Ontario. She's
an in-house architect for a New York-based real-estate investment
trust that owns and manages properties in 31 states. She loves her job.
She is working on a master's degree at New York University. And she
wants to return to Canada, get a master's degree in business administration and either establish her own firm or work for a company specializing in sustainable green development.

Therein lies her dilemma.

In New York she can find the sort of job she's looking for. In New
York she has connections, a network, recommendations from American
professors that carry weight. In Canada, she doesn't have the network
and she can't find the right job. Ms. Strauss has contacted a score of
firms in Toronto and Vancouver but none offers the opportunities that
are hers for the asking in New York. "I'd love to work on the Olympic
Games in Vancouver. I'd love to contribute to Canada, and," she adds,
"make it easier for other people like me to find what they're looking
for – rather than have to come south of the border for it."

Ms. Strauss, who just did the Terry Fox Cancer Research run – yes,
there's one in New York – says her years in the U.S. have only made
her fall more deeply in love with her country. Indeed, like most of the
young Canadians interviewed, she scans the Internet daily for Canadian

news, and she has discovered a cable-TV channel ("I pay a lot of money for it") that for 10 minutes every morning presents a Peter Mansbridge newscast. Of New York and the U.S. she says: "I just don't think it's the right place for me. The border is very real for me."

Real in these ways . . .

Ms. Strauss is struck by how Americans see America as a melting pot: "You come here, and it doesn't matter where you may have come from, because this is better. Whereas in Canada, it seems almost more important for you to take what you are and where you're from and go about your life, and you can still be Canadian and that's okay."

She is struck by the pervasiveness of racialism in the U.S., even in a place as liberal and progressive as New York. She encourages her gay American friends, struggling to find private health insurance that will cover their partners, to move to Canada.

She is struck by how much better public services work in Canada than in the U.S., whether it's health care or a simple matter of applying for a driver's licence or a library card. "I grew up skating free on ponds. Here it costs $12 for two hours at Chelsea Piers [a sports complex on the Hudson River]."

She is struck by how Canadians are more mild-mannered, soft-spoken, sedate, less showy – and so, she points out, are her American friends whom she periodically brings home to Canada on visits. She compares the panic and rage in Manhattan during the blackout to the grin-and-bear-it shrugs in Ottawa and Toronto.

She misses the beauty of the land.

Most of Ms. Strauss's friends are Canadian, from work and school. "I must know about 50 Canadians in New York," she says. "And I don't actually know any who are committed to staying here forever. In my age group, there is somewhat of a consensus to come here and get experience, work for a few years and then return. We get articles on the Canadian brain drain and why it happens, and it hurts a little bit. We're not just a bunch of kids running across the border . . ."

•

From the black-glass tower of JP Morgan Chase investment bank where he works, Sean Brown, 27, has sprinted across Park Avenue to the Starbucks at the corner of East 48th Street. He apologises three times for being late – all of 10 minutes – and explains he was at his desk until 5 a.m. before going home to his Manhattan apartment briefly to sleep.

"In corporate finance," he says, "it's miserable hours."

He is in Morgan Chase's power and natural resources group, working on transactions like raising equity capital for corporate buyouts. "The size of the transactions we work on, and the sheer responsibilities they put on me . . ." He puts in 100- to-110-hour weeks. Night after night he's at work until past 1 a.m.

Since Morgan Chase recruited him two years ago from his MBA class at University of Western Ontario, he's done little else except work – and find time for a few hours' sleep and a gym workout (he ran the New York marathon the previous weekend; time: 3:54) and fly home to Canada about once a month on rare days off or when he can get staffed on Canadian financial projects. "I try and get staffed on as many Canadian deals as I can, just for a free trip back." To friends' weddings in Toronto, to his parents' cottage-home in Nova Scotia and the family's skiing place, to his girlfriend Heather who works in the Calgary oil patch.

He has a timetable for returning home for good. Three years, he says. "Or less." And then he adds: "It's something I'll re-evaluate every year."

Because Mr. Brown, like Ms. Strauss, has a dilemma.

"I'm here right now and I have this wonderful opportunity to work at this massive institution which dwarfs any Canadian bank, and I get exposure to huge transactions. So it's really developing myself as a professional. The downside is that maybe I'll leave before the learning curve has started to plateau. My one fear is leaving before . . ." He pauses. "You know, the lifestyle can be pretty crappy down here. I want to keep on learning, and taking advantage of that learning, and I don't want to sacrifice that before I'm sure it's what I want to do."

Will he eventually be sure? He replies, simply: "Yes, it's Canada. I'm really fiercely Canadian. I just love the country. That's where I'd rather be. That's where the majority of my friends are. My family's there. I grew up in Canada and I like the values. I like the fact that we're not a superpower ... [that] Canadians are friendlier, a good more laid-back. I like the fact that Canada is a massive country, a natural resource ... an open space, and I'm big on camping and going on month-long canoe trips. I shattered my thumb two years ago, and you simply slide your health card across. Here it would be tons of specialists and thousands of dollars ..."

Mr. Brown sounds like he will be eventually sure.

In the meantime, he says, it's not the money that keeps him in New York. In fact, his friends in the Canadian financial industry – whose cost of living is in Toronto dollars, not New York dollars – may be better off. "It's just a lot bigger. There's more going on. And to be able to say when I want to go back to Canada, to say that I just spent three years in New York, and excelled, counts for a lot more than me having spent three years doing a similar thing in Toronto. It's just that much more rigorous, that much more intense."

Morgan Chase employs a lot of Canadians. "We sort of have our own little Canadian mafia here," Mr. Brown says. And the younger ones, the ones his age, the junior analysts and associates – Mr. Brown is an associate – all talk the same about staying just long enough to acquire professional experience and then head home. Head home before being trapped by promotions, marriage (often to an American or to someone with her or his own career in New York), children, a house in the suburbs. "The more senior ones – a senior associate and up, 30ish on average and up – you don't really hear much about them wanting to leave. But I think you could ask any of the Canadians in our group, except for the very senior ones, if they could have the same job in Toronto, they'd probably take it. Because I would ... you know, once I'd stayed here long enough, to get the most experience that I could."

Always that hedge: once he gets the right amount of experience, once he can decide when his learning curve has started to plateau, once the time is finally right to head home.

Tricky.

Mr. Brown knows that his American peers at Morgan Chase tend to be more clustered around life's survival values and that his Canadian colleagues think more about living a life that's more fulfilled. "Generally, I look at the guys in my group, and the Canadians are concerned with their personal lives as well as their professional lives. For me that's most important. And the thing that makes it easy to stay here until 5 a.m. is I know I have an option to move back to Toronto or Halifax or Calgary or wherever. Any second I want to. It's not a black hole for me. Whereas there are some people that are here, and they know they're going to do this for the rest of their lives in New York, and they just want to get to the top."

Mr. Brown, sitting in Starbucks, checks his palm pilot. The black tower at 277 Park Avenue is beckoning.

The Off-Broadway, 499-seat Daryl Roth Theatre is in a charming neo-classic 19th-century former bank building – the facade perfectly preserved, and resolutely protected by New York City heritage laws – on East 15th Street across from Lower Manhattan's Union Square. Reviews for its current production of De La Guardia are hot. The man who offers to lead the way to the general manager's office through a confusing warren of stairways and corridors makes, one guesses, a New York joke at a particular isolated corner: "This is where I rob you."

The Daryl Roth's general manager is Adam Hess, 28. He has sung and danced his way around the world into this job. (Literally. In 1999, Mr. Hess was lead performer in a musical revue on a round-the-world cruise aboard the flagship Rotterdam of the Holland America Lines. "It was," he says, "quite an experience.")

His curriculum vitae can be defined by a single word: "intentional." He has travelled his young life in an arrow-straight line – from child performances in Toronto's Young People's Theatre and the Shaw Festival's *Christmas Carol* to a dancer's role in the 1993-94 Toronto production of *Show Boat* just after high school graduation, to a bachelor of fine arts degree in musical theatre at University of Michigan, to a master's of fine arts degree in theatre management at Columbia, to jobs as dance instructor, choreographer, apprentice director and director for a score of productions at university and in and around New York and, finally, in 2001, to the Daryl Roth.

"I always knew I wanted to go into theatre," Mr. Hess says.

He left Toronto for the U.S. because he won a scholarship to Michigan. "But the second and probably more important reason was that there just wasn't the opportunity in Canada in terms of musical theatre that the States had. The Canadians had Sheridan College [just outside Toronto], but it didn't have the academic stature University of Michigan had. Michigan provided not only a musical theatre education but very much an academic education."

Most of his graduating class at Michigan went on to the master's program at Columbia, and so did Mr. Hess.

"I knew I wanted to get more into the business side, which is why I went to Columbia. They have a program in theatre management and producing, and it's excellent. It's all hands on. My courses were in Times Square. My professors were the top in the industry, in the not-for-profit theatre world and the commercial theatre world. It [provided] an excellent liaison into the business side of things."

What Mr. Hess leaves unspoken speaks volumes: What training, in Canada, could be remotely comparable?

Mr. Hess is definitely Canadian. He speaks of his ties to family, of regular trips home to Toronto – more frequent, four or five times a year, now that he has young nephews and nieces. He talks of the price paid in diminished quality of life by being outside Canada. He knows his standard of living would be higher in Canada. He misses the green spaces. He talks of Canada being a more cohesive community than the U.S., more accepting, more inclusive. He talks of the continuing violence around issues like abortion. "In Canada, it's still there but you don't have the bombing of clinics. It's a debate, a polite debate." He talks about Americans' almost blinding patriotism, about their ready willingness to give up their civil liberties after the attack on the World Trade Center – which Mr. Hess watched, standing in Union Square, calling friends on his cell phone to make sure they were all right.

And although New York, he says, is a charged environment, "it does get to be tiring. It's very inspirational at times, but it's also very draining at times."

Like all the other young Canadians interviewed in New York, he dreams of taking his talent and skills home. And he may be the least likely to accomplish it.

New York is closing in on him. His friends are mostly American. His business connections are almost all American. "I've lost my accent," he says (it's true, his diphthongs have fallen). He was told to lose it for performances. "But I still have the 'eh.' The 'eh' you can't get rid of."

Canada – at this point – doesn't have what he wants and, in fact, Mr. Hess wonders if Canada wants him. He tells of applying for a role at Stratford a few years back and not getting an audition. "That's not about talent. I put in my résumé, just after my college career, to see if I could come back to Canada, and I couldn't get an audition. And here I had for someone my age a pretty good résumé – and not to be seen to me says something. To be seen and not get hired, that's one thing. But not to be seen at all, that kind of signals something that's sort of strange.

"Because of my connection with *Show Boat*, which was an American production even though I was Canadian, and because of my education in American institutions, there was definitely a feeling – and I don't have any facts to back this up – but my feeling [from the Canadian theatre] community is that there was very much a feeling that I had deserted."

What Mr. Hess dreams of doing is coming home and starting something new in theatre.

"It doesn't have to be something big, but something where I can grow. I'd love it. Toronto's a wonderful town. If I can come in at the top . . ."

Which, for Mr. Hess, is the rub.

"The difficulty that I find now is that I'm in a position, because of my age and because of my skills set, where I feel that to go back to Toronto and do what it is I want to do, I have to come back at a leadership level and I don't feel like I'm there yet [for Toronto]. I think if I look at comparable institutions, with comparable positions to what I have now – and because of the size of New York, and the opportunity of New York, you scale it down to Toronto – and if you look at facility management, which is part of what I do . . . it's the Mirvishes or what? You know, David Mirvish [the Toronto impresario] really runs the theatre town."

Small Toronto puddle – compared to New York – with one big duck. How much room for a young, ambitious Adam Hess?

I say to him: "There's a risk we're going to lose you."

He replies: "I would hate to see that."

There is no risk that Canada will lose Axel Bernabe.

Every plan he has for his future is located north of the border – after, that is, he does a master's degree at London School of Economics on the politics of the world economy. He says politics is his passion. "I don't want to be in corporate law. I don't want to be a lawyer." Law, he says, is something you do to analytically and structurally train your mind.

Mr. Bernabe, the son and stepson of two senior Ottawa public servants, knows he is Canadian. He ticks off the differences between American and Canadian values as if he's read Michael Adams's book, which he hasn't. "Really? He uses those words, survival versus fulfillment? That's exactly it."

He knows he is going home. He sees himself teaching at a Canadian university. Or he sees himself at a Canadian think-tank. Or he sees himself as a policy specialist for a political party or for Ottawa's Privy Council Office. He has as many questions of his interviewer as his interviewer has for him. What's happening in Canadian politics? Is there any sense of a new, young guard moving in behind Paul Martin? Is there something stirring in Canadian politics?

He happily let himself be recruited out of McGill's law school into an international New York-based firm specializing in competition policy because he wanted to get to know the U.S. and to explore how transnational capital really works, to see if Canada in a global economy has to be merely a middle-class power that toes the line. ("What I'm taking back to Canada with me is that it doesn't.") Apart from a summer's internship with his law firm, he has been in New York for a year and two months. "I'm absolutely swept away by New York, by the energy of it, the arts and culture." And just as absolutely convinced that he would never permanently live there or anywhere else in America.

He describes the U.S. work ethic as psychotic. He talks about U.S. society as a culture of fear – fear of not surviving, fear of job security, fear of never getting out from under thousands of dollars of student debt before the arrival of mortgages and children and the cost of their education, fear of never acquiring sufficient social status.

"I don't think Canadians aspire to being part of a certain class the way they do here – the idea of making it into an Ivy League school and to be part of that club is enormous. That's one of the things that shocked me the most." Within five minutes of two Americans meeting, says Mr. Bernabe, they've ascertained what university each went to.

He finds Americans more deferential to authority than Canadians, more inclined to fall in line with their government but at the same time more alienated from government. "They have no illusion that government is going to provide them with any kind of service. It's one of the myths of Americans, that the less government is best. Three months' unpaid maternity leave? Three months? You wonder, what the hell?"

He sees a society that ascribes wealth and education and language along race lines. "It's so divisive, and such a reality."

He sees a society that has had idealism knocked out of it. "You have no time to dilly-dally. You have no time to engage in the pleasantries of being an idealist, or even of travelling as much.

"You know, two Canadians meet in New York, and they start to talk about where they've been and how many languages they speak, or they speak to each other in French [Mr. Bernabe speaks French and Italian as well as English and is learning Spanish from his Colombian sculptor girlfriend], and the American first is just struck. And then he's kind of resentful, because he feels he's been excluded from this possibility and he's the one who's supposed to have all the freedom in the world.

"But in fact we're a lot freer. We have the ability to pursue education for years and to live out a dream of a liberal world. We don't have to remake the nation."

It's a powerful statement.

20

SWAPPING PLACES

DOUG SAUNDERS

Americans are assertive, patriotic entrepreneurs, while Canadians are skeptical, deferential and shy? Not if young Canadians have anything to say about it. In fact, both casual observation and survey data reveal that individualism is on the rise here and in some decline south of the border. Contrary to what many people predicted after free trade, the values of the two countries seem to be becoming more different, not less – and not the way you might expect.

IT WAS SUPPOSED TO BE A FRIENDLY GAME of team Frisbee. But now fists are striking flesh, hands are gripping necks, two big men are rolling on the twilight playing field in a spasm of punching, choking and loud curses. As the flailing men are pulled apart by their teammates, the captains launch into their own screaming fight on the sidelines, each blaming the other's excessively assertive players. Much later, when calm play has returned to the field, one of the captains regains his composure enough to realize he's betrayed his national image. "Sorry you had to see that – that's really not supposed to happen in this sport," he says. "That really wasn't very Canadian of us."

Wasn't it? After days of observation and study, I am no longer very sure just what is supposed to be "Canadian."

A week later, in a nearly identical field in a very similar town 2,000 kilometres south in Virginia, I witness another game of Ultimate – the popular Frisbee sport that combines the rules of basketball and football. Also played by co-ed students in their 20s, this game is much more peaceful, with children running on the sidelines and the intense competition reduced to a chessboard calm. The Americans, in almost every other discernible way identical to the Canadians, are playing a much more peaceful game.

This I am willing to chalk up to coincidence. One game of pick-up Frisbee does not define an entire country. I am searching for more pro- found and fundamental distinctions, divergences between core beliefs and behaviours that have become shockingly apparent in surveys and polls. If the latest research is to be believed, young Canadians and Americans seem to be moving in dramatically different directions.

The game, a very casual but elegantly played affair, has taken place on a muddy field at the centre of the University of Virginia campus, whose showy brick buildings had been designed by the founder, Thomas Jefferson. Afterwards, the exhausted and dirty team join me for pizza at a strip-mall restaurant. For two hours, and in interviews at their homes and workplaces throughout the week, I question them about their lives and beliefs.

I had found two towns that were as similar as possible. Guelph, Ont., is about an hour from Toronto, has a population of around 100,000, and is home to a mid-sized public university. Charlottesville, Va., is just south of the Mason-Dixon line, about an hour from Richmond and two hours from Washington, D.C., has a population of 50,000, and is home to a mid-sized public university.

I settled on Ultimate players because their sport is casual, inter- national, universal, non-contact, co-ed and attracts people with many daytime pursuits. These weren't going to be average Canadians and Americans, but they would be similar in most respects.

Around the pizzeria table in Virginia, I learn that I have assembled a roughly equal number of Northerners and Southerners, urbanites and small-town folk, conservative Republicans and liberal Democrats, religious churchgoers and non-believers. After we've talked a while, I drop what I thought would be a simple question: "Do you trust the government?" One by one, the Americans blankly shake their heads. It is as if the idea of trusting Washington has never crossed any of their minds.

A week earlier, in another pizza place, I've put the same question to the Guelph students. Every one of them says yes reflexively, without a moment's hesitation, as if the idea of distrusting the government is utterly alien.

I ask a series of questions about loyalty: Are you loyal to your country? To your state? To your university, your family, your friends, the company you work for? Or to certain brand names? This, too, produces striking differences. One after another, the young Americans say they are not loyal to their country – of the 10, only four say they are, and one of them, 28-year-old Jake Altimus, makes it very clear that his national loyalty is trumped by his loyalty to his state: "In my heart," he says, "I live in Virginia." The Canadians all say, without reservation, that they are loyal to Canada. In individual interviews, this comes out dramatically: The Canadians, regardless of their political beliefs, are flag-waving patriots. The Americans are much more reserved about their national identity – family, church, corporation and pastimes are far more likely to draw their loyalty.

"Canadians consider themselves more Canadian than ever," writes Queen's University social researcher Matthew Mendelsohn in a review of dozens of polls and surveys. "The Canadian is stronger than the provincial in all provinces except Quebec."

In Guelph, I visit the comfortable apartment of Vince Filby, a 24-year-old who is studying the unlikely combination of classics and computer science – subjects he chose out of passion, rather than strict financial interest. Mr. Filby is stringing his guitar, and preparing to sew a maple leaf onto his backpack. "I'm very patriotic," he says, "but I'm against dogmatism in many ways." His is not a naive patriotism. He has spent time in the States, and says he likes Americans, although it would take "a lot of money" to get him to work there.

None of the Americans, even the loyal George W. Bush supporters among them, wears a stars and stripes, and most are highly skeptical of their government. Has the image of the flag-waving American and the dispassionate Canadian become obsolete?

Some other things stand out. Half of the American team members are married – one couple, aged 23 and 24, wed more than three years earlier, and one couple has a toddler – while none of the Canadians plans on marrying any time soon. Likewise, while half the Canadians say they are religious, none attend churches or temples regularly. Half the young Americans are regular churchgoers. The young married couple are Baptist (her) and Roman Catholic (him); she compromises by attending a Catholic church, which allows them both to worship every week.

Are these diverging allegiances a result of some deeper belief?

When I drop in on the Charlottesville architecture firm where 26-year-old Allison Hill works as a structural engineer, I expect to find a hard-driving woman devoted to her career. After all, she is an aggressive Ultimate player, a star engineering graduate and the wife of a fast-climbing doctor. Ms. Hill says she is working in engineering because it is her family's trade – but not for money. "I'd love to work 30 hours a week, and take a long maternity leave," she says. A family, which she plans to begin in two years, is far more important to her than her work.

When I ask her what she considers the biggest problem with America, she surprises me by answering, "The work ethic." Does she think people are becoming lazy? Quite the contrary. "There's too much work," she says. "Everyone's expected to spend all their time working,

to make it their entire life. If you're not working all night and thinking about work all the time, you're not considered successful. I think
this is really hurting the whole country."

Later, I drop in on Peter Gee, a 23-year-old from Massachusetts,
at the physics lab where he is working for the summer. A piece of
equipment was broken, so the project is moving slowly, which is just
fine by him. "I continued with school because I didn't want to get a
job," he tells me. "I just want to spend some time not doing too much."
When I ask him his country's problems, he can't think of any. "I don't
really deal with problems – I just like to live in my own little world
and I figure those things will take care of themselves."

In Guelph, I drop by the campus office of Avin Duggal, 27. An
environmental-science student, he is one of the more aggressive
Ultimate players, competing in matches across Ontario and in the
northern U.S. He is also involved in a number of student organizations
and a busy social scene, on top of his research into soil purification. "I
don't get much chance to see my family," he says. He feels close to them
– his parents are Indian immigrants who live in nearby Mississauga –
but his own trajectory does not allow enough time for visits.

He worked in the U.S. for four years for an environmental-con-
sulting firm, and noticed something about his American friends.
"They were way closer to their families," he says. "They were much
tighter-knit, they put family above career all the time and they wanted
to go out and have children as soon as possible." His own ambitions
are somewhat different. "I have a very specific plan for what I want to
do with the next 15 years," he says. His graduate work will lead to a
series of employment opportunities. He will start a family at 31.

Together, the Canadians seem to be devoted more to engaging
personally with the world, to setting themselves up as individual suc-
cesses. The Americans often do this, too, but they are trying to fight it:
For them, the hard work and sacrifice of their parents isn't worth it, and
it's preferable to escape into the comforts of family, community,
church and school.

This gets into the terrain of a controversial new thesis about Canadians and Americans, one popularized by Michael Adams in his book *Fire and Ice*. Mr. Adams believes that Canadians are becoming more individualistic, more entrepreneurial and autonomous, while Americans are "retrenching," rediscovering traditional values and institutions, becoming more deferential to authority and excluding themselves from larger society.

This is a dramatic change. The United States has always been based on collective projects driven by a sense of renegade individualism, while Canada has long relied on deference to a strong state and on employment, rather than entrepreneurship. "We're living in different worlds," Mr. Adams says. "The Canadians have tried moving away from the church, holding off having big families, reducing the size of government, and the younger generations have discovered that you can do this and the world doesn't cave in around you. But in America, the world seems much more dangerous, it's not to be trusted, and people are seeking the safety of family and church and secure communities."

Some of his data are impossible to refute. For example, he asked Americans and Canadians in every region whether they believe that "the father of the family must be the master in his own house." In Canada, "yes" answers range from 15 per cent in Quebec to 21 per cent in the three Prairie provinces. In the United States, they range from 29 per cent in liberal New England to 71 per cent in the Deep South.

Indeed, there is considerable indication that young Americans are far more anxious and uneasy about their world. A major survey of attitudes in five countries conducted last year by the Pew Research Center for People and the Press found that Americans aged 18 to 29 are twice as likely as young Canadians to worry about crime, ethnic and racial conflict and "moral decline." While the first two categories may reflect real political conditions, the third indicates that the anxiety may be rooted in deeper beliefs about the world. Other polls show young Americans are far less trustful of immigrants, international bodies such as the United Nations, and that they are more likely to believe that politics is corrupt.

Do my Frisbee players bear out the radical thesis that Canadians and Americans seem to be swapping places? Not entirely. None of them believe the father must be the master of the house (these are, after all, co-ed teams). And it would be a caricature to say that the Virginians are cocooning themselves and avoiding the nasty outside world, while the Ontarians are taking risks, abandoning comfortable institutions and discovering their roles in the larger community. But at the end of my travels, contrary to my own long-held prejudices, I am left with the distinct sense that young Canadians and Americans, indistinguishable as they may seem at first, really do see the world through different eyes. They look the same, talk the same and play the same, but their hearts occupy different lands.

21

A NEW FORK IN THE COUNTRY ROAD

DOUG SAUNDERS

Canada's rural and city dwellers used to be divided by social issues. But the latest generation of farmers are almost nothing like their parents, with views as liberal and cosmopolitan as any urbanite's. There is still an urban-rural divide, however, and it involves the world of money and work: Rural life nowadays is a business, not a lifestyle, and the young farmers are far more pro-trade and anti-government than their urban counterparts.

IF YOU WANT TO KNOW ABOUT THE TWO Canadas, pay a visit to the Spurr sisters. Each spent a few years living in Toronto before deciding to move back to Nova Scotia's Annapolis Valley to take up the family's apple and potato farming business.

They did not choose the easier life. These days, Melissa Spurr, 22, and her sister Lisa Jenereaux, 27, get up before dawn to tend the orchards seven days a week, working constantly until their nightly spraying is finished just before midnight. If you're lucky enough to

Photo Sandor Fizli

find them amid the 17 varieties of apples, they will be glad to tell you about the divide between Canada's urban and rural communities.

"People are different here, and I don't think people in the city really understand a lot of the issues involved in agriculture," Ms. Spurr says. "I didn't find it hard to get along with people in either place, but I don't know if they'd always understand us. People here have their own views."

Like most of the farmers in their 20s around here – and the ones who don't leave for the city are a small group, typically only two or three in a high-school class – the Spurr sisters decided to stick with the rural life because they love it. Their other four siblings have chosen urban lives. "I was very happy living in the city," says Ms. Jenereaux who, like her sister, has studied agricultural management and attends farming conferences in the United States. "But after a while I realized that I really wanted to get back here. The work is harder in agriculture, but it's far more rewarding to be working for yourself and see the results of your work all the time."

Are these young farmers part of an entirely separate Canada, one that is alienated from a nation run by urbanites? Is Canada deeply divided into a "red" rural heartland and a "blue" urban strip, as the United States has been since the polarizing 2000 election there? Are there really two Canadas?

There is a difference between city and country in Canada. But, according to the New Canada poll, it isn't the difference people expect. The latest generation of farmers are almost nothing like their parents. While Canada's rural residents used to be divided from city-dwellers by social issues, today's greatest divide involves the world of work, money and business. Rural life nowadays is a business, not a lifestyle, and young farmers are almost indistinguishable from their urban counterparts.

The question has deep political implications. "I think this is the sleeper issue . . . It's the new divide," says Donald Savoie, a veteran civil servant, economist and political adviser at the University of Moncton.

"If politicians don't learn how to handle the rural-urban divide, they're going to be in trouble." Mr. Savoie points to his province's premier, Bernard Lord, who was almost unseated in his 2003 bid for re-election by angry voters from New Brunswick's rural north. The federal Progressive Conservative party faced a serious challenge to its leadership, and a roadblock in its effort to unite with the Canadian Alliance party, mounted by a band of largely rural protectionists led by farmer David Orchard. Ontario's Conservatives have enjoyed a decade in office at the hands of largely non-urban voters.

In the 1997 federal election, the Canadian Alliance Party is believed to have won its Official Opposition status in large part on rural issues, including fury at Liberal gun-control policies.

But the rural vote has its limits. Canada is one of the most urbanized societies in the world, according to the Organization for Economic Co-operation and Development. Its large cities are home to almost 80 per cent of its population. Only city-states like Singapore and Hong Kong have smaller percentages of their population in the country. And only about 2.5 per cent of Canadians are directly involved in agriculture. Rural power tends to be regional: New Brunswick, for instance, is 50-per-cent rural (a threshold that Ontario has not seen since 1917, although Ontario and Quebec are home to most of Canada's agriculture).

It certainly isn't hard to find young farmers here in the Maritimes who are seeking a political voice for their rural identity.

"I have a lot of time for the Alliance Party's issues; those are a lot of things that I feel strongly about," says Sonny Murray, 25, who advises dozens of farmers on a large co-operative on pesticides, crop diseases, irrigation and other crop-science matters. He believes that gun control was a bad idea. He also feels that employment insurance has made it very difficult to run a farm. "You can't get anyone to work from around here, because they make more money sitting around collecting [EI] than you can pay them to pick anything," he says. It is a popular sentiment.

But Mr. Murray and his friends should not be mistaken for agrarian conservatives. On most social matters, their views are as liberal and cosmopolitan as any urbanite's. "I was surprised when I moved here," says Mr. Murray, who hails from Pictou, 200 kilometres away. "People here are pretty conservative. They're a bunch of religious fanatics." He is referring not to his fellow young farmers, who tend to share this view, but to their parents and grandparents.

While the Valley still has plenty of adherents to a variety of fire-breathing Pentecostal denominations, people in their 20s mostly say that religion doesn't govern their lives. The same applies to questions of race and immigration. These farmers are acutely aware they are living in a homogenous and somewhat intolerant community, but none of them actually exhibit any of that intolerance.

"I guess you would call this a pretty racist place, except that everyone looks the same so there isn't anyone to be racist towards," Ms. Jenereaux says. This isn't just an abstract issue for her. She and her family are among a small group of farmers who want to bring in workers from Mexico and the Caribbean for the intense picking season, but she is worried that local xenophobia would make this difficult. Like most people her age here, she feels that more cultural diversity would be a boon to the area.

This is the most startling thing about the latest generation of rural Canadians, according to the New Canada poll: Unlike any generation before them, their views on social matters are almost indistinguishable from those of urban Canadians. This new unity is especially startling on issues of immigration, race and diversity, issues that traditionally pointed out deep fissures in Canadian society. Now, rural and urban opinions are identical.

"Rural youth, despite their lack of contact, have fully embraced the Canadian mythology about multiculturalism," says Dr. Matthew Mendelsohn, who helped conduct and analyze the polling data.

Even tolerance of gays has become nearly universal in the countryside – slightly more than in the city, in fact: Asked if they would be "uncomfortable" learning that a close relative was gay, 30 per cent of rural residents said yes, compared with 32 per cent of big-city dwellers.

While rural young adults show only a slightly higher propensity to hold strong religious beliefs, they are far more likely to be tolerant of others with such beliefs. In the country, 92 per cent of people in their 20s said they would be comfortable working for a Christian fundamentalist boss, compared with 71 per cent in the city.

In other words, rural Canadians today have a high level of tolerance for the more traditional and conservative environment they live in – but they themselves are not very traditional or conservative at all. Not, at least, on the social matters that are supposed to divide city and country.

Some political figures have recognized this dramatic transition. "I think any politician would be making a big mistake if he acted on the belief that there are separate rural and urban views in Canada," says Ian Davey, a veteran federal Liberal Party strategist. "Mass communications have narrowed the gap between urban and rural communities, to the point that those kind of distinctions just don't hold any political water any more."

Yet there are differences between urban and rural Canadians, even the young ones. If they aren't the social and family-values issues that were supposed to divide us, then what are they?

To find out, it helps to hang around the barn for a while. Here is Alicia King, 24, tending to a healthy-looking herd of Limousin beef cattle. Ms. King and her husband Danny are beef and cattle farmers, businesses they learned from their families, and they are currently gathering money to open a daring agricultural tourism enterprise, in which visitors from the city would stay in chalets here and experience the agricultural life.

"Farming for me is a way to really get in touch with your own labour, and to have a relationship with the environment," she says. Ms. King minored in environmental biology at agricultural college, and like many of her farm friends, considers herself an environmentalist.

Her views on most social and environmental matters would be familiar to any young person in downtown Halifax or Vancouver. But ask her what is the biggest problem facing Canada: "Free trade, no question," she says. "We have to keep those borders open: If we can't be making money from export, then there's no future for Canada." And on the important rural question of who she trusts more, big business or big government, there is no hesitation: "I sympathize with big business a lot more, because the people in business are in it for the same things that we are."

You will be hard pressed to find any young farmers who answer differently. This is surprising, since farmers have traditionally trusted government (which offered grants and loan guarantees) over big business (typically represented by the bank that foreclosed on the farm). "Years ago, if you were on the farm, there were all sorts of things for the government to help you out with," Ms. King says. "Now there's no government involvement at all. If anyone helps us out, it's the companies who are suppliers and customers."

That's where the largest urban-rural difference surfaced in the New Canada poll: on the question, "Which is the biggest threat: big labour, big business or big government?" Hardly anybody (10 per cent in each group) answered "labour." But among rural young people, 60 per cent said big government and 28 per cent said big business. In the city, 49 per cent said big business and 38 per cent said big government. "The old rural populism, directed toward large corporate power, is not very prevalent," Mr. Mendelsohn says.

Rural young people were far more likely than urban ones to agree with the statement, "If you don't succeed, it's your own fault." The farmers here in the valley, like the rural Canadians who responded to the poll, generally agreed with the sentiment that poverty arises from a lack of effort. City dwellers were more likely to see it as a matter of victimization or circumstance.

Indeed, one issue that almost all the young farmers in the Valley mentioned was the difficulty of finding farm workers. Almost all said this stemmed from the employment insurance and welfare systems, which, in their view, keep Nova Scotians from wanting to work. "It's a real problem, the UI [EI]; it makes people lazy," Mr. Murray says. And, Ms. Jenereaux says, Maritime workers are substandard. "They haven't learned a work ethic. The standards of quality on the farm have really increased over the past 20 years, but when you get Nova Scotians picking, they're not willing to keep their quality control up."

This is the real rural-urban divide today: Young rural residents are far more pro-business, pro-trade and antigovernment than their urban counterparts. In other words, the cloistered ideology of the family farm has been replaced with the universal ideology of small business. The issues that concern these young farmers are the same ones concerning a small factory operator in the city: taxes, trade, red tape, provision of cheap and reliable labour.

"I can't say that I got into this because I wanted to make a lot of money," says Tom Oulton, a 29-year-old chicken farmer. "I do this because I love working for myself, and I know it's not going to make me rich. But it's all about business, and I have a 10- to 15-year plan to make it successful. I don't have the luxury of treating this like it's just a job, because it's my business."

22

VASTNESS AND BEAUTY

ROY MACGREGOR

For all that the nation's ethnic makeup has changed and its values have modernized in recent decades, our passion for the landscape still unites us. Our first expressions of awe might have been in French or English, Ojibwa or Korean, but the natural panorama in preserves such as Algonquin Park touches and humbles us all. No matter how urbanized we become, the Canada of our hearts is still water and wood, snow and sky and stone.

THEY FIRST BROUGHT ME TO ALGONQUIN PARK when I was all of three days old.

This rocky point along the north shore of Lake of Two Rivers has not changed at all. Even the roots and rocks feel much as they did a half-century back when smaller versions of these feet first danced along them in a complicated game of chase invented by an older brother and sister.

The old log cabin our ranger grandfather built – and where our mother, who was born in the Ontario park, spent the loneliest winters of her life before finally marrying our logger father – has been torn down and carted away. Yet the surrounding landscape is still the one Tom Thomson came to paint before his mysterious death not far from here in 1917, his vivid impressions of the land eventually finding their way into the imaginations of us all.

And the cool, tea-coloured water still runs east toward the Madawaska River and on into the Ottawa, just as it did back in 1837 when explorer David Thompson, 67 years old, nearly blind and impoverished, scribbled "Current going with us, thank God" in his journal and began the final leg of a lifelong journey that saw him map about 3.9 million square kilometres of this massive continent – and still see but a fraction of it.

I come back here often but have been mostly away. By grace of a dream job, I have seen the sun rise at Cape Spear, Nfld., and watched it set off Long Beach on Vancouver Island. I have touched salt water east, west and north – and even bathed in salty Manitou Lake in the heart of Saskatchewan. I have flown by helicopter over the harsh coast and breathtaking fiords of Newfoundland; I have travelled by bush plane over the wild, white rivers of Northern Quebec; and I have stared down from passenger jets to know what David Thompson meant when his eyes were still sharp and he thought that the startling Rocky Mountains looked rather like "the waves of the ocean during a wintry storm."

I have felt the wintry storm, too, and marvelled later at the beauty of sunlight on iced-over trees. I have stood by prairie fields in late summer and watched the wind play as it sometimes did over the Lake of Two Rivers water when we lived here on this rocky point.

I have driven from coast to coast, paddled rivers far from any highway, tossed on ferries at both ends of this vast continent and found, at times, places so small and lovely – a miniature waterfall at the end of a certain lake, a hardwood forest barely up the street in the city in which I live – that I have feared speaking of them would somehow cause them to disappear.

I have taken trains and buses along the Central Canada corridor and watched, over time, fields vanish into housing developments and yet still felt in even the largest cities that a Canadian always has some connection, usually visual, with something far more lasting than whatever might be built: Montreal and the mountain, Toronto and the lake, Calgary and the foothills, Vancouver and the sea.

But it need not be so dramatic. Even in the densest parts of cities there will be a ravine or a park, perhaps nothing more than a sweeping back-yard garden where space, somehow, seems to go on forever in this overwhelming country called Canada.

I have been fortunate to see much of it, and yet I am certain I have seen but a small fraction of the fraction David Thompson mapped out.

It is probably easier to cup the morning mist that rolls along the gunwales of the canoe than it is to fully grasp the width and breadth and astonishing variety of this land.

I have been lucky and know it. I have been privileged to see so much more of the vast Canadian landscape than my mother and more, certainly, than my children, all in their 20s, who are but four of her grandchildren. These young Canadians, however, have still been to both coasts, both with family and alone, and though they all four live in cities, and always have, they come here to Algonquin Park each summer to get back in touch with something they are convinced was once firmly within their grasp – a deep connection to the land, to the lakes and the rivers that are, in fact, the capillaries that feed both the country and our imagination.

These four children, all born in Canadian cities, are different again from the 14 per cent of their generation who were born else-where and have come to live here and become Canadian. They come, almost exclusively, to cities, and yet it is impossible to spend time in an isolated place like this and not see their faces – faces that announce every other part of the world – coming to see for themselves what it is about this huge and sprawling country that makes it so different from anywhere else on earth.

Perhaps we should all, from time to time, bump into the Dutch tourists who passed this way the day before and spoke, with amazement, on simply what it felt like to drive long stretches without another automobile in sight.

Canadians may not think constantly of such matters, but there is an appreciation – and it has nothing to do with whether one's family was always here, came shortly after Confederation, or arrived when there were more than 31 million others. Nor does it matter if the first expressions of awe were in Ojibwa, French or English, Arabic or Korean.

This country may have changed dramatically since I ran barefoot among these rocks – but in other ways it has not changed at all. We may be the most urbanized society in the world, yet when a survey conducted for *The Globe and Mail*'s New Canada project asked what best symbolized Canada, 89 per cent across all generations said the vastness of the land.

Here, size matters.

David Chang, for example, considers it his duty to "explore" this country, even if more is done in his red Volkswagen Golf than in the canoe he and his friend Derek Liang have rented from the outfitters on Lake Opeongo. The 22-year-old Toronto telecommunications salesman was born in Canada, the country of choice for his Hong Kong father and Indonesian mother, and though his life has been spent in the city, he has found something far beyond the urban borders that gives his working life balance.

"It's an opportunity to take off the electronic leash," he says. "I come here to not see people. I come to avoid traffic and talk to trees."

"It's a break from the Toronto bar scene," adds 21-year-old Liang, a full-time student and part-time telecommunications salesman. "It's so beautiful here. It doesn't look real – it's like it's on television or out of a movie."

The previous night the two barely slept, paddling out to a small island where they lay on their backs on the rocks and watched the northern lights dance over a sky that seemed unlike any cover that ever appeared over the cities where more than 80 per cent of the population now lives. "You think how huge this park is," says Chang, "but then you realize it's still just a small part of the country."

Down at the Smoke Lake docks toward the western entrance to Algonquin, 31-year-old Jonathan Proctor of Red Deer, Alta., and his girlfriend, Tanya Litwiller, 32, are heading out into the park interior for several days of canoeing.

Once a professional guide in British Columbia, Proctor has just returned from four years of studying optometry in Alabama and he is relieved, he says, to get back to empty spaces on the map.

"The biggest difference between the States and here," he says, "is that you can still find a nice place that isn't exploited. In the United States, everything they have that might have once been nice has been turned garish."

He turns at the dock, the water stretching out deep blue before him, the varied green hills of early summer in the distance.

"It's nice just knowing it's out there," he says.

It is shared knowledge for all Canadians. Is it not telling that when we wish to make a statement, we cross the country? As I write, a 51-year-old man named Malcolm Scott is sitting buck naked behind the wheel of a motor home in the hope of promoting the benefits of "naturism" as he drops in on nudist colonies between Halifax and Victoria. And if you think the drive between Sault Ste. Marie and Dryden a tough haul, clothed or unclothed, just try rolling across Canada in a wheelchair – or running across it on one leg, as 22-year-old Terry Fox so valiantly attempted in 1980. A return of cancer forced the incredibly young man to stop near Thunder Bay, 5,373 kilometres into his run – roughly *half* way home.

They called this endless landscape "The Great Lone Land" back in 1872 when, five years after Confederation, Sanford Fleming decided to lead a grand expedition across the new country to see what had come out of all that big talk in Charlottetown and Quebec City. The Fleming expedition went from Halifax to Victoria – the same distance the naked motor-home driver is trying – and calculated they covered 1,687 miles by steamer, 2,185 miles by horses, including coaches, wagons, packs, and saddle-horses, nearly 1,000 miles by train and 485 miles in canoe or rowboats.

The new Dominion, recorded George M. Grant in his account of that early trek, "rolled out before us like a panorama, varied and magnificent enough to stir the dullest spirit into patriotic emotion."

We do indeed feel very patriotic on Canada Day, but we also see it as the beginning of the best season and the release from winter, school and work. Perhaps we are just quieter and less demonstrative than Americans when it comes to national birthdays, but it may also be that Canadians are simply acting more in keeping with what they celebrate: the solitude and tranquillity of the land beyond the settlements.

Decades after Grant talked of patriotism springing from the landscape, a young Pierre Trudeau was sent to this same park to polish up his English. He came from Montreal to attend Taylor Statten Camps on Canoe Lake, the same lake Tom Thomson painted and died on, and it was here that Trudeau gained his lifelong love for the canoe, the paddle and the backpack filled with all the "worldly goods" one requires.

Years after those first canoe trips, Trudeau penned an essay he called "Exhaustion and Fulfillment: The Ascetic in the Canoe," in which he said, "I know a man whose school could never teach him patriotism, but who acquired that virtue when he felt in his bones the vastness of his land, and the greatness of those who founded it."

There have always been those, however, who felt that vastness must be filled to have true value. In 1887, promoter Edmund Collins told the Canadian Club of New York City: "Alone, the valley of the Saskatchewan, according to scientific computation, is capable of sustaining 800,000,000 souls."

So, too, is the head of a pin.

"If nature has anything to teach us at all," Saskatchewan writer Sharon Batula wrote in *The Perfection of the Morning*, "her first lesson is in humility."

Feeling slightly overwhelmed by it all is something that comes naturally to Canadians who live through five-and-one-half time zones, who know what it is to pass a last-chance gas station or wait for a winter road to firm up, people who can appreciate what Prairie poet Yvonne Trainer was getting at when she asked, "Where do you run/ when your mother can stand outside/ and look six miles in any direction?"

There is no such luxury in a place like Algonquin Park unless, of course, one climbs one of the old fire towers that are no longer necessary in this age of aircraft patrol and satellite. Here, and in bush from one end of the country to the other, the sensation is less one of staring at a landscape than of standing in one – and perhaps it is this singular Canadian experience that explains the continuing popularity of Tom Thomson.

There is something about *The West Wind* that blows through all Canadians, even those seeing Thomson's painting for the very first time. And yet no one attending the recent exhibitions of his works that have toured Canada would disagree with what Lawren Harris once said about his friend. It was here, along the same routes that David Chang travels today, that Harris believed Thomson felt finally free of "the machinery of civilization."

Some believe the landscape and climate form Canadians – reserved people who have to reintroduce themselves to their neighbours each spring, yet hardy people who play a game others think overaggressive – but it would be naive to think this northern expanse is for everyone.

"There are those who find the wilderness exhilarating," British travel writer Stephen Brook said in the late 1980s. "I am not one of them. The expanses and vistas of Canada frustrate those who, like myself, often prefer the detail to the grand design. Canada's mystique is its spaciousness, its northern emptiness. To me it is oppressive."

Other writers, almost invariably born and raised elsewhere and come to Canada late, have felt much the same. Susanna Moodie, who came out to the colony with such great hopes in the summer of 1832, eventually declared that "my love for Canada was a feeling very nearly allied to that which the condemned criminal entertains for his cell – his only hope of escape being through the portals of the grave."

Surely it was such writing that gave rise to Northrop Frye's famous theory of a "garrison mentality" among those who wrote down what they saw all about them – a collective imagination, Frye felt, formed by "a tone of deep terror in regard to nature." Frye, sitting at his desk at the University of Toronto's Victoria College, even postulated that such fear was the first experience of the traditional immigrant as ships edged into the Gulf of St. Lawrence "like a tiny Jonah entering an inconceivably large whale." Forgetting for the moment that there were few steerages with wall maps for immigrants to form such an educated impression, Frye should have realized that weeks and months at sea with typhoid and scurvy, vomit and death would make the calm waters and green banks of the St. Lawrence appear like heaven itself.

Even Susanna Moodie's initial response was one of delight. "Never had I beheld so many striking objects blended into one mighty whole!" she wrote in her journal as the *Anne* neared Quebec City. "Nature had lavished all her noblest features in producing that enchanting scene."

I prefer to think Frye, in letting his own imagination run away on him, got it wrong, at least among those who come to live more than to write. The immigrant experience has been far less to fear the new land than to appreciate it, deeply, to stand in awe, yes, but not ready to flee.

My own experience, so indelibly shaped by this rocky point, has been that people were far more alarmed by streetlights than by shadowed paths. In fact, if I took Frye's *Bush Garden* and substituted the word "city" every time he uses the word "nature," it would pretty well hold true for how my parents and most people we knew felt about their vast country.

It cannot, of course, hold quite so true for my generation, now almost entirely city settled, nor for almost all of those newly come to this land.

And yet, for reasons that are sometimes understandable – a distant family farm, aboriginal heritage, a history that somewhere includes fishing, mines, logging, the railway – and for reasons no one can quite understand, there remains this enormous connection with the land.

Some might call it false memory. Better, I say, to think of it as true roots.

On the hill back of the rocky point there is nothing left of the log cabin but remnants of the magnificent stone fireplace the old ranger put in with his own hands.

The quartz is missing, and the lovely granite stones with the fine mica flakings. And yet Canadians will understand when I say it still burns.

PART V

WHERE WE'RE GOING

23

TEN CHALLENGES FROM THE 20S

MICHAEL VALPY, ERIN ANDERSSEN AND ALANNA MITCHELL

They've been brought up to celebrate different lifestyles, believe in the value of individuals, get ahead through education, and make time for their families. Now they expect society to go along with it all. Is Canada up to the challenge?

IT IS A GENERATION OF MYTH-BUSTERS, these Canadians in their 20s. They have rewritten the idea of the Canada-to-come and dropped a set of prickly challenges in the laps of governments and other social institutions.

The myths they have buried? Canada, quite simply, is not a country in search of an identity, contrary to the polemics of poets, pundits and professors. It's not a country continually on the verge of something but never quite there. Canadians are not a people who have nothing in common except their diversity.

All that has been made irrefutably clear by Canada's newest adults. They have remarkably similar values, as *The Globe and Mail*'s New Canada project has demonstrated. They have attitudes and an approach to life that markedly distinguish them from young Americans and young Europeans.

They are pursuing democracy in the workplace and in marriage. They are global thinkers, committed to issues of tolerance and social justice, led by the women. They are, of course, the best-educated generation the country has ever produced, possibly the best-educated generation of young adults in the world.

Look at them on the streets. Love is bubbling across racial and ethnic lines, and the Canadian post-ethnic identity is on its way to reality.

Look into Quebec. You'll find young adults turning their backs on separatism.

Look elsewhere in Canada and see the 20s embracing a pan-national identity with an affection and a fervour not seen in the country for decades.

And always keep this in mind about them, because it is the generation's most significant characteristic: They are not a sudden sociological phenomenon; they are Canadians whose values have evolved from those of the generations preceding them.

The challenges they present? Here are 10 issues where the next generation can be expected to show dissatisfaction with – and ultimately challenge – existing government and institutional policies and cultural norms; or where the generation's experience may well result in change.

What happens, anyway, if no one shows up to vote?

Political scientists are getting closer to understanding why only one in five Canadians in their 20s vote and, as the saying goes, it's not a pretty answer. As Roger Gibbins put it to an Elections Canada-sponsored national forum on youth voting held in Calgary in the autumn of

2003, "We may be asking the wrong question. Rather than asking why many youth are not voting, we should be asking why so many *are* voting, given a political process with so little appeal or relevance. We should be asking why anyone – young or old – does vote."

Mr. Gibbins, president of the Canada West Foundation, a Calgary-based public policy research institute, likened young Canadians' aversion to the polls to the canary down the mineshaft of Canadian democracy. "Canadian youth, through their lack of participation, are sending a message about the health of Canadian democratic politics. . . . The Canadian political culture carries a strong and persistent message that elections don't count for much, that Parliament is irrelevant, that the courts are now the primary policy makers in the land." Indeed, on the last point, a healthy majority of young Canadians told the New Canada survey that they did put more trust in the courts than in elected politicians to deal with public policy issues.

Since the 2000 federal election, when only 61 per cent of the electorate cast ballots – a record-low participation rate caused mainly by stay-at-home younger citizens – Elections Canada and political scientists across the country have been beavering away at a blizzard of studies and conferences on why this should be happening.

It is, to begin with, not unique to Canada. If anything, young voters in countries like the United States and Britain are more alienated from political participation, and young Canadians – somewhat paradoxically – report themselves to be more satisfied with how their democracy functions than their peers elsewhere in the Western democracies. It is not primarily the result of political cynicism: Research shows older voters are more cynical. It does not seem to be based on the lack of partisan competitive politics in Canadian democracy. In fact, young voters were less likely than older voters to think that there was "no race" in their constituencies. (And therein lies the first clue to what is at the root of the problem: political ignorance.) Apathy is a factor. Young voters are more bored, more uninterested in politics than older voters. But political apathy has always been a factor among the young – although the University of Manitoba's Brenda O'Neill finds that it is increasing – and is an inadequate explanation in itself for today's atypical electoral participation. Busyness is a factor: Today's young voters really do appear to have more frenetic schedules than earlier generations. But, again, that in itself is an inadequate explanation for the worrisome absence of a sense of "civic duty" among the young.

But add lack of civic duty to some of the findings of respected political researcher Henry Milner at Montreal's Vanier College – that levels of "civic literacy" in Canada, meaning "the knowledge to be effective citizens," are relatively low in Canada compared to other western democracies – and the academics start coalescing around agreement on what's wrong.

Young Canadians are not so much apathetic toward Canadian civic engagement as they are withdrawing from it. They show low levels of knowledge of how democracy works, and it's not a concern to them because fewer and fewer of them think formal democracy is relevant to their lives. Moreover, as Mr. Gibbins and others point out – as, indeed, many others have pointed out inside and outside of Canada, including U.S. political scientist Robert Putnam, author of the land-mark study of civil society *Bowling Alone* – there is a correlation between their withdrawal from democratic participation and their lack of involvement in other forms of civic engagement. Too many young Canadians aren't merely bowling alone, they're not bowling at all.

Stephanie Higginson, 27, is a high-school civics teacher on leave from the Toronto school board to do a master's degree at University of British Columbia – "to make," as she says, "the classroom a better place." And one of the systemic changes she advocates is to lower the voting age to 16 so that the youngest citizens will still be in school for at least the first election of their voting lives, where they can be taught about the workings of democracy and civic engagement.

"I am not convinced that the low vote turnout means that people in my age bracket are not participating in our democratic system," she says. "I look at the increase in protesting and demonstrating and see a much more active participation in democracy than simply voting. But how can we make more young people vote?" Canada's current political culture, she says, is at odds with the dominant values of Canada's youngest adults. "The current system is simply not reflective of the values we have been raised to hold true – equality, equity, the environment, the importance of education and so on."

And on this point, political scientists are inclined to agree. They suggest that political parties and other advocacy groups do an inadequate job of getting the message to young adults about how their democratic participation might impact on public policy, whether it be on urban issues – cities are where most of them live, and cities are electorally underrepresented in the Canadian system – or issues touching the environment, family and work life, and equity. As Mr. Gibbins says, it's not just a problem to toss in Elections Canada's lap. It touches all of Canadian society.

A global generation with attitude, they want to export Canada

Mike Quinn represents the new generation of foreign aid worker. The 23-year-old Canadian engineer is a volunteer in Ghana, building multi-purpose diesel engines that will power corn mills and wood saws, and even Internet cafés, in impoverished rural villages. He wanted something that made him feel passionate, and wasn't just about profit. He survives on less than $3 a day – you cannot be an effective development worker, he says, and continue a western lifestyle. He lives in a one-room apartment that occasionally goes weeks without electricity, sharing a toilet and shower in the local compound, passing up on the restaurant meals and hot water in the ex-pat areas of nearby Accra.

For Canada, he talks about more support of grassroots operations, real debt relief, and holding Canadian companies to account when they earn profits in developing nations. "For me, development is just a buzzword mixed up in politics [that] lacks a human face," he writes in an e-mail from Ghana. He sounds a lot like Fahima Osman, studying to be a doctor in Hamilton, who was disheartened by the lack of real progress she saw while volunteering for development agencies in Somalia, the country of her roots. "We assumed that because we are Canadians, the whole world loves us," writes Mr. Quinn. "We have to question whether they love us because we are helping them develop or because we are a western country with a big chequebook."

Canada's newest adults want a country and a political leadership that mirror their own values of responsible global citizenship. They are not always inspired by what they see. Ben Parrin says the country has become complacent, resting on the "borrowed capital" of past accomplishments. "Empty words mean nothing to the people on the front lines of the greatest tragedies in the world," says Mr. Parrin, 24, the executive director of the Future Group, which sends young Canadians overseas to help with problems like child trafficking.

Dr. James Orbinski, former president of the Nobel Peace Prize-winning international public health agency Médecins Sans Frontières and a research scientist at University of Toronto's St. Michael's Hospital, says: "Citizenship for a nation is a new concept, a new way of imagining Canada's place in the world. It means trying to reflect in practice the pluralism – and I don't say the multiculturalism – the pluralism of Canada in the way we approach our presence in multilateral institutions."

It's a concept, he says, that has particular resonance with young Canadians. "We now have a visionary generation that sees itself in a fundamentally different way than [the] similar age-demographic of previous generations. And that's revolutionary in terms of the meaning of politics both domestically and internationally for Canada." Canada's newest adults expect their national government to act internationally in the same way they expect it to act domestically, Dr. Orbinski says – as the government of "a highly pluralistic society that almost unknowingly values and actively pursues tolerance, and values and actively pursues respect for the 'other.' They've deeply experienced this in their own daily lives with the reality of pluralism in this country, and it's something that the so-called multicultural vision of Trudeau and others created for us."

Dr. Orbinski says political reality – the influence of U.S. interests, perhaps – does not always give Canada a free hand to act globally. "Citizenship is about balancing, finding the right relationships between individuals and concentric layers of communalism and public interests. Political reality does not always allow that to be actualized. But what I'm saying is, particularly for this demographic [of Canadians in their 20s], there's a deep awareness that it should."

Former foreign affairs minister Lloyd Axworthy, now head of the Liu Institute for Global Issues at University of B.C., says good global citizenship "is something we once had a patent on." But much of the image has been lost, and when the country does take a position – such as signing the Kyoto accord or staying out of the way on Iraq – "it's not very well communicated."

Young Canadians not only want leaders who speak with passion about shaping a better world, they want a return to the peacekeeping of the past, with a streamlined military that can respond to conflicts with a humanitarian agenda. In their vision, a focused foreign-aid policy would commit long-term resources – money and people – to helping key areas, with the capacity to assist with sudden human catastrophes. They look for more examples of the government's move to give poor countries better access to cheap, generic drugs – which Dr. Orbinski calls a perfect example of Canada's global good-citizenship: "It's a very practical and concrete example of how Canada can lead."

Canada, observes Parker Mitchell, 27, is not capitalizing on its "competition advantage" – its reputation as an inclusive society welcoming to newcomers, its lack of baggage as a former colonial power, and the educated young people who want do something on the ground, like soon-to-be Dr. Osman, who plans to practice medicine part-time in Somalia. Mr. Mitchell heads Engineers Without Border, the organization that send Mr. Quinn to Ghana; they get 20 volunteers for every placement they can fund and organize. That's a lot of unused talent: trained engineers willing to travel unpaid to Africa, living as cheaply as they can, to bring water and electricity to villages where people die every day.

In fundraising speeches, Mr. Mitchell talks about Canada becoming the most "pro-development country in the world" – a nation that tops the list of per-capita funding of foreign aid, sets an example in environmental sustainability. The Canada he wants does not overindulge in applauding its values of equality and inclusion – it works to export them to the excluded.

Applying a little more style to being in bed with an elephant

Canada annoys the U.S. administration of President George W. Bush by not supporting the American-led invasion and occupation of Iraq. It annoys the administration by contemplating the legalization of marijuana. For the mouse in bed with the elephant, former prime minister Pierre Trudeau once said, every twitch of the big beast matters. Thus, it's one of those questions that transfix Canadians: If Canadian and American social and political values are diverging, as the evidence strongly suggests they are – especially the values of young adults in the two countries – while at the same time the two economies are merging, will management of the U.S.-Canadian relationship grow trickier? The question tends to divide generations: Younger Canadians are more inclined to want Ottawa not to be deferentially wussy around the Americans and to speak out with an independent and unfettered voice in support of Canadian domestic and global values; and older Canadians are not only more likely to see Canada's interests as similar if not identical to those of the United States but also more apt to be fearful of Canada taking actions that would put it at odds with U.S. policy – fearful that the elephant will whack the mouse where it hurts the most, in the economy.

Interestingly enough, the people who professionally study the cross-border relationship suggest that, by and large, Canadians have a distorted perception of the issue – overwhelmed by the trees, they don't see the forest. They say that, because of the *mutual* economic dependence of the two countries – something Canadians seldom if ever think about – Canada is largely insulated from being whacked by Washington when it disagrees with U.S. policy.

Jack Mintz, president of the C.D. Howe Institute and a former University of Toronto business school professor, suggests that so long as both countries are satisfying their mutual economic interests there is little reason to believe that the relationship will be undermined by different policy decisions in other areas. "In any relationship among countries, whether it's Canada or the United States, or, in some other context, the European Union – or going farther back into history – they'll always move ahead if it's in their own interests to do so, and they can have quite different values," he says. "Britain and France are still very different in their values, and certainly some of the Scandinavian countries versus Germany. The only reason we worry about our relationship [in this regard] with the United States is because it's a huge trading partner and our economies are linked." Or as Michael Byers, head of the Canadian studies program at North Carolina's Duke University (and a Canadian himself) puts it: "We tend to obsess about our own particular relationship with the country next door, and forget sometimes that [trade and economic integration] are global developments and what's happening to us isn't unusual. It's different to the degree that we've got only one 800-pound gorilla living next door, as opposed, say, to the Dutch who've got a couple of them, and that might affect the dynamic in some way."

Thus, the first point Mr. Mintz and Prof. Byers make is that the United States, like most countries, largely de-links trade and the economy from other issues in its international relationships. "So I'm not sure divergent values necessarily undermine relationships," says

Mr. Mintz, "so long as both countries are satisfying their own interests in terms of trade, or facilitating trade, or facilitating mobility of labour and things like that." And their second point is that the economic bond between Canada and the United States is a bridle on Washington as well as on Ottawa. Both Mr. Mintz and Prof. Byers cite the exceptionally close economic and political ties between Canadian provinces and northern border states, many if not most of which are political swing states in U.S. presidential elections. "At times," says Mr. Mintz, "to understand what's going on at the national level in the United States, you have to understand the local politics." Consider, he says, the fact that Illinois is Canada's fourth largest customer. Prof. Byers continues in the same vein: Consider, he says, that the largest international trading partner of North Carolina [where Duke is located] is Canada. "And I can tell you that if the President did anything to negatively affect that trade relationship, the business community of North Carolina would be up in arms. And that's small potatoes compared to Michigan or Washington state or New York state. The President is not going to do anything that's going to annoy the voters of Michigan. The trade relationship [between Canada and the U.S.] to a significant degree is insulated from other aspects of the relationship because it is so important to Americans, and important in ways that Canadians underestimate. The President is desperate to win every single state next November (2004), and Washington state and Michigan and so on are swing states."

Prof. Byers says the U.S. administration has only threatened punishment for non-economic issues against countries with which it doesn't have much of an economic relationship. Conversely, he points out that the U.S. showed no interest in retaliating against Mexico even though, as a member of the United Nations Security Council, it voted against the U.S. Iraqi action, and it didn't threaten to punish Brazil for leading the opposition to U.S. policy at the summer 2003 World Trade Organization ministerial meeting in Cancun. Both Mexico and Brazil have significant economic links with the U.S.

The fact that Canadians haven't become Americans in the face of economic convergence, Hollywood, American culture and the Americanization of not only Canada but also the world, is – says Prof. Byers – "bizarre." But that's the way things have turned out. And for older Canadians, quite willing to celebrate the newest adult generation's liberal and progressive values in most respects, there's a troubling discomfort around the cohort's lack of deference to the next-door neighbour.

Axel Bernabe, just turned 30, went to New York to practice corporate law after graduating from McGill law school because he wanted to better understand the Americans, and because he wanted to understand what freedom there was for a middle power like Canada to adhere to its own values in a global economy. "In a sense, it's about the way the debate is framed [between the countries]," says Mr. Bernabe. "Living on the south side of the border, the Canadians I know would appreciate a little more style in the way our politicians handle being in bed with the elephant. We get so hung up on what the Americans might think, we forget to conduct ourselves in our own distinctive manner; that's what I mean by 'style.' Most of the time we do not even register south of the border. We all recall being scandalized at being forgotten in Bush's speech thanking his 'friends and allies' following 9-11. In any courtship, a degree of cool indifference is essential to successful seduction – nobody likes a desperate courtesan."

In any event, says Prof. Byers, to risk a whacking from the U.S., "we'd have to do something so colossally unprecedented. On 99 per cent of all issues we're on the same page anyway."

"How ya gonna keep 'em away from Broadway, Jazzin' around, and paintin' the town?"

What the statistics show today is a far remove from the herds of Canadian university graduates who thundered through U.S. immigration posts in pursuit of the good American life in the 1960s, '70s and '80s. The most recent research says less than two per cent of young Canadians head south after collecting their degrees (with nearly one in five doing so for love, joining American or migrating partners). It indicates that at least 60 per cent of those who cross the border come home again, reflecting the marked preference among young Canadians for life in their own culture and country. And it suggests those graduates who head south after being recruited off Canadian campuses by American corporations is minuscule. It's all nice and positive-sounding and, indeed, in the past few years the brain drain has fallen off the table as an issue for debate.

But, as the punch-line writers say, not so fast. When the focus is narrowed to look at PhD and perhaps comparable professional graduates, the statistics show that about 12 per cent of them go south, that at least half of them graduated in the top 10 per cent of their class, and that a smaller percentage of them return. And perhaps more significantly, an assessment of the migration statistics done for Industry Canada in 2000 by policy analysts Serge Nadeau, Lori Whewell and Shane Williamson declares that, small numbers or not, there should never be complacency about who's turning in their zeds for zees.

Canada, the analysts point out, is investing heavily in knowledge-economy skills. It has the highest per-capita postsecondary enrolment in the world and is among the world's leaders on education spending. They write: "Retaining our skilled workers in Canada is vital to the global success of Canadian firms in the knowledge-based economy." In this regard, one statistic can serve to illustrate why complacency is a bad idea. While Canada had 20,000 job vacancies in the information technology sector in the late 1990s, the U.S. had 190,000 vacancies – with the North American Free Trade Agreement making it immeasurably easier for Canadians to slip across the border to take those jobs, quite likely market-sweetened by America's greater demand, with more attractive financial inducements than at home. Moreover, as we examine the ingredients that go into the stew of a "smart city" – an urban environment attractive to global knowledge-workers – it's not just the knowledge-workers themselves, or attractive jobs: It's also an attractive arts community along with vibrant health care and education communities, all of whose members have long felt the pull to the south.

The good news is that the brain-drain debate, however flawed its more alarmist arguments may have been (lower U.S. taxes hardly make it onto the radar screen of why Canadians go south), has ignited notions that "something must be done." The bad news is that far too little is being done, and, for the most part, it's uncreative and un-muscular.

On the plus side, the recently endowed Canada Research Chairs and other new federal and provincial funding are enabling major Canadian academic institutions to more aggressively attract Canadian post-doctoral researchers and doctoral students – particularly since Sept. 11, 2001, notes Vivek Goel, University of Toronto's vice-provost for academic recruitment: "Geo-political forces are helping us." As is young Canadians' awareness that living conditions are by and large better at home. The cake beneath that icing, says the vice-provost, is that the U of T has been very successful in offering opportunities to Canadians in the U.S., such as collaborative and cross-disciplinary research that they can't find elsewhere. He also points out that only in the past few years, since older professors have started retiring in significant numbers, has the university been in a position to actively recruit new faculty members

On the minus side, it's instructive to listen to young Canadians – such as Toronto's Adam Hess, 28, who spends a great deal of his time jazzin' around Broadway as general manager of an Off-Broadway theatre. Talented young Canadians in the States, he says, rarely if ever get approached by Canadian headhunters but are sought out by their American counterparts. They have difficulties finding out about job opportunities in Canada, although the Internet is helping.

Mr. Hess also suggests that if Canada is too small to support academic arts programs of the quality found in the U.S., it could take

advantage of them by offering young Canadians supportive opportunities to study abroad. "I didn't go to University of Michigan [and
later Columbia] because I was turning my back on the Canadian education system," Mr. Hess says. "I went because it offered me a musical
theatre program of a calibre that could not be found in Canada" – and
loaded him with American university debt that makes it harder for
him to turn his back on a U.S. salary. "What can you do when U.S.
salaries are greater?"

Finally, he says, "I believe the best time to capture the attention of
Canadians studying abroad is right after university. The more time we
have to establish roots in foreign cities, the harder it is to come home."

A national forum on the topic, hosted by a group of young policy-
minded Canadians called Canada 25, concluded that too often the
country is seen as the kind of place to which you'd retire, but short on
the economic energy that guarantees top-notch career opportunities
when you're starting out. The nation, they concluded, needs to get
more excited about new ideas. They proposed a high-profile mone-
tary award, bestowed by the Prime Minister for top young innovators,
and a program that employs fresh talent for "short bursts" of work in
the public service.

Ottawa's Jessica Strauss, 27, a New York architect, says young
Canadians in the U.S. come to believe there are more choices and
greater opportunity for them there "but the reality is different from
the perception" – there is a lot happening at home, but Canadian
companies generally do an inadequate job of telling anyone about it.
Similarly, she says, the country does a bad job of marketing itself to its
young citizens who have gone abroad. "Whenever I enter back into
Canada I'm struck by the incredible infrastructure that exists to facilitate life there. Basically, things work. I'm looking for assurances that
I'll be able to grow professionally and personally in a country that
wants to build for the future. Marketing, I tell you. . . ."

Bright lights, green spaces and everyone is welcome

In a country where 80 per cent of the population dwells in urban centres, it goes without saying that cities matter a great deal. Canadian 20s, more mobile than previous generations, are more deliberate about where they choose to live – especially the brightest among them. This creates an obvious challenge for cities that must compete against each other for the same talent.

Let's start with green spaces. Young Canadians tend to be more conscious of the environment and Canada's global responsibility. Those interviewed in Calgary, for example, almost always mentioned clean air as a leading plus about their city, and bemoaned the glut of SUVs on the streets. Dave Fortin, a 28-year-old intern architect in Calgary, waxes poetic about the mountains and wheat fields, walks to work at his firm, and balks at the very thought of distance commuting. "I can think of a lot better ways to spend 10 hours of my week – that's my guitar time," he says. Mostly, though, he gets a buzz from the contrasts in urban life. Where before there was a desire to be like your neighbour – he points to the sameness of suburbia – now people want to be accepted while being different.

But the cities must also work as diverse, vibrant places of equal opportunity for all residents. Successful urban centres will have healthy downtown cores, deep labour markets and affordable neighbourhoods. Cities need to promote everyday culture like parks and libraries and community centres – the infrastructure where people from all backgrounds naturally congregate – as much as the so-called high cultures of the symphony and museums. They need to fight against social gaps by pushing programs that allow new immigrants to afford housing in a wide range of neighbourhoods, and help them integrate smoothly into the workforce. University of Toronto professor Meric Gertler points out that Canada could be smarter on the issue of foreign credentials; he praises the program originated by the Toronto City Summit Alliance that links new immigrants with internships and mentors in the business community. Revitalizing public schools should be a priority, he says, since a second-rate school so often defines a neighbourhood's reputation and can cripple the poorest communities, where parents have fewer skills to organize and make up the difference.

Betsy Donald, an assistant professor of geography at Queen's University, says cities must consider their public policies of inclusion – the same way restoring heritage buildings in low-income neighbourhoods sends a positive message that the neighbourhood is valued. San Francisco did not become a successful, creative city only because artists moved into town – there was a clear political will to welcome them. Federal politics also have an impact on a city's ability to draw the desired mix of people, she says, citing Canada's full-year-maternity benefits, openness to same-sex marriage, and multiculturalism policy.

If people continue to move not to companies but to places, not to countries but to urban centres, then cities must consider what they say to the world. "Our cities are our lifeblood," says Dr. Donald, "and all our policies play out in them."

In the right position to demand a work-life balance, or else

Young Canadians have learned a few lessons from their parents about the nature of work. While they were growing up, their mothers and fathers were becoming the wealthiest generation of Canadians in history. Women jumped en masse into some of the best jobs. People worked longer and harder. In an economic downturn, they were rewarded with downsizing; at home, they were waging custody battles.

So young men like Jeff Canizares, a university graduate working as assistant manager in a box store, recalls clearly the Christmas he opened his presents over the phone with his doctor father. And young women like chartered accountant Trish Muraca, 28, and her husband's cousin Maria Muraca, also 28, a newly married medical resident, talk deliberately about planning a balance between home and office, so they can succeed at both. Trish says she became a chartered accountant in part because it offered the chance to scale down her work week, to work at home and perhaps run a business from there. "But I also see that you need to be assertive and aggressive in what it is you want [when integrating family and career], because you're never going to have anything handed to you on a silver platter."

In the *Globe*-CRIC survey, young women reported feeling the most stress of all Canadians; they were also far more likely than young men to say they would choose more family time over bigger pay-cheques. This generation will insist – not request – that workplaces allow them to integrate careers with family and personal lives; they are sensitive to not repeating the mistakes of the past, and frustrated with a snail's pace of change.

Sarit Batner, a 29-year-old civil litigator in Toronto, receives at least one e-mail a week from other female associates seeking advice on how to balance their family plans with their career goals. Ms. Batner is a rarity, even in these modern times: a rising, ambitious lawyer with a husband and a 17-month-old daughter, who makes certain that, barring emergencies, she gets home by six each night, and doesn't work weekends. Instead, she starts the day at 7:30 a.m., and concentrates on doing her best work efficiently – it is the balance in her life, she says, that makes her productive and keen as a litigator. She has a clear advantage with a husband who cooks breakfast and dinner, and handles the daycare drop-off and pick-ups, but she never intended to make the office her life. Generally, though, she says female associates who have young children still "flee private practice," and those who adopt part-time hours are typically "seen as less than 100 per cent committed."

"There's been a shift in society away from the commitment to work," she says. "People are not willing to tolerate the conditions their predecessors did. But it's a battle."

Then again, she observes, if you're valued, then your employer will make it work. It's a point well taken: Canada is on the edge of a labour shortage, with the first wave of baby boomers about to head off to retirement. More of the highest-skilled workers in the country will be young women, many of whom want families, and who live in a nation that needs them to have families. A blunt study commissioned by the Canadian Policy Research Networks warns that employers who drag their feet on flexible work policies – to say nothing of on-site child care, good benefits, and creative work space – will quickly find themselves losing valuable knowledge-economy workers.

Smart companies are hiring young 20s to build their experience base for when their senior staff leaves permanently for the cottage. They can expect to meet a new kind of worker, one with a mercurial loyalty to the company, a need to be inspired at work, who won't miss the school Christmas pageant to work late on a project. "This generation is in the driver's seat," says Nora Spinks, president of the consulting firm Work-Life Harmony Enterprises. "They can make demands – and expect their demands to be met – because of the pressure of the shrinking labour force."

Where the sun doesn't shine: left behind in New Canada

What will Canada do to help Sandy Banhidi dream her dreams of a future? When her mother died ten years ago, Ms. Banhidi, 27, quit high school without graduating to help pay the family bills. For a variety of reasons, she was never able to return. Today she is manager of a rental car agency in Toronto. Her customers love her. She usually surpasses her monthly business-volume targets. She is intelligent, articulate, a good employee. But she barely earns $25,000 a year. Her company offers higher salaries to new employees with university degrees or college diplomas than to Ms. Banhidi with three years' experience and a flawless work record. She cannot move up, she cannot move out to a better job, she cannot afford to start a family with her boyfriend. "Nobody wants you to move up in the company," she says. "They know you're going to leave, and that's okay, because they'll replace you. Do I feel stuck? Yeah."

In the society into which Ms. Banhidi and others like her are trying to fit, the space is widening dramatically between rich and creative, and poor and constricted. Canada now has more full-time, low-wage workers per capita than any country in the Organisation for Economic Co-operation and Development other than the United States. Women still comprise two-thirds of workers earning less than $8 an hour. The most economically vulnerable people in the labour market are single Canadians, single parents, aboriginals, and recent and particularly older immigrants.

It is getting harder and harder in many sectors of the service industry to get sufficient work hours and wages to keep families out of poverty, and indeed, while incomes are declining, family debt is growing. There are broad social implications, with young people either postponing children or raising them in poverty, along with a young workforce less able to support the needs of an aging population. "My mother was 21 when I was born," says Ms. Banhidi, "my boyfriend's mother was 26. I'm now 27 – and I'm not even close to thinking of having children. Because I can't afford it." But she is struggling as best she can to look after her father with whom she shares a house.

Ms. Banhidi and young Canadians like her are the underside of an economy that so heavily values skills and education. Ron Saunders, the director of work research at the Canadian Policy Research Networks, points out in a 2003 paper that what is being created is a class of employee with limited access to employment rights and benefits and less freedom to access them for fear of losing their jobs – an underclass of adult workers likely to earn low wages, not for transient life stages, but over the long term. The challenge, Mr. Saunders says, is to help these workers while maintaining the nation's ability to compete in a global market.

The case he makes is grounded more in pragmatism than in any big-hearted compassion. With Canada's labour force aging, he says, it simply makes no sense to have a large group of young adults underemployed. The country's ability to compete globally is impacted, he says, "if we end up discouraging people, paying them little, giving them little chance to improve their skills. That hurts them and it hurts the economy."

He advocates policies that would offer training and development to people who are the least likely to get it on the job; experts cite countries like Norway that concentrate investment training in the lowest-income workers. The debate over the minimum wage – whether increasing it costs jobs or maintaining the status quo forces more and more families into poverty – needs to be resolved. A 2003 statistical study by the Caledon Institute of Social Policy puts minimum-wage incomes across Canada at below-poverty rates, even assuming that workers are employed full time for a complete year, which creates a disincentive to work. "I have goals, you know," says Ms. Banhidi. "I just can't seem to attain them. And it's not for my lack of ability."

Where the boys are: It's not in school

Canadians in their 20s – especially the male half – may be forgiven if these days they contemplate the society around them and proclaim it to be a girls' world. Young women, more so than young men, are defining the liberal, inclusive, progressive values of their generation. Young women, in the past few years, have accounted for more than 75 per cent of enrolment at Canada's postsecondary academic institutions, overtaking male students in disciplines like law and medicine. Young women show up on surveys like the New Canada poll as more confident, more sure of where they're heading, more comfortable with the complexities of 21st-century postmodern life. *The Globe*'s interviews with young adults ten years out of high school found women much more inclined to have travelled a straight line on their chosen career-paths while the men drifted in and out of university and college, chopped and changed their choices on what they wanted to become.

Whenever there's evidence of a gap, a difference, it cannot be ignored, says Charles Ungerleider, professor of education at UBC and

B.C.'s former deputy minister of education. But, he adds, whether there's anything problematic with the way boys are being educated is another matter. There's no supporting evidence. If anything, the evidence points in the other direction: that feminism's daughters are merely catching up.

It's an analysis for the most part embraced by Jane Gaskell, dean of University of Toronto's Ontario Institute for Studies in Education and one of North America's foremost experts on education and gender. "Girls have always done better than boys in elementary and secondary education," she says. "Most girls graduated from high school right up through the 1960s in most places in North America. Only recently have girls gone on to postsecondary education in the same numbers as boys, and that reflects the women's movement and opportunities at work for women, as well as some restructuring of job entry to require more university education [which thus benefits girls]. The interesting question is when the public becomes concerned about it, and why."

One guess is that the concern is coming from parents of male offspring, although not, it seems, from young men themselves. Take Hamish Rhodes, 27, who planned to attend art school after graduating from high school in Vancouver, but instead followed a girlfriend north, and now manages a wildlife resort in the Yukon. He shrugs and grins: "I'm taking a longer path."

Not all behavioural scientists and educators are of one mind on the issue. Dr. Gaskell says: "Educators have been periodically concerned, for instance modifying texts in the early 1950s to appeal to boys and counteract the 'feminization of schools.'" Dr. Kenneth Zucker, psychologist in chief at Toronto's Centre for Addiction and Mental Health, wonders if the education system has shifted dynamics on gender imbalances over the past few decades: telling girls what they can do and boys what they can't, and leaving the boys a little confused. For her part, Bev Freedman, a Toronto-based schools consultant on gender issues, says, "It's the motivation and engagement of young men in school that troubles me – both in the short term and long term. The boys are just as capable but less compliant in a traditional sense." Less compliant to being moulded? "Yes, I think so. Males are also identified as [more in need of behavioural] special education than girls in terms of attention deficit disorder and attention deficit hyperactivity disorder. And a lot of the new reforms in education have increased demands [for] literacy and fewer boys are successful on this test. This may increase the percentage of girls in postsecondary."

What educators and behavioural scientists do know, however, is that boys are greater risk takers than girls, which may require – and in some cases already has required – structural changes in education. The post-high-school drift factor can be explained by male risk-taking behaviour, Dr. Gaskell says. Whereas young women can well be expected do better in disciplines requiring certification – education, law, medicine – young men will do better where certification is not required but risk is, like business. Would greater certification of business as a discipline benefit boys, she wonders. It might well benefit girls. Similarly, Dr. Gaskell is pleased that education ministries such as Ontario's are counter-balancing male risk-taking with policies such as apprenticeship training that begins in high school and continues on afterward, thus engaging more males before they wander loose. High-school-based apprenticeship should also benefit girls in time, she says. "Before, the unions controlled the apprenticeships. The girls could never figure out unions."

The right generation of natives to envision a better tomorrow

Alec Durocher was only 14 when he moved from his remote Métis community of Ile-à-la-Crosse to Saskatoon for Grade 9. He was one of just three aboriginal people going to the school at that time. He remembers feeling shut out, trying to fit into a world that was very different from the one he had grown up in. It wasn't that the other

kids said nasty things to him. "It was more of them not saying anything at all," he says. "I felt like a loner."

This search for identity – both as aboriginal and as Canadian – sits
at the heart of the staggering challenges faced by this generation of
aboriginal Canadians in their 20s. Among them: lower rates of education and employment than non-aboriginal Canadians, higher rates of
poverty, drug and alcohol abuse, family dysfunction, incarceration
and suicide.

Of all these, the most pressing is suicide, emblem of an absence
of hope and self-worth. Already five to six times higher among aboriginal youth (up to 25) than their non-aboriginal peers in the mid-
1990s, this rate is poised to go even higher this decade as a
demographic bump of aboriginals hits their late teens and early 20s.
In a special report on suicide called *Choosing Life*, the Royal
Commission on Aboriginal Peoples, which reported in late 1996, said
it had heard directly from this generation about why suicide and
attempted suicide are so common: "The causes, they told us, are all
around them all the time: in the confusion they feel about their identity, in the absence of opportunity to make a good life, in the bleak-
ness of daily existence where alcohol and drugs sometimes seem to
offer the only relief."

But this generation of native Canadians has a unique opportunity
to improve things. They are more likely than older generations to have
moved beyond identifying the causes of the problems to figuring out
practical ways to solve them, especially at the community level. Having
seen parents and peers fall into patterns of despair and self-destruction,
they are "rising above the psychology of grievance" with a vision of a
better tomorrow, the commission said. "It became clear that for young
aboriginal men and women, community development is not about
infrastructure, but about people, and about building a stronger community. By and large, they are not concerned with perceived political
or administrative impediments; they do not worry about overlapping
jurisdictions, competing programs or other bureaucratic hurdles.

They feel these political obstacles are immaterial, creations of a system that has largely failed aboriginal people."

"We know we can't go back to our original way of life," says Dwight Bird, 28, a second-year student in the aboriginal justice and criminology program at the University of Saskatchewan in Saskatoon, "but we still want to keep our culture alive and move ahead."

There may be reason for hope. A survey done by Ipsos-Reid for the New Canada project examined broad social acceptance of various groups in society. Among the questions was whether a person would feel comfortable with a close relative marrying an aboriginal or having an aboriginal teacher or boss. It's a traditional test of deep-seated racism. The percentage of Canadians who were comfortable all these scenarios was in the mid- and high-90s. "Canada has come a long way in understanding and appreciating many of the aboriginal issues," says Wanda Wuttunee, a professor of native studies at the University of Manitoba in Winnipeg. "It's important to look at the baby steps forward."

Still, the list of political and legal issues that the next generation of aboriginal leaders will need to address is long, and it is in addition to all the social and health problems. For example: the huge concerns over governance of First Nations, the move of aboriginals into urban settings, the fate of the environment, the settlement of land claims and hunting and fishing rights. To Keren Rice, director of aboriginal studies at the University of Toronto, this generation will be key in finding fixes. "They have an understanding of where they come from and what they can be," she says. "They've got a sense of how to put this all together. If they can do that, they're going to have an enormous effect."

To Mr. Durocher, now 25, who moved to Saskatoon for high school, access to education is at the centre of all the issues. Through education can come self-awareness and self-acceptance and faith in the future. He can see the changes in just the decade or so since he arrived at the big-city school. His daughter, Nichole Kyplain, 6, goes to an elementary school in Saskatoon where there is a large percentage of aboriginal and African-American children. Part of the curriculum is to learn about other cultures – including aboriginal culture – and to respect them. And when he reads the local newspaper, he consistently finds stories about aboriginal public-school students who are excelling at basketball, hockey and other sports.

While some are taking the traditional native route of entrepreneurship to reach success, Mr. Durocher says he'd like to see more emphasis on education. "It's going to open up a lot of doors," he says. Lloyd Barber, who was president of the University of Regina from 1976 until 1990, can't help but agree. One of his first acts as president was to welcome the Saskatchewan Indian Federated College into the university. Today, it has well above 10 per cent of the university's student population, a new name – the First Nations University of Canada – and a growing list of graduate programs. It's not enough. The key now is to help students from some of the isolated First Nations make the move to the city. "They won't go one by one. They'll go 10 by 20 by 30," Mr. Barber says. "They have to have colleagues, cohorts."

Celebrating the multicultural brew – or, time to make a fresh pot?

Travelling on Halifax public transit, engineering student Angelina Eghan, the 25-year-old daughter of Ghanaian émigrés, often notices with grief how the seat next to her on a crowded bus is the last to be filled. She knows this is not something Canadians want to hear, that racial prejudice still thrives in their country. But, she says, while Canadians deserve credit for building the principles of an inclusive society, they shouldn't close the door on talking about the problems that remain. "People feel that just by disagreeing with anyone of a different race, they'll be labelled a racist," she says. "And that's made it hard to have an open discussion about discrimination."

In fact, Canadians – especially Canadians in their 20s – are aware of continuing problems. In the New Canada poll, two-thirds of all respondents agreed with the statement that, in Canada, "there is a lot of

racism." But at the same time, only about one-third believed that people
were discriminated against in the workplace. Perhaps, this is sign of
the high value Canadians place on civility – as in Brooks, Alberta,
where general misconceptions about a group of African newcomers
contrast with individuals' courtesies towards one other. Or perhaps,
as Ms. Eghan says, this means Canadians accept that racism happens,
but do not see it in their own workplace or on their own street.

But a new generation of so-called visible minorities are reaching
adulthood in Canada – not hoping for equal treatment as their parents
hoped, but expecting it. Amanda Affonso, a 27-year-old Calgary business analyst whose parents came to Canada from Pakistan in 1973,
says she thinks it is too early to see discrimination blocking her career
path. But if it should happen, she stresses, she will not sit quietly by.
Three decades after her parents arrived here, she expects "that I'm not
filling a quota to illustrate that minorities are accepted."

As the colour of Canada's immigration changes – and the children
of those immigrants grow up – it is time to revisit the official policy of
multiculturalism.

To begin with, the notion of junking the multicultural policy
because it emphasizes diversity rather than what Canadians hold in
common is a non-starter with the 20s age-cohort. They *like* diversity
and, to a lot of Canadians' surprise, the common values have looked
after themselves. Those values are as concrete and durable as the Rockies
and diversity has impeded no one's definition of Canadian identity.

Nevertheless, as Bernard Ostry, the Trudeau-era senior public
servant who cobbled together Canada's multiculturalism policy
nearly 35 years ago, says, "The environment of 1970 is not the environment of 2003. We did not conceive [at the time] of an environment of
globalization." And Jeffrey Reitz, professor of ethnic, immigration
and pluralism studies at University of Toronto (and one of North
America's foremost experts on multiculturalism), notes that
Canada's policy was shaped in the context of European immigration
and not related to racism or discrimination or disadvantage. That

may well be a significant weakness now that the bulk of Canada's immigration is no longer European – that is, white – and assumptions can no longer be made with the same automatic surety that immigrants will be successful. There are increasing suggestions that Canadians are no longer as open to immigration as they once were. Adds Prof. Reitz: Any government action to legalize illegal immigrants in the country "may rebound and have an impact on the way people view the diversity of society."

Mr. Ostry suggests creating a royal commission to study how global migration and new economic patterns may be altering Canada, and with what implications – whether, for example, it makes continued sense to protect French in British Columbia when the second language spoken in the province is Chinese. It's a point supported by 27-year-old Ajay Chopra, of East Indian descent, who – in a truly Canadian blend of cultures – worked on Phil Fontaine's successful campaign to lead the Assembly of First Nations. "We should promote French and English, but we need to realize it's not just French and English anymore." In a globalized age, says Prof. Reitz, "it's untenable to treat issues as purely domestic."

24

CONTRADICTIONS IN THE NEW CANADA

MATTHEW MENDELSOHN

We want social policy, but we don't trust either market or state to implement it. Quebec has experienced a second "quiet revolution," but it remains different from the rest of Canada. How will we balance these contradictions?

IN THE OLD CANADA, THE SYMBOLS OF NATIONAL identity were institutional and government-driven: There was the Crown, the CBC, Air Canada, the auto pact, the wheat board, Cancon media regulations, Via Rail. As many of these have come under threat or vanished entirely, some Canadians worry about our survival. They shouldn't.

The New Canada's identity is not about what governments do, but about how Canadians live. It's evolving daily at interpersonal and societal levels. Young Canadians are less introspective about the Canadian identity, less likely to ruminate about what it means to be Canadian, but this is not because they feel little attachment to the country. It's because their Canadian identity is secure. Canada is a global network, a country where borders matter less and less.

This is a rapidly changing country, full of complexities and contradictions and challenges, as the New Canada survey shows. It seems clear where young Canadians want to go, but how we might get there is not. The path to the New Canada is not a perfectly linear one, and it would be a serious mistake to think the answers lie in the old mechanisms of government regulations and bureaucracy. Among the contradictions we face:

1. Young people have disengaged from formal, party, and institutional politics. They are more likely than older Canadians to believe there is nothing they could do if the government was taking an action they did not support. The courts, in fact, are more trusted than legislatures. To young Canadians, our high courts take their responsibilities seriously, while politicians dither. Young Canadians do not fret that courts are usurping the power of elected officials.

Yet Canadians still care about social problems and want to be engaged, if only they believed they would have an impact. A real agenda for democratic reform is necessary if we are to avoid becoming a managerial democracy without citizens.

2. The New Canada has little confidence in either the market or the state to address complex social problems, whether the issue is homelessness or aboriginal poverty. Governments could eliminate public-sector bureaucracies and most young Canadians would not bat an eye. The traditional connection between "a large state" and "social justice" has broken down.

Yet Canadians' social priorities haven't changed much in 30 years. This is tragic: A population that wants to act collectively on its social priorities, but believes that government action will not produce success. The test of a social program today for Canadians is: Does it empower all Canadians to make the most of their opportunities, and allow them to make their own choices? Programs that pass the New Canadian litmus test are those directed towards individual Canadians, rather than groups, and that provide all of us with equal opportunities to make choices to pursue education, training, small business start-ups, or opportunities for social entrepreneurship and volunteerism.

3. The New Canada is basically four metropolises: Vancouver, Edmonton-Calgary, Toronto, and Montreal. Half of us live in these four areas, and this proportion continues to grow. Their population is already about four times larger than that of the six smallest provinces and three territories combined. We are no longer a ribbon tucked up against the American border, but a small number of clusters of incredible social diversity and economic potential.

Yet our cities lack formal constitutional powers. Young Canadians are far more likely than older ones to say that their municipal government needs more power. An agenda that empowers the governments of large municipalities is overdue. But Toronto does not need the same powers as Winnipeg, which does not need the same powers as Kamloops. Call it "pragmatic asymmetry," but we're a long way from getting there.

4. Social liberalism, tolerance, and egalitarianism are the norm. The old battles over family structure and sexual orientation are things of the past, as foreign as debates over segregation. Young Canadians have a very high level of social liberalism and happily embrace diversity. Who you want to have sex with, which god you choose to worship, or how many parents you have are all non-issues. Young Canadians hold this social tolerance – this freedom – as a deeply felt moral principle. A radical change from our deferential past has occurred in Canada, producing a highly egalitarian, non-hierarchical political culture.

Yet Canadians' attitudes towards economic questions, such as whether taxes are too high or whether we should spend more money on education or health care, have changed little. The New Canada looks very much like the old Canada on these bread and butter issues.

5. Canadians' values are increasingly different from Americans' values. Every cliché turns out be true: Americans are more religious, more socially conservative, more materialistic, more supportive of market solutions and more comfortable with income inequality, more supportive of the military, more comfortable with violence, less supportive of ethnic and religious diversity, and more likely to feel socially excluded and alienated from society. Unlike in Europe, where a common European identity is developing, no common North American identity exists. The notion that Canadians and Americans are becoming indistinguishable because we watch the same television shows is a fiction.

Yet our economies, societies, security, politics, and entertainment cultures become more and more integrated. Our challenge as a country is to figure out how to avoid public displays of pique when we're annoyed that our values differ, how to accept that our closest ally, on whom we are terribly dependent, differs with us on some key values.

6. Canadians have adopted a new internationalist identity. We have embraced the idea that trade, based on a level playing field, is in our interest and the interest of the world's poor. A real trade liberalization agenda, where markets for goods and services both to and from the developing world are more open, would be fully embraced as an extension of New Canadian values. Canada is uniquely placed to help build civil society, trust, and the rule of law in the developing world, and this could be our contribution to global security. It would be consistent with the stories Canadians tell about themselves, but it would also be a large and significant contribution to ensure that other

countries, particularly the U.S., could not claim that we are not pulling our weight.

Yet there is a symbol-reality gap of enormous proportions. One of the features of the New Canada has been politicians who invoke the idea of an internationally engaged, caring, important "middle power," but who do not follow through in their actions. All countries have national mythologies, and mature countries may, paradoxically, have a whole series of national myths that they don't always live up to. But the gap may have grown too large, and finding money to make a difference internationally is essential.

7. Quebec has seen a second quiet revolution. The province today is a pluralistic society, and Quebeckers' attitudes toward ethnic and religious diversity are indistinguishable from the attitudes of those elsewhere in the country. Young Montreal has evolved into a multilingual community. Furthermore, young Quebeckers are far less likely to think that sovereignty is an important issue, or identify themselves as either "sovereigntist" or "federalist." Part of the second quiet revolution in Quebec is the decline in salience of the national question.

Yet Quebec remains quite different from the rest of the country. Quebeckers continue to identify themselves as Quebeckers first and Canadians second, which is different from the rest of the country. Also, many Quebec values remain different, as was powerfully demonstrated on issues such as the war in Iraq and same-sex marriage, where Quebeckers were much more liberal than other Canadians. Reflecting these values in the face of some opposition from the rest of the country will be an ongoing challenge.

The new Canadian identity is not tied to institutions created or maintained by the federal government. It is about how we live; it's about a unique set of values connected to multiculturalism, individual rights, the Charter, social egalitarianism, internationalism, bilingualism, peacekeeping, the environment, social liberalism, living within our means, and getting along with each other. If governments can help create an environment in which the New Canadian identity can flourish, great. But to many young Canadians, the linkage between these values, which they support, and government action ostensibly designed to further them, broke down a long time ago. That has to change if we are to live up to the promise of the New Canada.

BY THE NUMBERS:
A GRAPHIC LOOK AT THE NEW CANADA

RICHARD PALMER

Our great divide

This sample of 1,000 Canadians reflects the 2001 census results and shows just how dramatically society is changing. Almost 80 per cent of us are now city folk and the urban Big Four account for more than half of the population and the vast majority of immigrants, especially those who are much more likely to belong to a visible minority. Rural areas are defined as those with towns and villages of less than 1,000 population. The figures used in this chart do not include institutional residents, such as those in prisons, hospitals or shelters.

TOTAL RURAL:

20.4%

Population: 6,053,095

TOTAL URBAN:

79.6%

Population: 23,585,940

The urban areas outside the Big Four

Population: 8,731,785

9.5%

90.5%

Rural areas

6.3%

93.7%

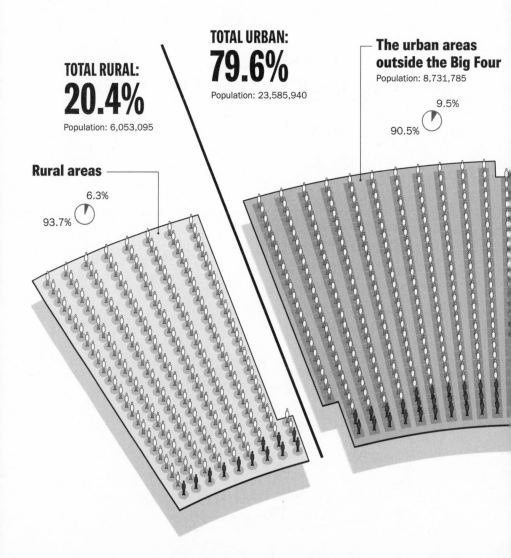

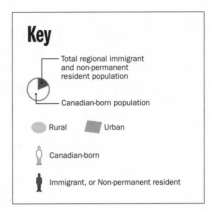

Key

Total regional immigrant and non-permanent resident population

Canadian-born population

Rural   Urban

Canadian-born

Immigrant, or Non-permanent resident

Vancouver
(Includes lower B.C. Mainland and southern Vancouver Island)
Population: 2,635,380

33.9%

66.1%

Calgary-Edmonton corridor
Population: 1,947,715

19.7%

80.3%

Montreal (and surrounding area)
Population: 3,630,585

18.2%

81.8%

Toronto (extended Golden Horseshoe)
Population: 6,640,475

37.6%

62.4%

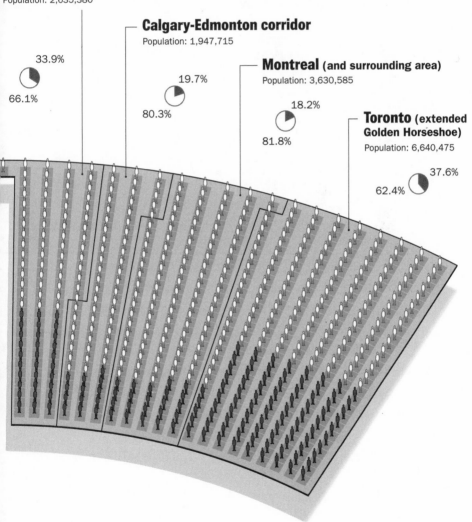

Where we live ...

The rural exodus

Here is how Canada's population has become the most urbanized in the world.

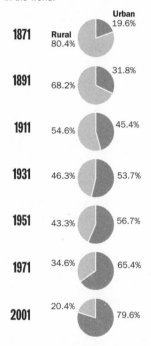

1871 Rural 80.4% / Urban 19.6%

1891 68.2% / 31.8%

1911 54.6% / 45.4%

1931 46.3% / 53.7%

1951 43.3% / 56.7%

1971 34.6% / 65.4%

2001 20.4% / 79.6%

Close quarters

The density of Toronto's population ranks 2nd among urban areas in Canada and the United States.

Population per square kilometre

Los Angeles 2,729.1

Toronto 2,639.1

SOURCE: 1
(SEE SOURCE PANEL)

Leaps and bounds

The population of Canada grew by 4.0% (1.16-million) between 1996 and 2001. Meanwhile, the population of the Big Four urban regions increased by 7.6%, almost double the national rate. Here is how both stack up in global terms.

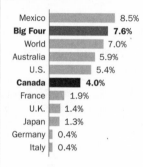

Mexico	8.5%
Big Four	**7.6%**
World	7.0%
Australia	5.9%
U.S.	5.4%
Canada	**4.0%**
France	1.9%
U.K.	1.4%
Japan	1.3%
Germany	0.4%
Italy	0.4%

But the highest rates of growth were found in the suburbs and outlying municipalities. Cochrane, Alta., near Calgary, grew by 58.9% while Vaughan and Richmond Hill, north of Toronto, increased 37.3% and 29.8% respectively.

Among major Canadian cities, Calgary's growth was well ahead of the pack.

Calgary	15.8%
Oshawa, Ont.	10.2%
Toronto	9.8%
Edmonton	8.7%
Vancouver	8.5%

Bright lights, big city

Migration

Between 1996 and 2001 the movement of Canadians within the country helped to boost the populations of mid-sized communities.

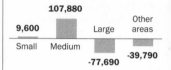

107,880

9,600 — Small

Large

Other areas

Medium

-77,690

-39,790

Immigration

But a massive flow of people into Canada hugely favoured the large centres.

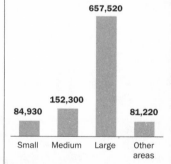

657,520

84,930 — Small

152,300 — Medium

Large

81,220 — Other areas

Concentration

More than 1.2 million immigrants came to Canada between 1996 and 2001. Here's where they went:

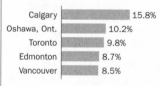

Other, **24.7%**

Montreal, **12.1%**

Vancouver, **17.1%**

Toronto, **46.1%**

SOURCE: 2

...who we are...

Return of the native

In 2001, 976,305 people identified themselves as aboriginal, a percentage of the population surpassed in only one other developed nation.

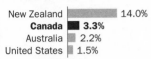

New Zealand 14.0%
Canada ■ 3.3%
Australia 2.2%
United States 1.5%

Rapid expansion

Although the aboriginal birth rate has slowed it is still 1.5 times that of non-aboriginals, whose population grew by 3.4% between 1996 and 2001. Growth within the native communities varied widely.

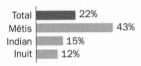

Total 22%
Métis 43%
Indian 15%
Inuit 12%

Youth

The aboriginal median age also was much lower than non-aboriginals' (37.6 years), especially in the West and the North.

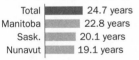

Total 24.7 years
Manitoba 22.8 years
Sask. 20.1 years
Nunavut 19.1 years

Planning for the future

Aboriginals make up 14% of the Saskatchewan population. But their representation among children is almost double that.

25% of children in Saskatchewan are aboriginal.

Diversity blooms

Canada's proportion of foreign-born people is second only to Australia's.

Australia 22%
Canada ■ 18%

The figure for Toronto, however, is double that of Australia. Canadian cities are among the world's most diverse communities.

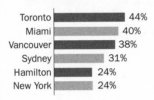

Toronto 44%
Miami 40%
Vancouver 38%
Sydney 31%
Hamilton 24%
New York 24%

Visible majority?

Visible minority in Richmond, B.C. **59%**

This Vancouver suburb leads the nation when it comes to visible minorities, with the largest proportion of Chinese-Canadians, the second largest of Japanese heritage and third largest of Filipino descent.

On the flip side, one Quebec region has a very tiny representation.

Visible minority in Chicoutimi-Jonquiere **0.6%**

Going grey

In 1966, the median age of Canadians was 25.4. It's now 37.6, which is an all-time high and means that half of the population is already older than the life expectancy the World Health Organization gives to people in 19 countries, such as Zimbabwe, Mozambique and Afghanistan.

Also worth noting is how close the overall median age has come to that of the labour force over the past century. Where have all the children gone?

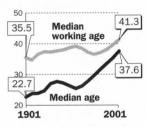

The median extremes

Trois-Rivieres in Quebec has replaced Victoria as the nation's oldest urban community while Saskatoon remains the youngest.

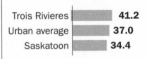

Trois Rivieres **41.2**
Urban average **37.0**
Saskatoon **34.4**

Out to pasture?

The age distribution of farm operators in Canada.

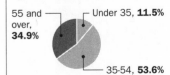

55 and over, **34.9%** — Under 35, **11.5%**
35-54, **53.6%**

Work in progress

In 2001, immigrants accounted for almost one-fifth of the Canadian work force, while in Toronto, almost half of all workers were born outside the country.

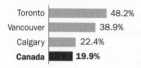

Toronto	48.2%
Vancouver	38.9%
Calgary	22.4%
Canada	**19.9%**

The gender divide

The labour force grew by 9.5% or 1.3 million jobs between 1991 and 2001. Women accounted for most of this growth:

New jobs held by men, **34.8%**

New jobs held by women, **65.2%**

But men still tipped the balance, holding 53.4% of Canada's 15.5 million jobs.

Can you see the glass ceiling?

The New Canada poll asked:

If two equally qualified people are being considered for a promotion, one man and one woman, whom do you think would get it?

Most men, both young and old, thought both candidates would have an equal chance. Almost half of the women disagreed.

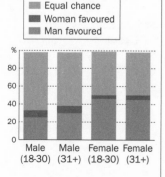

- Equal chance
- Woman favoured
- Man favoured

%
80
60
40
20
0

Male (18-30) Male (31+) Female (18-30) Female (31+)

Family values

Canadian households have changed radically. For one thing, they are less crowded. The proportion that have four or more members has dropped from one-third to one-quarter.

1981

2001

Traditional

Also on the decline are the proportions of households occupied by married couples and married couples with children.

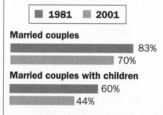

■ **1981** ■ **2001**

Married couples
83%
70%

Married couples with children
60%
44%

Non-traditional 1

More couples, particularly in Quebec, are living common-law.

Common-law families:

- 5.6% (Canada)
- 13.8% (Canada)
- 30% (Quebec)

Non-traditional 2

34,500 same-sex couples living common-law were counted in 2001.

Proportion of same-sex households

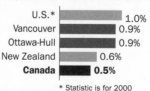

U.S.*	1.0%
Vancouver	0.9%
Ottawa-Hull	0.9%
New Zealand	0.6%
Canada	**0.5%**

* Statistic is for 2000

Race and sexuality

Our poll revealed:

Prejudice lives on ...

Which statement more closely reflects your own view: There is still a lot of racism left in Canada. OR: There isn't much racism left in Canada.

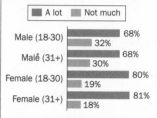

■ A lot   ■ Not much

Male (18-30)	68% / 32%
Male (31+)	68% / 30%
Female (18-30)	80% / 19%
Female (31+)	81% / 18%

but its power is fading ...

Which statement more closely reflects your own view: At work or at school in Canada, just about everyone succeeds or fails on the basis of how well they do their work. OR: Many people are judged at work and school on the basis of their ethnic background, with some having a harder time due to prejudice.

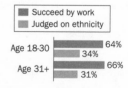

■ Succeed by work
■ Judged on ethnicity

Age 18-30	64% / 34%
Age 31+	66% / 31%

and more could be done

The Charter of Rights and Freedoms guarantees equal rights for women, ethnic and religious minorities and other groups. In your opinion, should the Charter also guarantee equal rights for gays and lesbians?

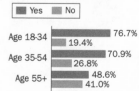

■ Yes   ■ No

Age 18-34	76.7% / 19.4%
Age 35-54	70.9% / 26.8%
Age 55+	48.6% / 41.0%

... and what we think

Things we agree on

Both young workers and old value security over salary ...

If you had to choose between a higher salary or greater job security, which would you pick?

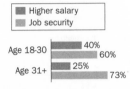

- ■ Higher salary
- ■ Job security

Age 18-30 — 40% / 60%
Age 31+ — 25% / 73%

and even more consider family time precious ...

Which would you prefer: Earning more money, even if that meant working more hours each week. OR: Having more time for yourself and your family, even if that meant earning less money?

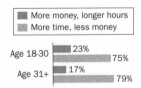

- ■ More money, longer hours
- ■ More time, less money

Age 18-30 — 23% / 75%
Age 31+ — 17% / 79%

and a sense of nationhood important

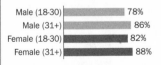

Male (18-30) — 78%
Male (31+) — 86%
Female (18-30) — 82%
Female (31+) — 88%

Things we disagree on

Is religion an important part of one's identity?
Older women think so ...

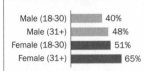

Male (18-30) — 40%
Male (31+) — 48%
Female (18-30) — 51%
Female (31+) — 65%

When choosing a spouse, is it important to look for a similar ethnic background?
Not according to young people ...

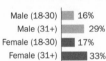

Male (18-30) — 16%
Male (31+) — 29%
Female (18-30) — 17%
Female (31+) — 33%

Do you support gay marriages?
Older people tend not to ...

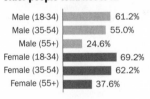

Male (18-34) — 61.2%
Male (35-54) — 55.0%
Male (55+) — 24.6%
Female (18-34) — 69.2%
Female (35-54) — 62.2%
Female (55+) — 37.6%

Who should pay for daycare?

Do you think parents should pay the full costs of daycare, or is it the government's responsibility to ensure there is affordable care for Canadian children?

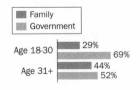

- ■ Family
- ■ Government

Age 18-30 — 29% / 69%
Age 31+ — 44% / 52%

The road ahead

Life is good ...

Suppose the top of the ladder represents the best possible life for you, and the bottom, the worst possible life for you. On which step of the ladder do you feel that you stand at the present time?
(10-rung scale)

High (7-10) — 67%
Medium (4-6) — 31%
Low (0-3) — 2%
SOURCE: 3

... and getting better

Just your best guess now: On which step do you think you will stand in the future, say five years from now?

High (7-10) — 77%
Medium (4-6) — 12%
Low (0-3) — 4%
SOURCE: 3

Predictions

Our poll suggested:

It is likely that ...

(Bars indicate percentage that agree)

1. Canada will adopt the U.S. dollar as its currency.

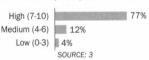

Age 18-30 — 24%
Age 31+ — 27%

2. There will be more peace in the world and less war.

Age 18-30 — 28%
Age 31+ — 34%

3. The quality of the environment in Canada will improve.

Age 18-30 — 52%
Age 31+ — 62%

The census also found Canadians have more than 200 ethnic origins

Canada – total single and multiple responses

British Isles
- English, 5,978,875
- Irish, 3,822,660
- Scottish, 4,157,210
- Welsh, 350,365
- Other, 150,585

French
- Acadian, 71,590
- French, 4,668,410

Aboriginal
- Inuit, 56,330
- Métis, 307,845
- North American Indian, 1,000,890

North American
- American (USA), 250,005
- Canadian, 11,682,680
- Newfoundlander, 13,715
- Québécois, 98,670
- Other, 4,375

Caribbean
- Antiguan, 2,435
- Bahamian, 1,585
- Barbadian, 23,725
- Bermudan, 1,845
- Carib, 1,330
- Cuban, 6,200
- Dominican, 6,865
- Grenadian, 7,995
- Guyanese, 51,570
- Haitian, 82,405
- Jamaican, 211,720
- Kittitian/Nevisian, 1,730
- Martinique, 605
- Puerto Rican, 1,045
- St. Lucian, 2,765
- Trinidadian/Tobagonian, 49,590
- Vincentian/Grenadinian, 7,450
- West Indian, 59,705
- Other, 10,990

Latin, Central and South American
- Argentinian, 9,095
- Belizean, 725
- Bolivian, 1,795
- Brazilian, 9,710
- Central/South American Indian, 8,965
- Chilean, 34,115
- Colombian, 15,865
- Costa Rican, 1,615
- Ecuadorian, 8,785
- Guatemalan, 9,550
- Hispanic, 7,850
- Honduran, 3,025
- Maya, 2,875
- Mexican, 36,575
- Nicaraguan, 6,190
- Panamanian, 2,075
- Paraguayan, 760
- Peruvian, 17,945
- Salvadorean, 26,735
- Uruguayan, 3,800
- Venezuelan, 5,925
- Other, 41,620

European

Western European
- Austrian, 147,585
- Belgian, 129,780
- Dutch (Netherlands), 92,3310
- Flemish, 11,665
- Frisian, 3,175
- German, 2,742,765
- Luxembourger, 2,390
- Swiss, 110,795

Northern European
- Finnish, 114,690

Scandinavian
- Danish, 170,780
- Icelandic, 75,090
- Norwegian, 363,760
- Swedish, 282,760
- Other, 32,730

Eastern European

Baltic
- Estonian, 22,085
- Latvian, 22,615
- Lithuanian, 36,485
- Byelorussian, 5,115

Czech and Slovak
- Czech, 79,910
- Czechoslovakian, 33,540
- Slovak, 50,860
- Hungarian (Magyar), 267,255
- Polish, 817,085
- Romanian, 131,830
- Russian, 337,960
- Ukrainian, 1,071,060

Southern European

Balkan
- Albanian, 14,935
- Bosnian, 15,720
- Bulgarian, 15,195
- Croatian, 97,050
- Kosovar, 1,200
- Macedonian, 31,265
- Montenegrin, 1,055
- Serbian, 55,540
- Slovenian, 28,910
- Yugoslav, other, 65,505
- Cypriot, 2,060
- Greek, 215,105
- Italian, 1,270,370
- Maltese, 33,000
- Portuguese, 357,690
- Sicilian, 2,465
- Spanish, 213,105

Other European
- Basque, 2,715
- Gypsy (Roma), 2,590
- Jewish, 348,605
- Slav (European), 6,810
- Other, 20,450

African
- Afrikaner, 1,250
- Akan, 750
- Angolan, 1,110
- Ashanti, 1,860
- Black, 53,090
- Burundian, 1,900
- Cameroonian, 2,070
- Congolese, other, 6,235
- East African, 2,270
- Eritrean, 7,165
- Ethiopian, 15,725
- Ghanaian, 16,935
- Guinean, other, 1,120
- Ibo, 1,200
- Ivoirean, 1,120
- Kenyan, 2,990
- Malagasy, 780
- Malian, 815
- Mauritian, 2,720
- Nigerian, 9,530
- Oromo, 1,030
- Rwandan, 3,060
- Senegalese, 1,675
- Seychellois, 980
- Sierra Leonean, 565
- Somali, 33,725
- South African, 18,925
- Sudanese, 6,525
- Tanzanian, 1,865
- Togolese, 755
- Ugandan, 2,125
- Yoruba, 1,875
- Zairian, 1,885

- Zimbabwean, 1,250
- Black, other, 97,185
- Other, 155

Arab
- Egyptian, 41,310
- Iraqi, 19,245
- Jordanian, 3,760
- Kuwaiti, 855
- Lebanese, 143,635
- Libyan, 1,180

Maghrebi
- Algerian, 15,500
- Berber, 5,570
- Moroccan, 21,355
- Tunisian, 5,325
- Maghrebi, other, 2,270
- Palestinian, 14,675
- Saudi Arabian, 1,080
- Syrian, 22,065
- Yemeni, 1,445
- other, 71,705

West Asian
- Afghan, 25,230
- Armenian, 40,505
- Assyrian, 6,980
- Azerbaijani, 1,445
- Georgian, 970
- Iranian, 88,220
- Israeli, 6,060
- Kurd, 5,680
- Pashtun, 1,040
- Tartar, 875
- Turk, 24,910
- Other, 8,805

South Asian
- Bangladeshi, 13,080
- Bengali, 7,020
- East Indian, 713,330
- Goan, 3,865
- Gujarati, 2,805
- Kashmiri, 480
- Pakistani, 74,015
- Punjabi, 47,155
- Nepali, 1,170
- Sinhalese, 3,560
- Sri Lankan, 61,315
- Tamil, 39,075
- Other, 49,205

East and Southeast Asian
- Chinese, 1,094,700
- Filipino, 327,550

Indo-Chinese
- Burmese, 2,840
- Cambodian, 20,430
- Khmer, 1,000
- Laotian, 16,950
- Thai, 6,965
- Vietnamese, 151,410
- Hmong, 595
- Indonesian, 9,700
- Japanese, 85,230
- Korean, 101,715
- Malaysian, 6,095
- Mongolian, 1,675
- Taiwanese, 18,080
- Tibetan, 1,425
- Other Asian, 2,010
- Other, 8,795

Oceania
- Australian, 25,415

Pacific Islands
- Fijian, 10,035
- Hawaian, 1,955
- Maori, 1,305
- Polynesian, 1,745
- Pacific Islander, other, 390
- New Zealander, 8,600

CONTRIBUTORS

The writers

Erin Anderssen and Michael Valpy were the lead writers on *The New Canada*. Erin is the social trends reporter for *The Globe and Mail*, and the winner of two National Newspaper Awards. Raised on the south shore of Nova Scotia, she currently lives in Ottawa. Michael, born in Toronto where he now lives but raised in Vancouver, has won three National Newspaper Awards and, in 1997, was awarded an honorary doctorate by Trent University.

Roy MacGregor, born in Whitney, Ontario – and brought to Algonquin Park for the first time when he was three days old – writes *The Globe and Mail*'s Page 2 column, "This Country."

Matthew Mendelsohn is director of the Canadian Opinion Research Archive and associate professor in the political studies department at Queen's University and was a consultant on the CRIC-*Globe* survey on the New Canada. He was born and raised in Montreal.

Alanna Mitchell is a senior feature writer at *The Globe and Mail* in Toronto. Raised in Regina, she served as a Calgary correspondent for several years. She has won three international awards since 2000 for her reporting on the environment.

Ingrid Peritz, a native Montrealer, has been observing life in that city as a reporter and feature writer for nearly 20 years. She worked for the *Ottawa Citizen* and the *Gazette* before joining *The Globe and Mail*'s Montreal bureau.

Margaret Philp, social policy reporter at *The Globe and Mail* in Toronto, has won a National Newspaper Award for feature writing. Born in Toronto, she was raised there and in Winnipeg.

Doug Saunders, an international affairs writer and columnist with *The Globe and Mail* in Toronto, has served as the paper's Los Angeles bureau chief, media reporter and editorial writer. He has won three National Newspaper Awards for his work. He was raised in Hamilton, Ontario.

Ken Wiwa is a *Globe and Mail* columnist and author of *In the Shadow of a Saint*. He was born in Lagos, raised in London, and now lives in Toronto.

The editors

Edward Greenspon is Editor-in-chief of *The Globe and Mail*.

Catherine Wallace, deputy national editor, and Cathrin Bradbury, weekend editor, were co-editors of The New Canada project in *The Globe and Mail*. Catherine adapted the material for this book.

Alison Gzowski is the assistant books editor at *The Globe and Mail*.

Jerry Johnson is editor of *The Globe and Mail*'s weekend Focus section.

Richard Palmer is graphics editor at *The Globe and Mail*.

David Pratt is *The Globe and Mail*'s editorial design director.
Carl Wilson is a senior features editor at *The Globe and Mail*, and writes a weekly music column for The Globe's Review section.

The photographers

Erin Elder is photo editor at *The Globe and Mail*.

Jayson Taylor, an assistant photo editor at *The Globe and Mail*, created the cover image.

Patti Gower, Tibor Kolley, John Lehmann and Fred Lum are *Globe and Mail* photographers.

Sandor Fizli, Darryl James, Christinne Muschi, Keith Moulding, Mackenzie Stroh and Don Weber are regular *Globe and Mail* freelancer photographers.